Redeemer Nation in the Interregnum

Redeemer Nation in the Interregnum

AN UNTIMELY MEDITATION ON THE AMERICAN VOCATION

WILLIAM V. SPANOS

FORDHAM UNIVERSITY PRESS

New York   2016

Visit us online at www.fordhampress.com.

Library of Congress Cataloging-in-Publication Data

Spanos, William V.
    Redeemer nation in the interregnum : an untimely meditation on the American vocation / William V. Spanos ; foreword by Donald E. Pease. — First edition.
        pages cm
    Includes bibliographical references and index.
    ISBN 978-0-8232-6815-3 (hardback) — ISBN 978-0-8232-6816-0 (paper)
    1. Exceptionalism—United States.   2. Political culture—United States.
    3. Democracy—United States.   I. Title.
    E169.12.S667   2015
    306.20973—dc23
                                        2015006039

Printed in the United States of America

18 17 16   5 4 3 2 1

First edition

Dedicated to Paul Bové, Daniel O'Hara, and Donald Pease,

the profane Trinity—
the nothing, the fire, and the unholy bird—
whose polyvalent force has guided me
in my destruction of the American world I live in
and my imaging of the polis that will arise from its ashes

Contents

*Foreword: Witness to the Critical Imperatives
of the Interregnum* by Donald E. Pease   ix

Preface   xv

Acknowledgments   xxi

1. The Nothingness of Being and the Spectacle:
   The American Sublime Revisited   1

2. American Exceptionalism in the Post–9/11 Era:
   The Myth and the Reality   42

3. "The Center Will Not Hold": The Widening Gyre
   of the New, New Americanist Studies   74

4. American Exceptionalism and the Calling:
   A Genealogy of the Vocational Ethic   105

*Appendix: The Debate World and the Making
of the American Political Class—An Interview Conducted
by Christopher Spurlock with William V. Spanos*   145

Notes   157

Index   177

Foreword

Witness to the Critical Imperatives of the Interregnum

DONALD E. PEASE

William V. Spanos's *Redeemer Nation in the Interregnum: An Untimely Meditation on the American Vocation* brings to fruition and provides the coda for a series of remarkable volumes—*The Exceptionalist State and the State of Exception: Herman Melville's "Billy Budd, Sailor"* (2011); *Herman Melville and the American Calling: The Fiction After "Moby-Dick," 1851–1857* (2008); and *Shock and Awe: American Exceptionalism and the Imperatives of the Spectacle in Mark Twain's "A Connecticut Yankee in King Arthur's Court"* (2013)—in which Spanos undertook a radical critique of American exceptionalism. In conducting that ongoing critique, Spanos brought together two critical dispositions—Gramsci's dismantling of hegemony as a "coercive ideological project that represents itself as universal truth and finds its fulfillment in the 'end of history'" and Heidegger's destruction of "the global triumph of the imperial logic of hegemony." This study continues Spanos's critical *destruktion* of American exceptionalism, but it differs from its precursors in that Spanos attests to the emergence of a way of being that coincides with the revocation of the American exceptionalist calling.

The phrase "An Untimely Meditation on the American Vocation" indicates what sets this volume apart from Spanos's preceding volumes. In *Redeemer Nation in the Interregnum*, Spanos engages the polyvalent ideological connotations that resonate around "American exceptionalism" when it is understood as the foundational trope of the American national identity. Whereas the vast majority of commentators on the term have interpreted American exceptionalism as an ideological mystification of imperial predation, Spanos constructs a genealogy of American exceptionalism that teases out its polyvalent ideological implications by finding them at once condensed yet concealed in the idea of an American calling or vocation. Spanos's genealogy of American exceptionalism as "*the* American calling" discloses how it functions simultaneously as an ontological, a moral, an economic, a racial, a gendered, and a political phenomenon.

According to Spanos, American exceptionalism is not a conscious and articulate ideology. It is an ethos in Rancière's sense of the word, a polyvalent discourse that works as an apparatus of capture—a whole way of life—that saturates the American body politic right down to its capillaries. In light of Spanos's genealogy, American exceptionalism should not be construed as a corrigible ideological screen. Its inordinate invisible power cannot be resisted by direct confrontation undertaken in the name of an identity, no matter whether working class, racial or gendered minority, or ethnic constituency. This exceptionalist ethos continues to determine the worldly mission of the U.S. imperial exceptionalist. But it cannot be opposed in the name of any of these identities because identities are the means whereby the exceptionalist state apparatuses are programmed to operate in a decisively effective way.

From the monograph's opening chapter, Spanos explicitly links this argument with claims he previously laid out in *Shock and Awe: American Exceptionalism and the Imperatives of the Spectacle in Mark Twain's "A Connecticut Yankee in King Arthur's Court."* Spanos specifically reveals the way in which the spectacular show of force Mark Twain staged in *A Connecticut Yankee in King Arthur's Court* uncannily anticipated the post–9/11 global American cultural-political occasion. Twain's Hank Morgan also prefigured Bush's desire to transform the exceptionalist national ordinance into an absolute spectacle. When it pursued the logic of American exceptionalism to what Spanos calls its "fulfillment" in an apocalyptic spectacle, the Bush administration revealed the sublime violence that the benign discourse of the "redeemer nation" had previously covered over.

Characterizing George W. Bush's War on Terror as the paradoxical fulfillment of the exceptionalist narrative, Spanos conducts a compelling reenvisioning of the whole arc of American culture. Spanos describes what's different about the discursive structure of the Bush administration's Project for the New American Century as its total reification of the temporality of being into an absolute spectacle. "At this liminal point, the nothingness of being, which is ontologically prior to its thingness, is *dis-*

closed for positive thought." When George W. Bush's shock-and-awe war in
the Middle East rendered the long-disavowed violence of the state spectacularly visible to Americans and the world, the entire buttressing logic
of U.S. exceptionalism "self-de-structed." In the interregnum precipitated
by its coming to its completion, that which American exceptionalism
always disavowed and rendered "invisible"—that specter which, in fact,
always haunted it—has manifested itself, *contrapuntally*, as the Other
that American exceptionalism covered over.

Spanos's exposure of the centrality of American exceptionalism to the
discourse of the American political class has been echoed in the work of
a generation of scholars in New American studies who endorse Spanos's
critique of U.S. exceptionalism. But after persuasively demonstrating
how the American exceptionalist ethos continues to determine the mentality of the policy-makers responsible for articulating America's mission
in the world, Spanos devotes the entire third chapter of this untimely
monograph to a prolonged chastisement of a constellation of "New,
New Americanist" scholars—Russ Castronovo, Malini Schueller, Brian
Edwards, Wai Chee Dimock, Paul Giles, Dilip Gaonkar, Paul Jay, and
John Carlos Rowe—for their premature celebration of the demise of
American exceptionalism.

Spanos generously acknowledges the praiseworthy achievements of
these transnational American studies scholars: in uncovering the underside of U.S. imperial exceptionalism, they exposed the violence that the
hegemonic exceptionalist discourse has disavowed; in interpreting the
history of U.S. imperial exceptionalism from the standpoint of its victims, they also enabled the silenced peoples of the world to speak for
themselves; and in so doing, they made it possible to think an alternative
to the U.S. imperium. But in Spanos's view, the antiexceptionalist discourse of these scholars remains too parochially within the American
exceptionalist problematic they call into question and too indifferent to
the critical imperatives of the voices of the exile or outside Others silenced
by imperial American exceptionalism.

Spanos is particularly incisive in his criticism of the tendency of scholars involved in transnational American studies—myself included—to
privilege the global at the expense of the local and thereby diminish the
significance of the new manifestation of post–9/11 exceptionalism. Arguing that transnational American studies' deterritorialized and panoptic
perspective is itself enabled by the exceptionalist standpoint of the imperial hegemon, Spanos goes on to characterize transnational "re-mappings"

of the field of American studies as one of the means whereby American exceptionalism has effected its acts of imperial capture in the post–9/11 epoch.

As warrant for this critique, Spanos represents the Global War on Terror as the harnessing of its exceptionalist calling to the U.S. imperial state's endless errand into the world's wilderness. For Spanos, the Global War on Terror cannot be distinguished from the planetary spectacle of the exception. In his view the global war and the planetary spectacle are equivalent outcomes of the universal adoption of the exceptionalist ethos. It was the local U.S. exceptionalist state, as the agency responsible for the post–9/11 Global War on Terror, that precipitated the ominous normalization of the state of exception. Although transnational American studies scholars may claim that the exceptionalist center has been decentered, it is in fact the imperial state's exceptionalist center that has made possible their positioning themselves outside the local. According to Spanos, rogue states, the wilderness of failed states, and transnational Americanists' deterritorialized perspective were all made possible by the exceptionalist ethos. By collapsing the distinction between U.S. imperial exceptionalism and the exceptionalisms that defined other nation-states, transnational American studies scholars have refused to acknowledge the fact "that their deterritorialized panoptic perspective is facilitated by the exceptionalist paradigm of the imperial hegemon they have disavowed." Transnational Americanists' tendency to overdetermine the global perspective all but obliterated the actual history of a post–9/11 world, which is "bearing witness to an uneven struggle between the United States and a multitude of deracinated people, unhomed by the depredations of exceptionalist nation-state imperialism."

On encountering this compelling critique, a reader might wonder, as I did, how Spanos excepted his exposition from the impasses to which he consigned transnational American studies scholars. Spanos engaged this question head-on in the chapter that rests at the theoretical core of his "untimely meditation." Spanos begins "American Exceptionalism and the Calling: A Genealogy of the Vocational Ethic" by restating his foundational insight: the global war's "fulfillment" of the United States' "errand" effected a universalized state of exception that revealed the *nothing* at the core of the U.S. exceptionalist calling. Then Spanos describes the interregnum that emerged in and as a revelation of this nothingness as "humanity's radically secular ontological condition, its total untethering of its fate from any transcendental higher cause, whether deity or history." Spanos believes that it is from the existential now-time of this interregnum that we must take our critical directives addressing the globalizing occasion.

Spanos has written *Redeemer Nation in the Interregnum: An Untimely Meditation on the American Vocation* from within and as an attestation to the truth of the interregnum in the present destabilized planetary occasion. From the time of the nation's founding, the American exceptionalist calling to a higher cause effected the postponement of the "untimely" time of the now. Spanos's study describes the real event of the post–9/11 occasion as the emergence of "the now-time" of the interregnum as what is disclosed as and through the nothingness at the core of America's global exceptionalist calling. The interregnum is unlike the American calling in that it brings about the vocation of the "exilic consciousness"—the calling to be both inside and outside the world, at home yet not at home, at once a part of and apart from the world. By disrupting the relay between the elect, exceptionalism, and the vocation of the calling, the exilic consciousness renders inoperative the interpellating ethos of American exceptionalism.

Spanos's critique of transnational American studies scholars was necessitated by his conviction that their fascination with the globalized world order blinded them to the emergence of the interregnum and rendered them deaf to the vocation of the exilic consciousness. Spanos designed his critique to awaken the exilic consciousness that lies dormant within transnational American studies scholars so that we might join him, as this foreword has, in bearing witness to the critical imperatives of the interregnum.

Preface

Call me Ishmael.

—Herman Melville, *Moby-Dick*

I

This book had its immediate origins in President Barack Obama's fulfill-ment of President George W. Bush's promise to the American people in the wake of September 11, 2001, that he would "track down" Osama bin Laden and "get him" in the end. The ensuing "search-and-destroy" mis-sion reminded me in an uncannily precise way of what has been a guid-ing ontological directive of my criticism of the Western onto-theological tradition from virtually the beginning of my career. I am referring to the Kierkegaardian/Heideggerian notion that anxiety or dread (*Angst*), unlike fear (*Furcht*), has no *thing*, which is to say, nothing (*das Nichts*) as its object, and its corollary, that the West, from its origins, has defined itself as that global space that has had as its fundamental vocation the objec-tification of this nothing to render it comprehendible (take-holdable, manageable):

> In anxiety, we say, "one feels ill at ease [*es ist einem unheimlich*]." What is "it" that makes "one" feel ill at ease? We cannot say what it is before which one feels ill at ease. As a whole it is so for one. All things and we ourselves sink into indif-ference, this, however, not in the sense of mere disappearance. Rather, in this very receding things turn toward us. The receding of beings as a whole that

closes in on us in anxiety oppresses us. We can get no hold on things. In the slipping away of beings only this "no hold on things" comes over us and remains. Anxiety reveals the nothing.[1]

This contemporary American search-and-destroy mission also reminded me of what I take to be the enabling moment of Herman Melville's fiction, the moment when, with the American exceptionalist ethos in mind, Ishmael informs the reader of the origin of the name—Moby Dick—that Captain Ahab gave to the white whale:

> All that most maddens and torments; all that stirs up the lees of things; all truth with malice in it; all that cracks the sinews and cakes the brain; all the subtle demonisms of life and thought; all evil, to crazy Ahab, *were visibly personified, and made practically assailable in Moby Dick.* He piled upon the white whale's hump the sum of all the general rage and hate felt by his whole race from Adam down; and then, as if his chest had been a mortar, he burst his hot heart's shell upon it.[2]

The more general origin of this book, intimately related to the immediate one, was my uneasiness about the tendency of recent New Americanist studies to overdetermine the global perspective at the expense of the local in its effort to place America in the present destabilized planetary occasion. As I observed in the Preface of my last book, *Shock and Awe: American Exceptionalism and the Imperatives of the Spectacle in Mark Twain's "A Connecticut Yankee in King Arthur's Court"*:

> [I]n attempting to demonstrate that American culture is not historically exceptional or, to put it alternatively, is multicultural and geographically diverse, unstable, and fraught with tensions—this revisionary critical initiative has tended to efface the *reality* that the fiction of American exceptionalism became in the process of American history by way of the power of what I will call, with Antonio Gramsci and Louis Althusser in mind, interpellation. It is, therefore, imperative, at least, for the foreseeable future (that is, as long as the waning concept of the nation-state survives), that American studies address the local (national) / global (transnational) opposition not as an ontological binary, as it now tends to be, but as an indissoluble dialectical relation. It is, indeed, true that America is plural in its origins, that the exceptionalist national identity it has claimed for itself is myth. And these origins should not be minimized. But it is equally true that *this myth had become reality in the sense that it has contributed fundamentally and enormously to the making of (an unjust) historical reality on an increasingly global scale.*[3]

This book is essentially a sequel to that Twain book and three of my previous works in American studies: *American Exceptionalism in the Age of Globalization: The Specter of Vietnam* (2008); *Herman Melville and the American Calling: The Fiction after "Moby-Dick," 1851–1858* (2008); and *The Exceptionalist State and the State of Exception: Herman Melville's "Billy Budd, Sailor"* (2011), all of which were intended to trace the origins of the American exceptionalist ethos—a way of life, a vocation (in the Puritan sense of the word)—that surfaced as an ideology at the liminal point of the development of its exceptional logic—that is, in the wake of September 11, 2001, and the United States' brutal, spectacle-oriented global War on Terror and the tacit normalization of the state of exception in the name of homeland security. Unlike its predecessors, however, which were devoted to studies of heretical literary texts of the American past that were proleptic of the disclosures of post–9/11 American globalization, this study addresses the complex polyvalent role American exceptionalism continues to play in the world in the present post–9/11 occasion. I mean the in-between time I call the "interregnum" to underscore, against the tendency of the New Americanist studies to overdetermine the global (world literature), the indissoluble relationship of the local and the global, the national and the transnational, that constitutes the historical reality of the time in which we precariously live.

2

The chapters of this book can be read independently of each other, since they treat semi-autonomous topics—the reduction of the sublime (the nothingness of being) to spectacle (a simulacrum that robs the spectator of speech) in behalf of America's "errand in the [world's] wilderness"; the universal adoption of the exceptionalist ethos by the Americana political class in the wake of 9/11, when the term emerged as an ideological concept from its invisible hegemonic status; the tendency of recent New Americanist studies to overdetermine the global at the expense of the local; a critical genealogy of the contemporary discourse on the American calling; and an interview concerning the American debate world and the making of the American political class. But because the deeper purpose of the individual chapters is to tease out the complex, polyvalent ideological implications of the term "American exceptionalism" in the face of the prevailing simplistic meaning that posits the United States as superior to the nations of the rest of the world, "the nation of nations," I have organized the many facets of language pertaining to the exceptionalist ethos to incrementally accumulate this polyvalent ideological resonance around the idea of the "America calling" or "vocation," which is the topic of the last summary chapter. Thus, I think, reading the chapters consecutively would be preferable.

Chapter 1, "The Nothingness of Being and the Spectacle: The American Sublime Revisited," as the subtitle suggests, constitutes a genealogy of the highly prized American sublime that locates its origins in the *exceptionalist* logic of the American exceptionalist ethos—that is to say, in the reduction of the wonder-provoking sublime to the spectacle in Guy Debord's sense of the word—the enchanting simulacrum that strikes the spectator dumb (robs him/her of speech and thus of a polity)—and the harnessing of its inordinate power to the American exceptionalist imperial "errand in the [world's] wilderness." Beginning with a survey of the canonical American literature (prose and poetry) and painting from the Puritan era to the present post–9/11 occasion that spectacularizes (nationalizes) the sublime in the name of the American errand, this genealogy then goes on to epitomize the cultural history of the American sublime by way of an extended comparative analysis of representative works of two "quintessential American writers": Herman Melville's *Moby-Dick* and *Pierre* and Mark Twain's *A Connecticut Yankee in King Arthur's Court*, which address the question of American exceptionalism in the light of its relation to the sublime and its simulacrum, the spectacle. This comparative reading shows that, in deliberately distinguishing between the sublime and the spectacle, Melville's texts were proleptic not only of Twain's later canonical appropriation of the spectacle (his signature narrative strategy of staging for effect), whose origins extend back through the conquest of the Wild West to the Puritans' extermination of the Pequots, but also of the post–9/11 America's exceptionalist "errand [in the contemporary world's] wilderness."

Chapter 2, "American Exceptionalism in the Post–9/11 Era: The Myth and the Reality," demonstrates the pervasiveness of the reality of the myth of American exceptionalism in the discourse of the contemporary American political class (Republican and Democrat) even after the fall of the Bush administration. Undertaking close readings of speeches delivered at the Republican and Democratic presidential conventions of 2012 by prominent members of both parties (Republican Senators John McCain and Marco Rubio and Democratic Senator John Kerry and President

Barack Obama), this chapter shows not only the solidarity within the political class to its commitment to the American exceptionalist ethos but also its incredible obliviousness to its violent dark side, exposed by President George W. Bush in the aftermath of 9/11 and recorded and theorized by the growing counter-mnemonic scholarship of the New Americanists.

Chapter 3, " 'The Center Will Not Hold': The Widening Gyre of the New, New Americanist Studies," undertakes a symptomatic critique of the tendency of recent New Americanist studies (under the influence of proponents of world literature [*Weltliteratur*]) to overdetermine the global at the expense of the local, the planetary over the national. It shows that this transnationalizing tendency overlooks the stark realities of the contemporary post–9/11 occasion: that we live in an interregnum, an unstable in-between time characterized by the dying (but not yet death) of the nation-state and a new, alternative world struggling to be born. As a consequence of this disabling oversight, this new New Americanist initiative not only deflects attention from the urgent task of avowing the mythic status of American exceptionalism—and the violence that it has always disavowed; in minimizing the Puritan and the frontier theses about the origins of the American national identity, it also suggests, erroneously, that America has always been pluralistic, multicultural, hybrid—that is, not exceptionalist.

Chapter 4, "American Exceptionalism and the Calling: A Genealogy of the Vocational Ethic," constitutes a genealogy of American exceptionalism that finds its source in the Puritan concept of the "calling." I mean specifically the election by God that not only gave the Puritans their exceptionalist status but also rendered their vocation as a covenantal people unequivocally a matter of servitude to a higher cause. This genealogy is undertaken by way of the witnesses of three prominent continental theorists of modernity—Max Weber, Louis Althusser, and Giorgio Agamben—all of whom locate the origins of the spirit of democratic capitalism in the Protestant work ethic and of that minoritarian American counter-memory that is embodied in the Melvillean tradition, which includes Ralph Ellison, Thomas Pynchon, Robert Coover, William Gaddis, Donald Barthelme, Kathy Acker, Don DeLillo, and Toni Morrison. What this genealogy discloses is that the American exceptionalist calling (interpellation) produces subjected subjects whose vocation in life is undeviating service to a higher cause or *telos*: not only the postponement of the profane or existential time of the now, "*ho nyn kairos*," in Giorgio Agamben's radically subversive reading of St. Paul's calling (*klēsis*) by the

Messiah on the road to Damascus, but also the ruthless elimination of all those infidels who interfere in their redemptive errand in the world's wilderness. As such, the last chapter brings the particular topics concerning the exceptionalist ethos explored contrapuntally in the previous three chapters into its polyphonic orbit.

The last section of this book, "Appendix," consists of an interview with Christopher Spurlock, a member of the American college debate world, who, in opposition to its disinterested framework, asked me to speak to this issue on behalf of the multitude of high school and college students who enter the debate circuit without any awareness of the mind-numbing consequences of the protocols of this traditional framework. My main point in this interview is to show that the disinterested framework of the institutionalized debate world is, in fact, ideological, that it reproduces what throughout this book I call "the American political class," a class that makes its decisions on the basis not of the actual radically uneven conditions of modern American life, but according to the naturalized supernatural imperatives of the American vocation.

Acknowledgments

I have no language capable of adequately expressing my gratitude to my colleague Susan Strehle, not only for easing my disabled life in countless yet always special ways but also for helping me to clarify and enrich, in the process of listening to, my inchoate insights on the American calling in the process of writing this book. I also want to thank my incredible son, Adam, with all my heart for encouragement when my spirits were flagging and, not least, for being, as always, my archive. I am also grateful to my graduate students, Guy Risko, Bob Wilson, Shawn Jasinski, and Mahmoud Zidan for kindnesses above and beyond the call of duty, not to say for all the conversations about American literature that deepened my thinking about the unexceptionalism of American exceptionalism.

I dedicate this book to my *boundary 2* colleagues Paul Bové, Dan O'Hara, and Don Pease. Whatever our disagreements about the intellectual life in the United States over the many remarkable years of our close and always intense relationship, they were always there in the last instance to encourage my unerring errancy.

What's up, Ramal, I'm an American boy, a father, two children, graduate of Whitman High, where I was a member of the Science Club and Student Council, then I got to be the youngest elected officer ever in history of my town's Rotary chapter. I'm in charge of fund-raising, which hasn't been easy the past few years, what with the economy and all, but we're hanging in there. I hope you won't take this the wrong way, because I don't want to assault your sensibilities, or anything like that, but want to be up front with you because I believe that honesty is the best policy. So, I'm going to put a pointed plastic hood on your black and blue head and then I'm going to stand your caped body on a milk box, with live wires taped to your outstretched hands, and then I'm going to count to ten, you, witch-like Arab freak, and maybe I'll flip the switch and maybe not, it all kind of depends. By the time you get to MI, you'll be softened up, and you'll tell us where the terrorists are.

—Kent Johnson, "Lyric Poetry after Auschwitz, or: 'Get the Hood Back On'"

CHAPTER I

The Nothingness of Being and the Spectacle

The American Sublime Revisited

Unlimited power is the ideal thing when it is in safe hands.

—Hank Morgan, in Mark Twain, *A Connecticut Yankee in King Arthur's Court*

At the end of my first week in-country I met an information officer in the headquarters of the 25th Division at Cu Chi who showed me on his map and then from his chopper what they'd done to the Ho Bo Woods, the vanished Ho Bo Woods, taken off by giant Rome plows and chemicals and long, slow fire, wasting hundreds of acres of cultivated plantations and wild forest alike, "denying the enemy valuable resources and cover."

It had been part of his job for nearly a year now to tell people about that operation: correspondents, touring congressmen, movie stars, corporation presidents, staff officers from half the armies in the world, and he still couldn't get over it. It seemed to keep him young, his enthusiasm made you feel that even the letters he wrote home to his wife were full of it, it really showed what you could do if you had the know-how and the hardware. And if in the months following that operation incidents of enemy activity in the larger area of War Zone C had increased "significantly," and American losses had doubled and then doubled again, none of it was happening in any damned Ho Bo Woods, you'd better believe it.

—Michael Herr, *Dispatches*

I

The concept of the American sublime emerged in the late 1980s and early 1990s by way of the retrieval of the sublime by Continental theorists of postmodernity, mainly deconstructionist and Lacanian psychoanalytic critics pursuing the revolutionary implications of the linguistic turn in the face of the discovery of the undecidability of language. These new Americanists, that is, thought the emergence of the sublime from the prevailing textual perspective that Edward Said, in his paradigm-changing essay "Reflections on American 'Left' Literary Criticism,"[1] condemned as "unworldly." Despite their productive departure from the myth and symbol school that, in inaugurating American studies in the United States, had harnessed the American sublime to the Cold War against the Soviet Union, they by and large, as a result of their indifference to the "worldliness" of the text, saw no connection between the sublime and the American sociopolitical sphere—particularly its perennial self-representation as "redeemer nation" that was eventually to be articulated as the American exceptionalist ethos. This relatively large archive on the American sublime focused primarily on American lyric poetry, not the more worldly novel, and therefore overdetermined the textual/psychoanalytic site at the expense of the equally important sociopolitical sites on the continuum of being. This is borne witness to by the predominance of Harold Bloom's Freudian version of the sublime, which internalized the ontological sublime in the subject,[2] and its deconstructive affiliate, which, in asserting with Jacques Derrida that *"Il n'y a pas de hors-texte"*—there is nothing outside the text—rendered the nothing a universal rhetorical phenomenon.[3]

Since that time, the destabilizing postmodern global conditions that precipitated the retrieval of the sublime and enabled its rethinking have been greatly exacerbated, particularly in the wake of America's inauguration of its War on Terror following the bombing of "the American Homeland" on September 11, 2001. For the liminal extremity—"shock and awe" tactics—of that global initiative not only revealed the always disavowed violence of America's errand in the world's wilderness—that is, disclosed the ideological status of America's hegemonic self-representation as exceptional, but in doing so also brought to fulfillment its perennial use of the spectacle, *that social phenomenon so similar in appearance yet so radically different from the sublimity of being as such.* Given this triumph of the spectacle (and its confusing resemblance to the sublime) in postmodernity, particularly in an America self-righteously and unerringly bent on Americanizing the planet (by means of "preemptive wars" and "regime change") in the name of its redemptive exceptionalism—a triumph way beyond that imagined by Guy Debord when, in the 1960s, he called his contemporary capitalized occasion "The Society of the Spectacle"[4]—it becomes an urgent task of American criticism to revisit the American sublime. The following chapter constitutes a prolegomenal gesture in behalf of that urgent task.

2

Despite identifying the sublime with the political entity called America, the Americanists of the late 1980s and early 1990s generally seem indifferent to the worldly implications of the sublime—that it is both onto-logical—a representation of the continuum of being, from being as such, through the self, to its cultural, social, and political sites—and a psycho-logical affect. Unlike theirs, therefore, the point of departure of my revisitation of the American sublime will not be Longinus (who, I suggest, on the analogy of the Romans' reduction of the Greek *a-lethéia* [truth as unconcealment] to *veritas* [the adequation of mind and things] reduced his unknown Greek predecessor's ontological account of the sublime [*Peri Hupsous*] to a [contradictory] system of rules for the composition of "sublime" literature); nor will it be Edmund Burke and Immanuel Kant, whose versions of the sublime, along with Joseph Addison and Anthony Ashley-Cooper (third Earl of Shaftesbury), enabled the *self*-aggrandizing British "Romantic sublime";[5] nor Sigmund Freud, whose psychological "uncanny," through the mediation of Harold Bloom, the new Americanists harnessed to the American sublime at the expense of its polyvalent "worldly" implications. Rather, my point of departure will be Martin Heidegger's postmodern (or post*structural*) ontological destruction (*Destruktion*) of the Western philosophical ("onto-theo-logical") tradition, the exceptionalist tradition, that is, that, "in thinking the unnamable be-*ing* of being *meta-ta-physica* (from above or beyond the things themselves: panoptically), has had as its perennial purpose the spatialization or reification of its *unpresentable* temporal dynamics—that is, the reduction of its anxiety (or dread)-provoking incomprehensible essence to comprehensible form (from the Latin *com* and *prehendere*, "to take hold of," "grasp with the mind").[6] More specifically, I mean the exceptionalist Western metaphysical tradition that culminates in modernity with the apotheosis of man, the *Anthropologos*, and his empirical scientific mode of knowledge production, which has willfully reduced the temporality of being to total "world picture,"[7] and, in thus bringing the spatializing logic of anthropo-logical thinking to is fulfillment (liminal point), has self-de-structed: disclosed the radical temporality—that is, the sublime—what Heidegger had the courage to call the *nothing* (*das Nichts*)—that is ontologically prior to Being.

Heidegger inaugurated his de-struction of anthropological knowledge production and retrieval (*Wiederholung*) of the radical temporality of being/the nothing /the sublime in *Being and Time*, particularly in his repeated distinction between anxiety (*Angst*) and fear (*Furcht*). But, I suggest, it is in the widely known but still to be fathomed essay "What Is Metaphysics?" that the "worldly" implications of this destruction and retrieval begin to manifest themselves. In this post–*Being and Time* essay, Heidegger begins by showing how obsessively the modern, anthropological West has been committed to the nullification of the nothingness of being by way of reducing "it" to something take-holdable, which is to say, how insistently the specter of the nothing continues to haunt modern Western man's reductive objectifying effort:

> Man—one being among others—pursues science [modern knowledge production]. In this "pursuit" nothing less transpires than the irruption by one being called "man" into the whole of beings, indeed in such a way that in and through this irruption beings break open and show what they are and how they are. The irruption that breaks open in its way helps beings above all to themselves.
>
> This trinity—relation to the world, attitude, and irruption—in its radical unity brings a luminous simplicity and aptness of Dasein to scientific existence. If we are to take explicit possession of the Dasein illuminated in this way for ourselves, then we must say:
>
> That to which the relation to the world refers are beings themselves—and nothing besides.
>
> That from which every attitude takes its guidance are beings themselves—and nothing further.
>
> That with which the scientific confrontation in the irruption occurs are beings themselves—and beyond that nothing.
>
> But what is remarkable is that, precisely in the way scientific man secures to himself what is most properly his, he speaks of something different. What should be examined are beings only, and besides that—nothing; beings alone, and further—nothing; solely beings, and beyond that—nothing.
>
> What about this nothing? Is it an accident that we talk this way so automatically? Is it only a manner of speaking—and nothing besides?[8]

Indeed, this obsessive effort to annul (the "play" of) the nothing that haunts Western knowledge production (the "truth") assumes, for Heidegger, the telling proportions of monomania (paranoia):

However, what trouble do we take concerning this nothing? The nothing is rejected precisely by science, given up as a nullity. But when we give up the nothing in such a way do we not concede it? Can we, however, speak of concession when we concede nothing? But perhaps our confused talk already degenerates into an empty squabble over words. Against it science must now reassert its seriousness and soberness of mind, insisting that it is concerned solely with beings. The nothing—what else can it be for science but an outrage and a phantasm? If science is right, then only one thing is sure: science wishes to know nothing of the nothing. Ultimately this is the scientifically rigorous conception of the nothing. We know it, the nothing, in that we wish to know nothing about it. (WM, 95–96)

What is it about the nothing (or the sublime) that, according to Heidegger, precipitates this kind of monomaniacal will on the part of the modern scientific mind to nullify "it"? Here, Heidegger, taking his directives from the anti-Hegelianism of Søren Kierkegaard,[9] introduces his phenomenological account of the difference between anxiety or dread (*Angst*) and fear (*Furcht*). Fear is an emotion triggered by a threatening but *determinate object*. Anxiety, on the other hand, has no (determinate) thing as its object: "Anxiety is indeed anxiety in the face of . . . , but not in the face of this or that thing. Anxiety in the face . . . is always anxiety for . . . , but not for this or that. The indeterminateness of that in the face of which and for which we become anxious is no mere lack of determination but rather *the essential impossibility of determining it*" (WM, 100). Anxiety, that is, has the nothingness of being (*das Nichts*) as its object. In putting humanity's primordial relation to the indeterminateness of the be-ing of being in this way, Heidegger underscores its primordial thrownness (*Geworfenheit*)—its not-at-homeness in the world (*Unheimlichkeit*): the uncanniness that is the consequence of this thrownness. In so doing, he is also underscoring what previous versions of the sublime, whether Longinus's, Burke's, Kant's, or Bloom's and the early New Americanists', shrink back from: humanity's radically secular ontological condition, its total untethering of its fate from any form of transcendental higher cause, whether God or History.

Seen in the counter-light of this phenomenological retrieval of the nothing/sublime, it becomes manifest that modern knowledge production has had as its fundamental—and monomaniacally willful—purpose the *objectification* of the indeterminateness of the nothingness of being— the (play of) the sublime—to render "it" comprehendible (take-holdable: manageable). But precisely because of its monomaniacal (liminal) will to power over the nothing/sublime—its paranoid "wish to know nothing of the nothing"—modern knowledge production has disclosed the nothing/sublime—and the ontological reality of humanity's *infinite finitude.*

> In anxiety, we say, "one feels ill at ease" [*es ist einem unheimlich*]. What is "it" that makes "one" feel ill at ease? We cannot say what it is before which one feels ill at ease. As a whole it is so for one. All things and we ourselves sink into indifference. This, however, not in the sense of mere disappearance. Rather, in this very receding things turn toward us. The receding of beings as a whole that closes in on us in anxiety oppresses us. We can get no hold on things. In the slipping away of beings only this "no hold on things" comes over us and remains.
>
> Anxiety reveals the nothing. (WM, 101)

This disclosure of the sublime nothing is not, however, an espousal of nihilism. On the contrary, it is an opening of its anxiety-provoking decentered indeterminacy—its disconcerting play—for positive thought, which the Western tradition has compulsively denied "it." It is true, as Heidegger notes, that anxiety, instigated by the awesomeness of the sublime nothing, "robs us of speech" (WM, 101). This, however, should not be taken literally. Rather, it should be understood as an imperative to rethink the metaphysical idea of language that has dominated the West since the Romans' reduction of the creative errancy of the Greek *a-lethéia* to the reductive unerring *adequaetio intellectus et rei* (the adequation of mind and thing: correctness): the idea of language that has had as its purpose the annulment of the nothing and the sublime by reducing its dislocating play to a take-holdable and manipulable—and consumable—it. I mean, for example, the language of naming intrinsic to the bourgeois fathers of Bouville that Jean-Paul Sartre, taking his directives from Heidegger, destroys in his great novel *Nausea* in his effort to think a language that is adequate to the imperatives of the nothingness of existence. I am referring, of course, to the scene in the novel in which Roquentin, Sartre's postmodern antitype of the enabling paradigmatic Old Testament image of Adam who, endowed with God's *logos*, names and domesticates the beasts, sitting in the "*jardin public*" of Bouville before a chestnut tree, undergoes a visitation of the nothingness of being:

> Oh, how can I put it in words [the sudden transformation of the roots of the chestnut into an oozing motion]? Absurd: in relation to the stones, the tufts of yellow grass, the dry mud, the tree, the sky, the green benches. Absurd, irreducible; nothing—not even a profound, secret upheaval of nature—could explain it. Evidently I did not know everything, I had not seen the seeds sprout, nor the

tree grow. But faced with this great wrinkled paw, neither ignorance nor knowledge was important: the world of explanations and reason is not the world of
existence. A circle is not absurd, it is clearly explained by the rotation of a
straight segment around one of its extremities. But neither does a circle exist.
This root, on the other hand, existed in such a way that I could not explain it.
Knotty, inert, nameless, it fascinated me, filled my eyes, brought me back
unceasingly to its own existence. In vain to repeat: "This is a root"—it didn't
work anymore. I saw clearly that you could not pass from its function as a root,
as a breathing pump, *to that*, to this hard and compact skin of a sea lion, to this
oily, callous, headstrong look. The function explained nothing: it allowed you to
understand generally that it was a root, but not *that one* at all. This root, with its
color, shape, its congealed movement, was . . . below all explanation. Each of its
qualities escaped it a little, flowed out of it, half solidified, almost became a
thing; each one was *in the way* in the root and the whole stump now gave me the
impression of unwinding itself a little, denying its existence to lose itself in a
frenzied excess.[10]

Following Heidegger's directives, in short, we are enabled to say that the
nothingness of the sublime is an ontological condition that instigates, not
a passive contemplation or awe, but, as the early Greeks put it, an active
wonder, the alienated (*ek-sistent*) faculty of the human that, in humility
before its immensity, mobility, and variety asks questions about being
rather than, as in the Western tradition, imposes answers on its ontological indeterminacy.

This retrieved sublime is, thus, both the abyssal ontological difference
that, unlike its subordinated status in the Western onto-theological tradition, is in reality prior to a sovereign transcendental or imminent identity
(or principle of presence) and the destabilized psychological condition that
is its dislocating imperative: that is, the anxious or dreadful but also pleasurable sense of possibility as such. In Giorgio Agamben's radicalized
version of Heidegger's destruction of the onto-theological tradition, the
sublime, however dreadful, is the liberating affect of the infinite finitude
of being that precipitates in humans not silence—the bereavement of language—but a wonder-ful speech that renders the binarist language of the
Western tradition—the reifying language that would annul the sublime
nothing—inoperative. And it achieves this affect by identifying the prior
universal identity of the metaphysical tradition (the truth) as a fiction or a
construction (a re-presentation) that, in the name of the prior ontological
difference, can be reconstructed when it no longer corresponds to historical reality. The speech intrinsic to the sublime, that is, is a decentered

speech in which, like that of the Greeks according to Heidegger, "thought and being are the same thing" (Parmenides: "*To gar auto noein estin te kai einai*").[11] As such, it frees potentiality—the question—from its traditional subordination to the act (the answer). And, in so doing, it renders dialogic speech the fundamental condition of human being-in-the-world the *sine qua non* of a polity.

3

Whereas the sublime is an ontological condition of liberation from the Word, the spectacle, which resembles the sublime in its precipitation of awe in the spectator, is, in fact, an insidious apparatus of capture. It had its ontological origins in the West's inaugural metaphysical will to "*re-present*" the anxiety- provoking temporal phenomena of being from after or above them—panoptically, or, to put it alternatively, to substitute the sign for what it signified, the copy (simulacrum) for the original, or, more precisely, the spatial image for the dynamic and open-ended reality of being and its fulfillment in the modern (anthropological) era in which the temporality of being has been *totally* spatialized (re-presented): what Heidegger, anticipating Guy Debord, has appropriately called the mind-numbing or speech-negating "age of the world picture." Responding to the question "What is a world picture?," Heidegger writes:

> With the world picture we think first of all of a copy of something. Accordingly, the world picture would be a painting, so to speak, of what is as a whole. But "world picture" means more than this. We mean by it the world itself, the world as such, what is in its entirety, just as it is normative and binding for us. "Picture" here does not mean some imitation, but rather what sounds forth in the colloquial expression, "We get the picture" [literally, we are in the picture] concerning something. This means the matter stands before us exactly as it stands with it for us. "To get into the picture" [literally, to put oneself into the picture] with respect to something means to set up in this way. But a decisive determinant in the essence of the picture is still missing. "We get the picture" concerning something does not mean only that what is, is set before us, is represented to us, in general, but that what is stands before us—in all that belongs to it and all that stands together—*as a system*. "To get the picture" throbs with being acquainted with something, with being equipped and prepared for it. Where the world becomes picture, what is, in its entirety, is juxtaposed as that for which man is prepared and which, correspondingly, he therefore intends to bring before himself and have before himself, and consequently intends in a decisive sense to set in place before himself. Hence world

picture, when understood essentially, does not mean a picture of the world, the world conceived and grasped as picture. What is, in its entirety, is now taken in such a way that it first is in being and only in being *to the extent that it is set up by man, who represents and sets forth.* Wherever we have the world picture, an essential decision takes place regarding what is, in its entirety. *The Being [its temporality] of whatever is, is sought and found in the representedness of the latter.* (AWP, 129–30; my emphasis)

In "The Age of the World Picture," Heidegger overdetermines the sovereign power that man achieves over the being of being by re-presenting being as total image. He becomes a subject who, in objectifying/spatializing being, becomes its master. But this is a self-deception. For in objectifying being into world picture, he also objectifies himself, becomes, as Heidegger puts this epochal reduction in "The Question Concerning Technology," like the being he has mastered through the (spatializing) apparatus of enframing (*Ge-stell*), an object of mastery, *Bestand*: standing reserve, on call, which is to say, an entity that is disposable:

Yet when destining reigns in the mode of enframing, it is the supreme danger. This danger attests itself to us in two ways. As soon as what is unconcealed no longer concerns man even as object, but exclusively as standing reserve, and man in the midst of objectlessness is nothing but the orderer of the standing-reserve, then he comes to the brink of a precipitous fall; that is, he comes to the point where he himself will have to be taken as standing reserve. Meanwhile, man, precisely as the one so threatened, exalts himself and postures as lord of the earth. In this way the illusion comes to prevail that everything man encounters exists only insofar as it is his construct. . . . Man stands so decisively in subservience to the challenging-forth of enframing that he does not grasp enframing as a claim, that he fails to see himself, as the one spoken to, and hence also fails in every way to hear in what respect he ek-sists, in terms of his essence, in a realm where he is addressed, so that he *can never encounter himself.*[12]

Under the aegis of this apparatus of capture, human life is utterly bereaved of speech and a polity, or, in Giorgio Agamben's later biopolitical formulation of Heidegger's *Bestand*, ek-sistent/in-sistent man is reduced to bare life (*homo sacer*: life that can be killed without the killing being condemned as homicide).

Whereas Heidegger by and large overdetermines the first phase of the transformation of the sublime being into spectacle to be looked at and mastered by the panoptic gaze of man, Guy Debord, taking his directives from the Marxist interpretation of modernity as the late capitalist commodification—and quantification—of being (the fetishization of the commodity), emphasizes the second phase. Debord's Situationist analysis of the commodified "society of the spectacle" and its "Marxist" approach to warding off this apparatus of capture is too complex to be summarized in this limited space. Here I will restrict my remarks to a brief commentary on its fundamental ontological base in order to thematize the "political" aspect that is fundamental to his text, but not fully articulated (including its relation to the sublime), and that is pertinent to the question of American exceptionalism and the American sublime: the spectacle's reduction of the fully human being to a mere spectator.

The late capitalist commodification of being, according to Debord—and here he is at one with Heidegger—has its origins in the metaphysical West's privileging of the panoptic spatializing eye:

> The spectacle inherits all the *weaknesses* of the Western philosophical project which undertook to comprehend activity in terms of the categories of *seeing*; furthermore, it is based on the incessant spread of the precise technical rationality which grew out of this thought [in anthropological modernity]. The spectacle does not realize philosophy. It philosophizes reality. (SS, 19)

Under the aegis of this late capitalist commodification of being, humanity is radically separated from the reality—the be-*ing*—of being by way of the paradoxical *realization of re-presentation*—that is, by rendering the real a (visual) simulacrum and the simulacrum the real, thus reducing the human ability to act (*praxis*) to contemplation (*theoria:* seeing):

> The images detached from every aspect of life fuse in a common stream in which the unity of this life can no longer be reestablished. Reality considered *partially* unfolds, in its own general unity, as a pseudo-world *apart, an object of mere contemplation.* The specialization of images of the world is completed in the world of the autonomous image, where the liar has lied to himself. The spectacle in general, as the concrete inversion of life, is the autonomous movement of the non-living. (SS, 2; my emphasis)

In other words, the rendering real of the spectacle dehumanizes the human, or, more to the point, reduces the being who is capable of speech to pure spectator:

> The spectacle presents itself as something enormously positive, indisputable and inaccessible. It says nothing more than "that which appears is good, that which is good appears." The attitude which it demands in principle is *passive acceptance* which in fact it already obtained by its manner of appearance *without reply*, by its monopoly of appearance. (SS, 12; my emphasis)

Unlike the ontological sublime (Debord surprisingly does not mention it), which activates wonder in the human—the sense of potential and thus speech in the form of the anxious and pleasurable question—the spectacle is its simulacrum. It is, in short, a strategic apparatus of capture, enabled by *seeing* temporal reality from the end of the dominant modern capitalist/democratic order that, we might say, *calculatively stages the spectacle for effect*: to produce enchantment or to anticipate a shocking awe, which is to say, to strike the spectator dumb, to rob humans of language. And, in doing so, this bereavement of speech deprives humanity, if we recall Hannah Arendt's insistence on the indissoluble relation between speech and act,[13] of a polity: a space inhabited by everyone where the potentiality of speech prevails.

It is this "depotentiation of life," the bereavement of speech, and the deprivation of a polity that Giorgio Agamben thematizes in his increasingly intensive meditations on Guy Debord's critical analysis of the late democratic capitalist "society of the spectacle" from the vantage point of a half century later, when the spatializing logic of the age of the spectacle arrived at its liminal point. Returning to Debord's analysis of Marx's identification of the essence of capitalism with the "commodity fetish," Agamben invokes the spectacle of the Crystal Palace Exhibition of 1851 in London as the historical moment of the apotheosis (monumentalization) of late capitalism and the triumph of the age of the spectacle. This epochal event in the history of Western knowledge production, it should be remembered, was the imperial West's spectacular—awe-inspiring—image of its superiority and power—its exceptionalist status—over the other benighted regions of the world. "In the exposition catalogue," he writes, "Merrifield wrote that the Crystal Palace 'is perhaps the only building in the world in which the atmosphere is perceivable . . . by a spectator situated either at the west or east extremity of the gallery . . . where the most distant parts of the building appear wrapped in a lighter blue halo.' The first great triumph of the commodity thus takes place under the sign of both transparency and phantasmagoria.'"[14] To underscore the transparent and phantasmagoric—extreme or exceptional—essence of this symbolic/monumental architecture and its appeal to the dependent, purely spectatorial eye of commodity capitalism, Agamben adds, "Furthermore, the guide to the Paris Universal Exposition of 1867 reinstates this contradictory spectacular character: *'Il faut au [public] une conception grandiose qui frappe son imagination . . . il veut contempler un coup d'oeil; féerique et non pas des produits similaires et uniformement groupés'"* [The public needs a grandiose conception that strikes its imagination . . . it wants to behold a wondrous prospect rather than similar and uniformly arranged products] (MN, 74.5).

This impression of the Crystal Palace, Agamben adds, is probably what Marx had in mind "when he wrote the chapter of *Capital* on commodity fetishism. It is certainly not a coincidence that the chapter occupies a liminal position. The disclosure of the commodity's secret was the key that revealed capital's enchanted realm to our thought—a secret that capital always tried to hide by exposing it in full view" (MN, 74.5). Thus, against the Marxists of the 1960s, who, like Althusser, dismissed Marx's analysis of the commodity fetish as a "flagrant" and "extremely harmful" trace of Hegelian philosophy," he writes:

> It is for this reason that Debord's gesture appears all the more remarkable, as he bases his analysis of the society of the spectacle—that is, of capitalism that has reached its extreme figure—precisely on that "flagrant trace." The "becoming-image" of capital is nothing more than the commodity's last metamorphosis, in which exchange value has completely eclipsed use value and can now achieve the status of absolute and irresponsible sovereign over life in its entirety, after having falsified the entire social production. In this sense, the Crystal Palace in Hyde Park, where the commodity unveiled and exhibited it as mystery for the first time, is prophetic of the spectacle, or, rather, the nightmare, in which the nineteenth century dreamed the twentieth. The first duty the Situationists assigned themselves was to wake up from this nightmare. (MN, 75.5)

Despite Debord's overdetermination of the spectacle, the rhetoric he by and large uses to characterize its effects—"contemplation," "passive acceptance," "negation of action"—obscures the spectacle's apotheosis of the visual—and its resulting annulment of human speech. It is this foregrounding of the visual and its negation of language that constitute Agamben's significant contribution to the urgent task of waking up from the nightmare of the spectacle that Debord assigned his fellow Situationists in the 1960s. For, in doing so, he gave the spectacle the inordinate importance it commands in the age of globalization, particularly in the aftermath of September 11, 2001, when that staging for effect it called "shock and awe" became the United States' principle apparatus of capture:

> How can thought collect Debord's inheritance today, the age of the complete triumph of the spectacle? It is evident, after all, that the spectacle is language, the very communicativity and linguistic being of humans. This means that an

integrated Marxian analysis should take into consideration the fact that capitalism (or whatever name we might want to give to the process dominating world history today) is not only aimed at the expropriating of productive activity, but also, and above all, at the alienation of language itself, of the linguistic and communicative nature of human beings, of the *logos*, in which Heraclitus identifies the Common. The extreme form of the expropriation of the Common is the spectacle, in other words, the politics in which we live. (MN, 81.2)

In short, the spectacle, in its extreme avatar (unlike the sublime), strikes us dumb, robs us of speech and thus of a polity of the common.

But this dire modern condition of the human species is, for Agamben, not necessarily the end of the matter. For, in fulfilling its spatializing logic, in arriving at its liminal point, the age of the spectacle (not unlike the age of the world picture, which discloses the nothing for positive thought), self-de-structs: discloses the very language, the "communicative nature of human beings," that it must efface to triumph:

But this [extreme form of the spectacle] also means that what we encounter in the spectacle is our very linguistic nature inverted. For this reason (precisely because what is being expropriated is the possibility itself of a common good), the spectacle's violence is so destructive; but, for the same reason, the spectacle still contains something like a positive possibility—and it is our task to use this possibility against it. (MN, 81.2)

Understood in the context of this end point, it is not difficult to read Agamben's rethinking of Debord's analysis of the society of the spectacle in the 1990s as remarkably proleptic not only of the contemporary global occasion but also, despite the absence of reference to "America," of the United States' ferocious response to al Qaeda's attacks on the American homeland. I mean specifically the liminal occasion bearing witness to the United States' unleashing of its spectacular global War on Terror in the name of its exceptionalist and redemptive errand in the world's wilderness, a "preemptive war" that employs the spectacular—shock-and-awe—tactics intended to achieve "regime change" and the reduction of "rogue states" to ventriloquized (American-style) democracies—which is to say, an unending war on an unidentifiable enemy that has not only normalized the spectacular state of exception in the name of "homeland security," but also, analogous to Agamben's final opening gesture, the consequent disclosure—for positive thought—of the violence of the speech-robbing spectacular discourse American exceptionalism has always disavowed.[15]

4

What I want to argue in the following in taking my directives from Agamben's radicalized Heideggerian reading of Debord is not simply that the so-called American sublime, in almost all its historical literary and artistic manifestations, is not, as earlier Americanists claimed, an expression of the sublime but, rather, of the spectacular. More basically, but indissolubly related, I also want to propose that this spectacular simulacrum of the sublime *is intrinsic to the American national identity*, which is to say, to the "exceptional" logic—its proneness to excess—of the American exceptionalist ethos. To put it provisionally and all too summarily, the dominant— "chosen"—culture in the United States—from the inaugural "errand in the [New World] wilderness" of the founding Puritans (God's "chosen people"); through the era of westward expansion, which secularized the Puritans' Word and its providential history as "Manifest Destiny"; to the Vietnam War and post–9/11 age, which has borne witness to America's extension of its divine- or History-ordained "errand in the wilderness" to include the wilderness of the world at large—has re-presented the awesome immensity, the vastness, the majesty, the mystery of the world's wilderness in terms of a twofold ideological strategy directed inwardly toward the covenantal community and outwardly toward its threatening enemy. On the one hand, it has represented (staged) the anxiety-provoking awesomeness of the wilderness as a spectacular threat to the security of the covenantal people that is intended to rejuvenate its youthful energies and to remobilize its unity in the face of the recidivism—the backsliding and the disintegration of the unifying sovereign *logos*—intrinsic to the civilizing process. This is the national ritual, brilliantly foregrounded by Sacvan Bercovitch as the American jeremiad, inaugurated by the founding Puritans, that the dominant culture perennially stages (as spectacle) particularly at times of national crisis (threats to homeland security), and, above all, when the people's commitment to the nation's errand shows signs of flagging.[16] On the other hand, the dominant exceptionalist culture has represented this appalling vastness and mystery of the wilderness as an extraordinarily efficient means of gaining power over its alleged enemy Other. It has characterized the wilderness as the evidence of its Other's civilizational inferiority—which, when confronted with the exceptionalist covenantal people's superior practical empirical knowledge of natural phenomena—the staging of their magical ability to turn its wilderness into disposable reserve, as it were— would strike these superstitious savages dumb: cow them into subservience to their higher cause. This exceptionalist strategy, not incidentally, was the apparatus of capture of the early explorers/colonizers of the New World epitomized by Hernando Cortés, who, as Tzvetan Todorov has forcefully observed in his magisterial *The Conquest of the Americas* (1984), invoked their modern high-tech weapons of destruction, enabled by their superior "Western" (empirical/scientific) knowledge of nature, to awe the benighted natives into awed submission:

> Throughout the campaign [in Mexico] Cortés shows preference for spectacular actions, being very conscious of their symbolic value. For example, it is essential to win the first battle against the Indians, to destroy their idols during the first challenge to the priests, in order to demonstrate his invulnerability, to triumph during a first encounter between his brigantines and the Indian canoes; to burn a certain palace located within the city in order to show how irresistible his advance is; to climb to the top of a temple so that he may be seen by all. . . .
>
> The very use Cortés makes of weapons is of a symbolic rather than a practical nature. A catapult is constructed which turns out not to work; no matter: "Even if it were to have had no other effect, which indeed it had not, the terror it caused was so great that he thought the enemy might surrender." At the very start of the expedition, *he organized veritable* son et lumières *[sound and light] spectacles with his horses and cannons* (which then served for no other purpose); his concern for staging is remarkable. He conceals a mare at a certain point, then brings in his Indian guests and a stallion; the latter's noisy manifestations terrify these persons, who have never seen a horse. Selecting a moment of relative calm, Cortés has the nearby cannons fired. He has not invented such stratagems, but he is doubtless the first to employ them systematically.[17]

Indeed, the phrase "American sublime," coined by the early New Americanists, is itself a telling contradiction of terms, particularly if the identifying nationalizing adjective "American" is understood, as it should be, as a synonym for exceptionalism, since it does what the sublime in its essence resists: it names (nationalizes) and thus domesticates its anxiety-provoking ineffability, renders "it" an apparatus of capture, a voice-numbing spectacle.

I cannot, in this limited space, authoritatively demonstrate the deeply structured and enabling persistence in the history of American cultural production of this strategic reduction of the sublime to a spectacular apparatus of capture. I will, instead, first, simply refer tentatively to a number of what I take to be relatively obvious and decisive, though largely overlooked (or misrepresented), examples in American art, music, prose, poetry, and fiction from this history of the representation of the

American sublime in the hope that other Americanist scholars, pursuing this urgent question, will expand and deepen this preliminary insight, and, then, for the sake of brevity, focus on two exemplary "American" novelists whose fictions, self-consciously "American," obsessively engage the question of the sublime. I am referring to Herman Melville, who, from the beginning to the end of his career, as I have shown elsewhere, committed his writing to the interrogation of the American exceptionalist ethos and calling,[18] and Mark Twain, the quintessential American writer, who, from the beginning to the end of his career, was the spokesperson of the American exceptionalist ethos and calling.[19]

The American sublime—the conversion of the ineffable sublime to the effable spectacle—has its origins in the founding Puritans' discourse about their divinely ordained comportment to the wilderness of the New World. Despite the awesomeness of its vastness and the indefiniteness of its form, they did not understand the unhoming anxiety it instigated as an ontological imperative to rethink their *logos*. On the contrary, as Sacvan Bercovitch has decisively shown, they harnessed this anxiety in the face of the sublime wilderness to the task of rejuvenating the endless at-homing process:

> The American Puritan jeremiad was the ritual of a culture on an errand— which is to say a culture based on a faith in process. Substituting teleology for hierarchy, it discarded the Old World ideal of stasis for a New World vision of the future. Its function was to create a climate of anxiety that helped release the restless "progressivist" energies required for the success of the venture. The European jeremiad also thrived on anxiety, of course. Like all traditionalist forms of ritual, it uses fear and trembling to teach acceptance of fixed social norms. But the American Puritan jeremiad went much further. *It made anxiety its end as well as its means. Crisis was the social norm it sought to inculcate.* The future, though divinely assured, was never quite there, and New England's Jeremiahs set out to provide the sense of insecurity that would ensure the outcome. Denouncing or affirming, the vision fed on the distance between promise and fact.[20]

Armed with the unerring Word, like the Adam of Genesis who names and domesticates the wild beasts—which is to say, assumes an absolute total order behind the appearance of an immense and anxiety-provoking, chaos—the spokespersons of God's chosen people, the American Adam, *re*-presented the New World wilderness in their sermons and justificatory tracts: separated human beings from the be-*ing* of being by way of reducing them to spectators of a dazzling and enrapturing (captivating) total image—that is to say, as I have noted, their sermons, prose, and poetry, despite the proscriptive commitment to the "plain style," ritualized and staged the sublime, spatialized its unnamability into awesome spectacle that, on the one hand, guaranteed the perpetual unity and youthful energies of the covenantal people, and on the other, enabled the Word-wielding American Adam to assert his sovereign power over the savage denizens of the New World wilderness.[21]

This dual-phased worldly intent of the American sublime inaugurated by the Puritans—the sublime informed by the (American exceptionalist) Word—is manifest in some degree or other in the various arts, religious and secular, both early and late, that the myth and symbol school of Americanists canonized as representative of the American exceptionalist national identity in the Cold War era.[22] A few obvious examples from the multitude of works that combine the two phases of this art of the spectacle, besides the numerous Puritan sermons (as well as other prose and poetry) that have their source in John Winthrop's jeremiad on board the *Arabella*, "A Model of Christian Charity" (1630) or Mary Rowlandson's *The Sovereignty and Goodness of God* (1682) (often entitled *A True History of the Captivity and Restoration of Mrs. Mary Rowlandson*), are the following, which span the history of American cultural production from the eighteenth to twenty-first century: the Leatherstocking novels of James Fenimore Cooper, particularly *The Pioneers* (1823), which inaugurates the secularized theme of the rejuvenating frontier (Templeton and the Western wilderness beyond its border) and the "doomed Indian" (Chingach-gook);[23] the poetry of Timothy Dwight (*The Conquest of Canäan*, 1785) and Joel Barlow (*Colombiad*, 1807); the histories of colonial America of George Bancroft (*History of the United States* [1854–77]; Francis Parkman, particularly *The Conspiracy of Pontiac* (1851); Frederick Jackson Turner ("The Significance of the Frontier in American History" (1893); and Samuel P. Huntington, *Who Are We?: Challenges to the American National Identity* (2004), all of which are, in structure and content, American jeremiads calling for a rejuvenating frontier or enemy;[24] the journalism of John O'Sullivan ("The Great Nation of Futurity" [1839]); John Filson's biography of Daniel Boone in *The Discovery, Settlement and Present State of Kentucke* (1784); the paintings of George Caleb Bingham ("Daniel Boone Escorting Settlers through the Cumberland Gap" [1852] and "Washington Crossing the Delaware" [1856]); John Gast ("American Progress or Manifest Destiny" [1872]);[25] and Thomas Cole, which celebrate the immensity, grandeur, and primordiality of the American landscape in

the early and mid-nineteenth-century period while often pointing spectacularly to the diminished and doomed natives or the degenerating consequences of overcivilization.[26]

Though in the history of the American sublime in American exceptionalist cultural production, one phase of this dual function of the
spectacle is often emphasized over the other, this overdetermination,
given its motivating source in the American exceptionalist ethos, necessarily alludes—contrapuntally as it were—to its other. Examples of the
first, the overdetermining of rejuvenation (by violence), include the prose
of Ralph Waldo Emerson; the poetry of William Cullen Bryant and
Walt Whitman ("Brooklyn Bridge"); and the paintings of the Hudson
River Valley School (Albert Bierstadt, Thomas Cole, Frederic Edwin
Church, John Frederick Kensett, and Asher Brown Durand, among
others),[27] who often portray the American wilderness, whether of New
York or the American West, from the awed perspective of the American
Adam. Examples of the second, which overdetermine the spectaculariza-
tion of the sublime to achieve power over the native inhabitants, include
Thomas Jefferson's *Notes on the State of Virginia* (1785) and his letters on
Indian removal; Benjamin Franklin's *Autobiography* (1868), William
Gilmore Simms's novels, particularly *The Yemassee* (1835), and Robert
Montgomery Bird's *Nick of the Woods or The Jibbernainosay: A Tale of
Kentucky* (1837).

5

This entire cultural history of the American sublime, which bears witness
to the domestication of the sublime—its appropriation by the dominant
culture for ideological use, specifically, to facilitate the American "empire
of liberty,"[28] by way of reducing its wonder-provoking ineffability into
awe-inspiring spectacle—is synecdochically epitomized by the radical
difference between the marginalized or normalized anti-exceptionalist
fiction of Herman Melville, beginning with *Moby-Dick*, which radically
calls into question the American penchant, inaugurated by the "chosen"
Puritans, to stage the sublime as spectacle in behalf of imperial aggran-
dizement, and the insistently American exceptionalist fiction of Mark
Twain, particularly *A Connecticut Yankee in King Arthur's Court*, whose
narrative signature, as many Americanist commentators have noted,
without, however, attending to its resonant ideological function, is precisely that of staging for effect, indeed, one might say, on the basis of the

troubled history of the reception of Melville's fiction in the United States, that its unerring errancy—its courageous acknowledgment of the narrative imperatives of the ineffable sublime—is precisely that which has spectrally haunted the spectacular exceptionalist linguistic, plastic, and musical arts of the American canonical tradition.[29] I mean, specifically, the American vernacular tradition that Mark Twain, attuned to the hyperbolic narrative imperatives of the expansive and expanding "Wild West," brought to its fulfillment (and demise) at the end of the nineteenth century in fulfilling the spectacle-oriented logic of the American exceptional ethos.

It is no exaggeration to say that in his fiction, from *Moby-Dick* on, Melville's supreme theme is the interrogation of the democratic American exceptionalist ethos inaugurated by the Puritans and, above all, of the spectacular staging of the sublime that constituted the cultural imperative of the exceptionalism of their exceptionalist logic. It is no accident, for example, that in *Moby-Dick*, Ishmael, Melville's questing narrator, introduces the protagonist Captain Ahab long after his errant retrospective story has begun, thus hinting at the possibility that the dour and mysterious captain of the Pequod (the American ship of state) is orchestrating his sudden appearance on the quarterdeck to produce an awe-striking effect on the motley crew of "meanest mariners, renegades, and castaways"[30]—a symbolic cross section of the plurality of American society—one that, "before its tremendous centralization," would galvanize them into performing an unforeseen task in his behalf. Ishmael, in fact, despite his deep attraction to Ahab, intuits this strategic possibility—that the exceptionalism of this quintessential American man requires such a spectacular staging—at the very outset of his encounter with him:

> Nor, perhaps, will it fail to be eventually perceived, that behind those forms and uses [the ritual of command of the whale vessel], as it were, he sometimes masked himself; incidentally making use of them for other and more private ends than they were legitimately intended to subserve. That certain sultanism of his brain, which had otherwise in a good degree remained unmanifested; through those forms that same sultanism became incarnate in an irresistible dictatorship. For be a man's intellectual superiority what it will, it can never assume the practical, available supremacy over other men without the aid of some sort of external arts and entrenchments, always, in themselves, more or less paltry and base. That it is, that forever keeps God's true princes of the Empire from the world's hustings; and leaves the highest honors that this air can give, to those men who become famous more through their infinite inferiority to the

choice hidden handful of the Divine Inert, than through their undoubted superiority over the dead level of the mass. Such large virtue lurks in these small things when extreme political superstition invest them, that in some royal instances even to idiot imbecility they have imparted potency. But when, as in the case of Nicholas the Czar, the ringed crown of geographical empire circles an imperial brain; then, the plebeian herds crouch abased before the tremendous centralization. Nor, will the tragic dramatist who would depict mortal indomitableness in its fullest sweep and direst swing, ever forget a hint, incidentally so important in his art, as the one alluded to. (M-D, 148)

This reduction of the sublime to a spectacular apparatus of capture is graphically exemplified immediately following Ishmael's intuition in the scene—one of the greatest in American literature—of the oath-taking on the quarterdeck of the Pequod. To convey the immense—and disconcerting—power of this spectacular concerting moment would require quoting the chapter in its entirety. For every detail of Ahab's staging process—the cumulative ritual repetitions, the spatial arrangement (high/low, center/periphery), the timing that incrementally recalls the primal scene (the reaping of Ahab's leg by the white whale), the antiphonal call and response, the symbolization of the objects such as the gold doubloon and the harpoon chalices, the glorification of the powerless, the harnessing of the sun itself, and even the detail that registers doubt (Starbuck's resistance)—is orchestrated by Ahab to produce the awe-inspired galvanizing effect—the enthusiastic collective assent—he preconceives. For brevity, however, I will simply quote the conclusion in which he accomplishes this "tremendous centralization" that strikes the crew dumb and thus diverts a whaling voyage in behalf of the Nantucket market into a monomaniacal fiery pursuit of an objectified being in the name of humanity:

And now, ye mates [Flask, Stubbs, and Starbuck] I do appoint ye three cup-bearers to my three pagan kinsmen there,—yon three most honorable gentlemen and noblemen, my valiant harpooneers [Dagoo, Tashtego, and Queequeg]. Disdain the tasks? What, when the great Pope washes the feet of beggars, using his tiara for ewer? Oh, my sweet cardinals! Your own condescension, *that* shall bend ye to it. I do not order ye; ye will it. Cut your seizings and draw the poles, ye harpooneers!"

Silently obeying the order, the three harpooneers now stood with the detached iron part of their harpoons, some three feet long, held, barbs upright, before him.

"Stage me not with that keen steel! Cant them over! Know ye not the goblet end? Turn up the socket! So, so; now ye cup bearers, advance. The irons! Take them; hold them while I fill!" Forthwith, slowly going from one officer to the other, he brimmed the harpoon sockets with the fiery waters from the pewter.

"Now, three to three, ye stand. Commend the murderous chalices! Bestow them, ye who are now made parties to this indissoluble league. Ha! Starbuck! But the deed is done! Yon ratifying sun now waits to sit upon it. Drink, ye are harpooneers! Drink and swear, ye men that man the deathful whaleboat's bow—Death to Moby Dick! God hunt us all, if we do not hunt Moby Dick to his death!" The long, barbed steel goblets were lifted; and to cries and maledictions against the white whale, the spirits were simultaneously quaffed down with a hiss. Starbuck paled, and turned, and shivered. Once more, and finally, the replenished pewter went the rounds among the frantic crew; when, waving his free hand to them, they all dispersed; and Ahab retired within his cabin. (M-D, 166)

That Melville's intent in this quarterdeck scene is, indeed, to highlight Captain Ahab's staging of a spectacle that would bereave his spectator crew of their speech is underscored a few pages later, at the beginning of Ishmael's retrospective account of the naming of the white whale, when a sobered and now reflective Ishmael recalls the primal scene of persuasion to which he had borne rapt witness:

I, Ishmael, was one of that crew; my shouts had gone up with the rest; my oath had been welded with theirs; and stronger I shouted, and more did I hammer and clinch my oath, because of the dread in my soul. A wild, mystical, sympathetic feeling was in me; Ahab's quenchless feud seemed mine. With greedy ears I learned the history of that murderous monster against whom I and all the others had taken our oath of violence and revenge. (M-D, 179)

In this immediate aftermath of the electrical spectacle that robs him and his fellow shipmates of their speech, Ishmael begins the agonizing process of disaffiliating himself from his beloved American captain. Though, as he confesses, "My shouts had gone up with the rest," the liminality of the awesome scene—its histrionic excess—stirs ambiguities in him that instigate his return to the origins of Captain Ahab's furious desire for vengeance against the white whale—that is, for the answer to the troubling paradox that the epitome of the exceptionalist American democratic man becomes a "sultanic" totalitarian—and his gaze, a "tremendous centralization." This incremental disaffiliation from Ahab's democratic "sultanism," which is to say, from the captain's fiery exceptionalist pursuit of the white whale in the name of redeeming mankind, begins to unfold in the form of Ishmael's compelled retrieval and rethinking of that inaugural event in the distant past when Captain Ahab *names* the white whale "Moby Dick."

His three boats stove around him, and oars and men both whirling in the eddies; one captain, seizing the line-knife from his broken prow, had dashed at the whale, as an Arkansas duelist at his foe, blindly seeking with a six inch blade to reach the fathom-deep life of the whale. That captain was Ahab. And then it was, that suddenly sweeping his sickle-shaped lower jaw beneath him, Moby Dick had reaped away Ahab's leg, as a mower a blade of grass in the field. (M-D, 184)

At this point in his retrieval of that evental moment,[31] Ishmael begins, however tentatively, to distance himself from Captain Ahab, sensing not only the dark—the paranoid—side of his sovereign's fiery pursuit of the white whale (this "concentering" [M-D, 185] is enacted in the cumulatively expressive repetition of the word "all") and its symbolic significance for the idea of exceptionalist America (the analogy with America's racial and religious inferiors), but also intimating an *alternative* understanding of the inscrutable whiteness of the whale. I requote (in expanded form) the passage cited in my Preface to underscore the decisive importance of Melville's inaugural identification of Ahab's exceptionalist understanding of the truth of being with an apocalyptic violence-producing monomania for my reading of American exceptionalism in this chapter and in the rest of this book:

> No turbaned Turk, no hired Venetian or Malay, could have smote him with more seeming malice. Small reason was there to doubt, then, that ever since that almost fatal encounter, Ahab had cherished a wild vindictiveness against the whale, all the more fell for that in his frantic morbidness he at last came to identify with him, not only all his bodily woes, but all his intellectual and spiritual exasperations. The White Whale swam as the monomaniac incarnation of all those malicious agencies which some deep men feel eating in them, till they are left living on with half a heart and half a lung. That intangible malignity which has been from the beginning; to whose dominion even the modern Christians ascribe one-half of the worlds; which the ancient Ophites of the east reverenced in their statue devil;—Ahab did not fall down and worship it like them; but pitted himself, all mutilated, against it. All that most maddens and torments; all that stirs up the lees of things; all truth with malice in it; all that cracks the sinews and cakes the brain; all the subtle demonisms of life and thought; all evil, to crazy Ahab, *were visibly personified, and made practically assailable in Moby Dick*. He piled upon the whale's white hump the sum of all the general rage and hate felt by his whole race from Adam down; and then, as if his chest had been a mortar, he burst his hot heart's shell upon it.[32] (M-D, 184; my emphasis)

It is at this liminal point of the logic of Ahab's American exceptionalist ethos, when Ishmael recognizes *naming* (personifying, identifying, objectifying the unnamable and unpresentable) to be an apparatus of capture—a means of rendering the dread-provoking dynamics of being "practically assailable," that his redemptive errand self-de-structs: discloses the violence it always disavows, and thus compels Ishmael to rethink his American calling—his vocational servitude—to his exceptionalist American captain:

> What the white whale was to Ahab has been hinted; what, at times, he was to me, as yet remains unsaid.
>
> Aside from those more obvious considerations touching Moby Dick, which could not but occasionally awaken in any man's soul some alarm, there was another thought, or rather vague, nameless horror concerning him, which at times by its intensity completely overpowered all the rest; and yet so mystical and well nigh ineffable was it, that I almost despair of putting it in a comprehensible form. It was the whiteness of the whale that above all things appalled me. But how can I hope to explain myself here; *and yet, in some dim random way, explain myself I must, else all these chapters might be naught.* (M-D, 188; my emphasis)

Ishmael, it is true, does not at this moment disassociate himself entirely from Ahab's monomaniacally vengeful quest. In fact, he ends the chapter that struggles to convey the dreadful sublimity of the whiteness of the whale by way of piling one suggestive but inadequate example on top of another with the question to the reader: "Wonder ye then at the fiery hunt?" However, given his stark juxtaposition of the chapter that names the whale with that which attempts hopelessly to articulate its wondrously terrifying unnamability, it is impossible not to read this reference to the *Pequod*'s "fiery pursuit" as an ironic ambiguity that at the liminal moment of the voyage will disclose to Ishmael the insanity and abominable violence of such an unerring pursuit undertaken in the "concentering" exceptionalist name (the *logos*) of American man and the redemption of mankind.

That disclosive liminal moment—that "event"—occurs in the appropriately entitled "Epilogue," after Ishmael's account of the white whale's attack on the (now, we realize, appropriately named) American ship of state; the consequent death of Captain Ahab, who, to the last, "spit[s] my last breath at thee" (M-D, 572); and the perishing of the entire crew of "isolatoes." There and then Ishmael, tacitly explaining his (biblical) name,[33] tells his appalled reader that he alone "survived the wreck": "On the second day [after having been saved by Queequeg's coffin], a sail drew near, nearer, and picked me up. It was the devious-cruising Rachel, that in her retracing search after her missing children, only found another orphan" (M-D, 573). In this epilogue, that is to say, Ishmael undergoes a "resurrection," or, more accurately, a "de-struction" or "decentering." He does not rise from the sublime abyss of death as the same person he was before the event, but as one alienated from his American exceptionalist homeland—and from the exceptionalist language, the language that names the ineffable sublime be-*ing* of being in order to render it "practically assailable." This orphaned Ishmael rising from the abyss, in short, is the "errant" ("epi-logic") Ishmael who, having learned that the American exceptionalist *logos* becomes an annihilating monomania at this liminal point of its mono-logic, has been telling the errant story of Ahab's exceptionalist fiery pursuit of the white whale.

Ishmael, apparently, does not attempt to articulate the positive possibilities concerning language that his agonizing incremental acknowledgment of the ineffable sublime discloses—that is, his alienation from the American exceptionalist homeland. But this absence of overt reference is only apparent. For, I submit, it is forcefully enacted in the very revolutionary (postmodern) "errancy" of his narrative or, rather, analogous to his name, of the nomadic narrative incumbent on his acknowledgment of the "appalling" (dread-provoking) whiteness of primordial being, in Melville's language, the "diving," the immersion in the destructive element. I mean ultimately that interrogative / explorative linguistic openness that, unlike the unerring closed narratives of the American exceptionalist tradition that, as the narrator of *Pierre* puts them, constitute "false inverted attempts at systematizing eternally unsystemizable elements,"[34] exists to engage the reader in radical democratic dialogue about the unnamable sublimity of finite being. Indeed, if we are attuned to Edward Said's liberating commitment to contrapuntal reading, we might say, without exaggerating, that at play in Ishmael's catastrophic liminal narrative about the fate of the American ship of state under the aegis of its exceptionalist captain is another, antithetical narrative—the potential one that the overdetermined narrative must suppress to enact itself—in which the Pequod, the American ship of state, constitutes an alternative polity to those of both the Nantucket owners and its captain: a polity of the commons—of "isolatoes," the "meanest mariners, and castaways, and renegades" (M-D, 117). It is no accident that it was a black man, incarcerated on Ellis Island during the Cold War in the process of being deported by the U.S. government, who, long ago, saw this contrapuntal narrative at play in Ishmael's dark story. I mean, of course, C. L. R. James, the author of *Mariners, Renegades, and Castaways: The Story of Herman Melville and the World We Live In* (1953).[35]

The sublime (and the critique of the American sublime) was not a passing concern to Melville but an intense and abiding one in all his fiction following *Moby-Dick*, including *Billy Budd*, where he famously extols "fact" over "fable," "ragged edges" over the Orphic "symmetry of form"— that is, the sublime over the beautiful.[36] For the purposes of this general chapter on the sublime and spectacle in American literature and art, however, it will suffice to comment briefly on his other (controversial) counter-mnemonic masterpiece, the appropriately entitled *Pierre; Or the Ambiguities*, the offenses against the American exceptionalist ethos which compelled the custodians of the American cultural memory to "freeze him into silence."[37] I mean Melville's proleptic Nietzschean narrative about another Ishmael, a young American, that is, who is "orphaned"—exiled and estranged—from his hitherto rocklike American exceptionalist homeland (Saddle Meadows: post-revolutionary America), when he suddenly discovers that its "sublime" truth, symbolized by the portrait of his apotheosized father, is a monumentalized lie—or, to anticipate, a dumbfounding spectacle. I am referring, of course, to Pierre Glendinning's "extraordinary emergency," when the young American discovers that his monumentalized father has sired an illegitimate daughter and thus realizes that his doting mother—"formed chiefly for the gilded prosperities of life"—will not be able to acknowledge this decentering disclosure that the world of Saddle Meadows is, in fact, nothing but a simulacrum—a spectacle—of what it is represented to be:

> Thus with Pierre. In the joyous young times, ere his great grief came upon him, all the objects which surrounded him were concealingly deceptive. Not only was the long-cherished image of his father now transfigured before him from a green foliaged tree into a blasted trunk, but every other image in his mind attested the universality of that electrical light which had darted into his soul. Not even his lovely, immaculate mother remained entirely untouched, unaltered by the shock. . . . She well might have stood all ordinary tests; but when Pierre thought of the touchstone of his immense strait applied to her spirit, he felt profoundly assured that she would crumble into nothing before it.
>
> She was a noble creature, but formed chiefly for the gilded prosperities of life, and hitherto mostly used to its unruffled serenities; bred and expanded, in all developments, under the sole influence of hereditary forms and world-usages. Not his refined, courtly, loving, equable mother, Pierre felt, could unreservedly,

and like a heaven's heroine, meet the shock of his extraordinary emergency, and applaud, to his heart's echo, a sublime resolve, whose execution should call down the astonishment and the jeers of the world. . . . Then he staggered back upon his self, and only found support in himself. Then Pierre felt that deep in him lurked a divine unidentifiableness, that owned no earthly kith or kin. Yet was this feeling entire lonesome, and orphan-like. Fain, then for one moment, would he have recalled the thousand sweet illusions of Life; tho' purchased at the price of Life's Truth; so that once more he might not feel himself driven out an infant Ishmael into the desert, with no maternal Hagar to accompany and comfort him. (P, 89)

But Pierre's "extraordinary emergency," however life-damaging, is not entirely negative. As the noun suggests, especially if the first syllable is understood as a prefix, it also points, however darkly, like Ishmael's resurrecting immersion in the destructive element, to the possibility of liberation from a prior metaphysical (panoptic) interpretation of being and the debilitating social collectivity that it had produced. As in the case of Ishmael, Pierre's extraordinary emergency manifests itself at first dimly as an intuition of the dread-provoking sublime that is beyond a human's grasp: the disclosure of the "appalling" nothingness that lies in the "whiteness"—at the absent center—of being and the human self produced by the spectacular monumentalized American exceptionalist world of Saddle Meadows. Echoing Ishmael's account of the whiteness of the whale, the narrator, pointing to what the "enthusiastic [American] youth" intuits but cannot quite perceive, writes:

> But, as to the resolute traveler in Switzerland, the Alps do never in one wide and comprehensive sweep, instantaneously reveal their full awfulness or amplitude—their overawing extent of peak crowded on peak, and spur sloping on spur, and chain jammed behind chain, and all their wonderful battalionings of might; so hath heaven wisely ordained, that on first entering into the Switzerland of his soul, man shall not at once perceive its tremendous immensity, lest illy prepared for such an encounter, his spirit should sink and perish in the lowermost snows. Only by judicious degrees, appointed of God, does man come at last to gain his Mont Blanc and take an overtopping view of the Alps; *and even then, the tithe is not shown; and far over the invisible Atlantic, the Rocky Mountains and the Andes are yet unbeheld. Appalling is the soul of a man!* (P, 284; my emphasis)

This is not the self-aggrandizing sublime of the English Romantics and of the Americans, writers like Ralph Waldo Emerson and Walt Whitman or painters like Thomas Cole, who appropriated its awesome immensity for their nationalist—American exceptionalist—purposes. It is, rather, like

Ishmael's, the *Self*-diminishing, dread-provoking sublime—the unpresentable nothingness of being—that, as, it will be recalled, Heidegger observed, modern knowledge production will obsessively have nothing to do with, that is to say, that haunts modernity's spectacular onto-sociopolitical edifice and demands to be thought positively. This diminution of (American exceptionalist) man—and Pierre's inability at this stage to register its philosophical, social, and political significance—that is, its implications for language—is underscored by the narrator in what immediately follows, this time, however, in the pointedly resonant terms of the pervasive metaphor of the novel that refers to the American nation and its national identity: the monument—that is, the inaugural image of the prevaricating act that reduces the ineffable sublime to a simulacrum of itself, to a spectacle intended to strike the spectator dumb—to reduce him/her to silence.[38] The implicit parallel the narrator draws between the Old World and the New should not be overlooked:

> But not now to consider these ulterior things, Pierre, though strangely and very newly alive to many before unregarded wonders in the general world; still, had he not as yet procured for himself that enchanter's wand of the soul, which but touching the humblest experiences in one's life, straightway it starts up all eyes, in everyone of which are endless significancies. . . . Ten million things were as yet uncovered to Pierre. The old mummy lies buried in cloth on cloth; it takes time to unwrap this Egyptian king. Yet now, forsooth, because Pierre began to see through the first superficiality of the world, he fondly weens he has come to the unlayered substance. But, far as any geologist has yet gone down into the world, it is found to consist of nothing but surface stratified on surface. To its axis, the world being nothing but superinduced superficies. By vast pains we mine into the pyramid; by horrible gropings we come to the central room; with joy we espy the sarcophagus; but we lift the lid—and no body is there—appallingly vacant as vast is the soul of a man. (P, 285)

This appalling decentering of Pierre, so reminiscent of Ishmael's troubled account of the dreadful whiteness of the whale, is, of course, far from suggesting the inauguration of an alternative language to that of Saddle Meadows. But insofar as Pierre's ontological crisis ("e-mergency") and exile disclose the falseness—and the accompanying violence, the will to power—of the naming/monumentalizing function of the exceptionalist language of Saddle Meadows, it does pointedly suggest the possibility of a language that acknowledges rather than violates the irreparable imperatives of the unspeakable sublime—the nothingness of being. This possibility is underscored later in the novel when, on his way into exile from Saddle Meadows, Pierre finds the pamphlet, written by one Plotinus Plinlimmon, entitled "Chronologicals & Horologicals," which instigates a return to his intuition of the sublime—the "appalling" vast vacancy of man's soul. Here, in a manner that interprets his immediate Saddle Meadows past contrapuntally—from the perspective of the dreadful "ambiguities" precipitated by his extraordinary emergency (his exile from his homeland)—Pierre begins to call into question, indeed, in a remarkably proleptic gesture, to de-structure the Western philosophical tradition. I mean the exceptionalist tradition, including its unexceptionalist exceptionalist American imitators, that has monomaniacally assumed that a *logos*—a "transcendental signified," or "principle of presence," in Jacques Derrida's terms—informs the contingency of being (thus reducing "it" to a realm of mere "appearance") and, in so doing, compels "it" to speak:

> Hereupon then [when Pierre is confronted with the opposition between a "true world" and a "world of lies"] in the soul of the enthusiast youth two armies come to the shock; and unless he prove recreant, or unless he prove gullible, or unless he can find the talismanic secret to reconcile this world with his own soul, then there is no peace for him, no slightest truce for him in this life. Now without doubt this Talismanic Secret has never yet been found; and in the nature of human things it seems as though it never can be. Certain philosophers have time and again pretended to have found it; but if they do not in the end discover their own delusion, other people soon discover it for themselves, and so those philosophers and their vain philosophies are let glide away into practical oblivion. Plato, and Spinoza, and Goethe, and many more belong to this guild of self-imposters, with a preposterous rabble of Muggletonian Scots and Yankees, whose vile brogue still the more bestreaks the stripedness of their Greek or German Neoplatonical originals. That profound Silence, that only Voice of our God, which I before spoke of; from that divine thing without a name, those imposter philosophers pretend somehow to have got an answer; which is as absurd, as though they should say they had got water of stone; for how can a man get a Voice out of Silence? (P, 208)

Pierre, of course, as the narrator pointedly intimates from the beginning, does not follow the anti-essentialist directives of his extraordinary emergency, as his vestigial allegiance to "the Voice of our God" (albeit an eternally silent one) in this passage suggests. Indeed, as the narrator asserts, he fatally misinterprets them. The "enthusiastic youth" reads his decentering as a Titanic imperative to "regospelize the world anew" (P, 273)—that is, to write a "comprehensive compact book" (P, 283), which, as the first adjective is intended to make clear, arrogantly—ironically, like the "preposterous rabble of Muggletonian Scots and Yankees" and their "Greek or German Neoplatonic originals" who would find the "Talismanic Secret"—substitutes one *logos* for another. And it is a decision that, in the end, leads Pierre's regospeling efforts to a devastatingly dead end. Before he has the opportunity to rethink his decision, the custodians of the exceptionalist Saddle Meadows ethos, like the enchanted crew of the Pequod who relentlessly pursue the white whale, hound him and his potential inchoate community to their violent deaths. But this terrible failure to adequately think the absence he intuits at the center of the exceptionalist American *polis* is by no means the end of Pierre's and his community of alien exiles' story. The possibility of this impossible "new beginning" is echoingly announced in the last sentences of the novel, uttered appropriately by his illegitimate sister, Isabel, who speaks them spectrally to his "triumphant" pursuers—and to the contemporary audience:

> "All's o'er, and ye know him not!" came gaping from the wall, and from the fingers of Isabel dropped an empty vial—as if it had been a run-out sandglass—and shivered upon the floor; and her whole form sloped sideway, and she fell upon Pierre's heart, and her long hair ran over him, and arbored him in ebon vines. (P, 362)

At this liminal point, Saddle Meadows, the spectacular discourse of American exceptionalism, silences Pierre and destroys his potential alternative community of preterites—the "passed over," in the binarist providential language of the Puritans to which Melville is referring. (I will return to the relationship between this resonant American Puritan term and its modern avatars later in this book, particularly in Chapter 4.) But, as Isabel's last words resonantly testify, his silence—the voice he had been trying to get out of the awful silence of being—will return to haunt the monumentalized Saddle Meadows' world's life-damaging certainties. In the uncannily appropriate language that Giorgio Agamben uses to bring Guy Debord's meditation on the modern "society of the spectacle" into the contemporary occasion, where the state of exception is the rule and life is threatened to become bare life,

> How can thought collect Debord's inheritance today, in the age of the complete triumph of the spectacle? It is evident, after all, that the spectacle is language, the very communicativity and linguistic being of the human. This means that an integrated Marxian analysis should take into consideration the fact that

capitalism (or whatever other name we might want to give to the process dominating world history today) not only aimed at the expropriation of productive
activity, but also, and above all, at the alienation of language itself, of the linguistic and communicative nature of human beings, of the *logos* in which Heraclitus identifies the Common. The extreme form of the expropriation of the
Common is the spectacle, in other words, the politics in which we live. But this
also means that what we encounter in the spectacle is our very linguistic nature
inverted. For this reason (precisely because what is being expropriated is the
possibility itself of a common good), the spectacle's violence is so destructive;
but, for the same reason, the spectacle still contains something like a positive
possibility—and it is our task to use this possibility against it.[39]

It is this "linguistic and communicative nature of the human" and the
"Common"—the phenomena of being that are available to everyone—
intrinsic to it, I submit, that Melville is proleptically attempting to retrieve
in *Moby-Dick* and *Pierre* (as well as in the other fiction after 1850) by way
of thinking the sublime—the nothingness of being—that the enclosing
progress of the spectacular logic of the American exceptionalist ethos (the
American sublime) discloses at its liminal point.

6

As I have observed, however, Melville's is a minority voice in the long
history of the representation of the American sublime. On the other
hand, his younger contemporary, Mark Twain (whose resonantly nationalist name Samuel Langhorne Clemens adopted for his writing), epitomizes the predominant American literary/artistic representation of the
sublime: that which transforms the unspeakable nothingness of being to
spectacle, which, in rendering the spectator speechless, harnesses its awesomeness to the imperial purposes of the American exceptionalist ethos.
From the beginning of his career as a reporter of the American experience, Twain, a Southwesterner with a strong memory of the origins of the
American Puritans' "errand in the wilderness" of the New World and
conscious of the recidivism of the modern American East—its becoming
a "Gilded Age," as he observes in the novel he wrote with Charles Dudley
Warner—extolled the exceptionalist virtues of the rejuvenating and mobi-
lizing Wild West. As he put this perennial American jeremiadic impulse
(it is intended to recall Daniel Boone's mythical rejuvenating flight from
[over]civilization) at the end of his quintessential American novel, *The
Adventures of Huckleberry Finn*, "But I reckon I got to light out for the

Territory ahead of the rest, because aunt Sally she's going to adopt me and sivilize me and I can't stand it. I been there before."[40]

Despite his highly touted criticism of American society, Twain's exceptionalism is evident in his writing until the last years of his life, when, it is alleged by recent commentators,[41] he became disillusioned in a democratic America taken over by the "robber barons" and become an imperial power in the Pacific. As I have argued elsewhere, however, this late critical turn was not radical; rather, it was, in the spirit of the perennial American jeremiad, a call for the recuperation of the American errand in the face of backsliding into Old World values.[42] Twain's exceptionalism is most explicitly—and offensively—manifest in his popular journalistic texts such as *The Innocents Abroad* (1869), in which, in the process of reporting a pilgrimage to the Holy Land, he pits the youthful and dynamically progressive New World against the decadent Old World (Europe and the Arab Middle East):

> The plows the people [Arabs of the Lebanon Valley] use are simply a sharpened stick, such as Abraham plowed with, and they still winnow their wheat as he did—they pile it on the housetop and then toss it by shovelfuls into the air until the wind has blown all the chaff away. They never invent anything, never learn anything.[43]

and *Roughing It* (1872), in which, in a manner not unlike Francis Parkman's rehearsal of the rejuvenating pioneer experience in his autobiographical *The Oregon Trail* (1847), Twain celebrates the invigorating rawness of the perennially youthful American West.

What, remarkably, has not been noticed by the legion of critics and commentators—from T. S. Eliot and Ernest Hemingway to Henry Nash Smith and the myth and symbol school of Americanists—who identified Twain (his undeviating commitment to the American vernacular) as the quintessential American novelist, is the indissoluble relationship between Twain's American exceptionalism and his nationalization of the unpresentable sublimity of being by reducing it to presentable spectacle (the American sublime). Much, of course, has been written about Twain's signature narrative strategy: his penchant to stage (and hyperbolize) a scene for dramatic effect. But this characteristic Twainian gesture has almost universally been read simply as a narrative device whose origin lies in the "tall tale" humor of the American West. I, on the other hand, am arguing that it is a hegemonic/ideological strategy that is as old as and fundamental to the founding of America. More specifically, I, following

Melville's de-structive and errant directives, am claiming that Twain's aesthetic technique of staging for effect is intrinsic to the founding *exceptionalist* logic of the American exceptionalist ethos and that its essential purpose, therefore, is to shock and awe—to bereave its subjects of speech, which is to say, to subject its human subjects to its higher cause, or, in the language of the Puritan calling, to entice them into willing servitude to its divinely (or historically) ordained "errand in [the world's] wilderness."

This perennial American hegemonic/ideological strategy is, in some significant degree, evident in such essential Twain novels as *The Adventures of Tom Sawyer* (1876), *The Prince and the Pauper* (1881), *Pudd'nhead Wilson* (1894), and, not least, of course, *The Adventures of Huckleberry Finn* (1885). But for the sake of brevity, I will restrict my commentary to a brief discussion of two related and determining scenes from *A Connecticut Yankee in King Arthur's Court* (1886), which, because they are liminal manifestations of Twain's penchant for staging the sublime, graphically disclose both the spectacle's indissoluble relation to the exceptional logic of American exceptionalism and the inordinate violence intrinsic to its errand. I am referring (1) to the famous—indeed, legendary—scene in which Hank Morgan, the modern Connecticut "Yankee of the Yankees,"[44] who wakes from a blow on the head in modern Hartford, Connecticut, into sixth-century England (528 A.D.), not only saves his life, but also, against the magic of Merlin, the magician, wins a commanding position in King Arthur's court by predicting the eclipse of the sun; and (2) the climactic Battle of the Sand Belt, in which, in the name of his errand in the medieval wilderness—to establish an American-style capitalist democracy in the feudal world—the Yankee, under siege by a recalcitrant English knight-errantry, unleashes his modern high-tech weapons of mass destruction (Gatling guns and electrical wiring) to exterminate his inhibiting enemy.

The indissoluble affiliation between the Connecticut Yankee's American exceptionalism and the staging of the spectacle—the reduction of the awe-inspiring sublime to practical (ideological) use—is manifestly evident in the first example by way of Morgan/Twain's meticulous staging of this inaugural scene of an eclipse of the sun that will obliterate the world in terms of a struggle between the modern Yankee and the medieval Merlin—that is, empirical/scientific knowledge against magic/superstition. That Twain is pointing to the exceptionalist ethos in this inaugural episode is made manifest by his invoking of its paradigmatic expression, identified by Tzvetan Todorov, in the strategy employed by the early Western colonizers of a "primitive' America, from the Spanish conquistadors and the English Puritans to the American pioneers, to cow the superstitious natives into submission:

> You see [the Yankee writes at the point when he is notified of his pending execution], it was the eclipse. It came into my mind, in the nick of time, how Columbus, or Cortez, or one of those people, played an eclipse as a saving trump once, on some savages, and I saw my chance. I would play it myself, now; and it wouldn't be any plagiarism, either, because I should get it in nearly a thousand years ahead of those parties. (CY, 29–30)

The exceptionalist "knows" the awesome mysterious operations of nature beforehand in a way that his native spectators cannot. This is not only because he is a product of the modern age, an enlightened age that is over a thousand years in advance of the benighted (superstitious) medieval world of King Arthur's England he finds himself in, but also because he is a modern—practical—American who, unlike his Old World counterparts, is endowed with the attributes of human progress: practical scientific and technological knowledge. Nothing in being, no matter how awesome, is ultimately mysterious to him (to his panoptic eye)—escapes his grasp, as it were—as it is to his superstitious adversaries. Thus his worldly perspective in the face of the recalcitrantly superstitious natives is fundamentally calculative, a matter of staging that empirical knowledge for dramatic effect.

Twain begins his meticulous orchestration of Morgan's playing this powerful "trump card" before the entire population of medieval Englishmen from the very beginning of his novel, when, in what appears to be a casual reference to the time of his protagonist's waking up in medieval England, he informs the reader that that year is 528 A.D. and that an eclipse of the sun "had occurred on the 21st of June, A.D. . . . and began at 3 minutes after 12 noon" (CY,17). And, after a number of suspense-producing delays (including a "discouraging" turn precipitated by Morgan's ventriloquized page, Clarence, that upset the timing of the eclipse) in which the struggle between the practical Yankee and the magician Merlin is intensified, it culminates in the advent of the "calamity" Morgan had predicted. I quote this passage, in which the Connecticut Yankee, like a deity (and Captain Ahab, not incidentally), orchestrates the transformation of the sublimity of the phenomena of nature to self-aggrandizing spectacle at some length to convey the essence of this moment of the triumph of his awesome and stunning exceptionalist scientific knowledge over Merlin's pedestrian magic: its silencing—indeed petrifaction—of the spectatorial mass—that is, its bereavement of the people's speech (the contrast of the bodily gestures of the monk and those of the Yankee should especially be noted):

> As the soldiers assisted me across the court the stillness was so profound that if I had been blindfolded I should have supposed I was in a solitude instead of walled in by four thousand people. There was not a movement perceptible in those masses of humanity; they were as rigid as stone images, and as pale; and dread sat upon every countenance. This hush continued while I was being chained to the stake; it still continued while the faggots were carefully and tediously piled about my ankles, my knees, my thighs, my body. Then there was a pause, and a deeper hush, if possible, and a man knelt down at my feet with a blazing torch; the multitude strained forward, gazing, and parting slightly from their seats without knowing it; the monk raised his hands above my head, and his eyes toward the blue sky, and began some words in Latin; in this attitude he droned on and on, a little while, and then stopped. I waited two or three moments: then looked up; he was standing there petrified. With a common impulse the multitude rose slowly up and stared up into the sky. I followed their eyes; as sure as guns, there was my eclipse beginning! The life went boiling through my veins; I was a new man! The rim of black spread slowly into the sun's disk, my heart beat higher and higher, and still the assemblage and the priest stared into the sky, motionless. I knew that this gaze would be turned upon me next. When it was, I was ready. I was in one of the most grand attitudes I ever struck, with my arm stretched up pointing to the sun. It was a noble effect. You could *see* the shudder sweep the mass like a wave. Two shouts rang out, one close upon the heels of the other:
> "Apply the torch!"
> "I forbid it!"
> The one was from Merlin, the other from the king. Merlin started from his place—to apply the torch himself, I judged. I said:
> "Stay where you are. If any man moves—even the king—before I give him leave, I will blast him with thunder, I will consume him with lighting!"
> The multitude sank meekly into their seats, and I was just expecting they would. Merlin hesitated a moment or two, and I was on pins and needles during that little while. Then he sat down, and I took a good breath; for I knew I was master of the situation now. The king said:
> "Be merciful, fair sir, and essay no further in this perilous matter, lest disaster follow. It was reported to us that your powers could not attain unto their full strength until the morrow; but—"
> "Your majesty thinks the report may have been a lie? It *was* a lie."

That made an immense effect; up went appealing hands everywhere, and the king was assailed with a storm of supplications that I might be bought off at any price; and the calamity stayed. The king was eager to comply. He said:

"Name any terms, reverend sir, even to the halving of my kingdom. But banish this calamity, spare the sun!"

My fortune was made. I would have taken him up in a minute, but I couldn't stop an eclipse; the thing was out of the question. So I asked time to consider. . . .

After further delay orchestrated to build further suspense, during which he gains the authority he demands of the king, the Yankee concludes:

It grew darker and darker and blacker and blacker. While I struggled with those awkward sixth-century clothes, it got to be pitch dark, at last, and the multitude groaned with horror to feel the cold uncanny night breeze fan through the place and see the stars come out and twinkle in the sky. At last the eclipse was total, and I was very glad of it, but everybody else was in misery, which was quite natural. I said:

"The king, by his silence, still stands to the terms." Then I lifted up my hands—stood just so a moment—then I said, with most awful solemnity: "Let the enchantment dissolve and pass harmless away!"

There was no response, for a moment, in that deep darkness and the grave-yard hush. But when the silver rim of the sun pushed itself out, a moment or two later, the assemblage broke loose with a vast shout and came pouring down like a deluge to smother me with blessing and gratitude; and Clarence was not the last of the wash, be sure. (CY, 35)

Thus, like Ahab, whose spectacularization of the sublime endows him with "sultanic" power over the crew of the Pequod, Hank Morgan's enables him to become "THE BOSS" (CY 40–44) of feudal England.

The second instance of Twain's strategic reduction of the sublime to spectacle is, in fact, a liminal manifestation of the spectacular logic driving the suspense-producing structure of the first. Its decisive disclosive threshold function, not incidentally,[45] is prefigured by the scene earlier in the novel (shortly after Morgan's staging of the eclipse) that narrates the highly advertised tournament pitting the Yankee against the formidable champion of British knight-errantry, Sir Sagramore le Desirous (but in fact is another epochal contest between his "enlightened" scientific/technological knowledge and Merlin's "dark age" magic). At the climactic moment of this spectacular episode, characteristically represented by Twain in the hyperbolic Western tall-tale tradition, the Connecticut Yankee, threatened by the formidable weaponry of his adversary, pulls out his hidden "magical"(virtually invisible), high-tech revolvers and shoots his adversary dead, the bullet that kills him remaining invisible to the spectators' eyes.[46]

It is this relay between the logic of American exceptionalism, the speech-numbing orchestrated spectacle, and the (pleasurable) violence, which is always disavowed as simply collateral damage or rightly deserved, that dramatically manifests itself at the climatic "Battle of the Sand Belt"—the liminal point of the Connecticut Yankee's redemptive errand, his effort to establish an American-style republic in medieval England. I again quote at length from the concluding pages of his narrative of the battle to convey the indissoluble nature of this relay—and its disclosive force:

> I sent a current through the third fence, now, and almost immediately through the four and fifth, so quickly were the gaps filled up. I believed the time was come, now, for my climax; I believed that that whole army was in our trap. Anyway, it was high time to find out. So I touched a button and set fifty electric suns aflame on the top of our precipice.
>
> Land, what a sight! We were enclosed in three walls of dead men! All the other fences were pretty nearly filled with the living, who were stealthily working their way forward through the wires. The sudden glare paralyzed this host, petrified them, you may say, with astonishment; there was just one instant for me to utilize their immobility in, and I didn't lose the chance. You see, in another instant they would have recovered their faculties, then they'd have burst into a cheer and made a rush, and my wires would have gone down before it; but that lost instant lost them their opportunity forever; while even that slight fragment of time was still unspent, I shot the current through all the fences and struck the whole host dead in their tracks! *There* was a groan you could *hear*! It voiced the death-pang of eleven thousand men. It swelled out on the night with awful pathos.
>
> A glance showed that the rest of the enemy—perhaps ten thousand strong— were between us and the encircling ditch, and pressing forward to the assault. Consequently we had them *all*! and had them past help. Time for the last act of the tragedy. I fired the three appointed revolver shots—which meant:
>
> "Turn on the water!"
>
> There was a sudden rush and roar, and in a minute the mountain brook was raging through the big ditch and creating a river a hundred feet wide and twenty-five deep.
>
> "Stand to your guns, men! Open fire!"
>
> The thirteen gatlings began to vomit death into the fated ten thousand. They halted, they stood their ground a moment against that withering deluge of fire,

then they broke, faced about and swept toward the ditch like chaff before a gale. A full fourth part of their force never reached the top of the lofty embankment; the three-fourths reached it and plunged over—to death by drowning.

Within ten short minutes after we had opened fire, armed resistance was totally annihilated, the campaign was ended, we fifty-four were masters of England! Twenty-five thousand men lay dead around us. (CY, 254–55)

Indeed, the relay between the Yankee's American exceptionalist ethos, his appropriation of the sublime as spectacle, and the horrific violence that manifests itself in this highly orchestrated climactic episode of the "Battle of the Sand Belt" could be put alternatively and without exaggeration in the following proleptic way: In order to fulfill his redemptive errand in the feudal English wilderness, the Connecticut Yankee is compelled by the very progressive—forwarding—logic of his exceptionalist ethos to normalize the state of exception, a gesture of his sovereignty that thus justifies a biopolitics—his earlier creation of "Man factories" to produce "freemen" (CY, 68)—preemptive war, and regime change. In the end, then, this "Yankee of the Yankees," unerringly pursuing the exceptionalist logic of his Yankee (nationalist) vocation in behalf of establishing a humane American-style republic in the England of the "Dark Ages," in fact produces its dehumanized antithesis. In the resonant current and appropriate language Giorgio Agamben uses not only to characterize the Nazis' concentration camp but also, with the United States especially in mind, the increasing biopolitics of the triumphant democratic capitalist states, the neoliberal Yankee reduces the human life he encounters in the Old World to *homo sacer* or "bare life" (*vida nuda*), *bios* to *zoé*, life that can be killed without its being called murder:

Along with the emergence of biopolitics [in the post–World War II era], we observe a displacement and gradual expansion beyond the limits of the decision on bare life, in the state of exception, in which sovereignty consisted. If there is a line in every modern state marking the point at which the decision on life becomes a decision on death, and biopolitics can turn into thanatopolitics, this line no longer appears today as a stable border dividing two clearly distinct zones. This line is now in motion and gradually moving into areas other than that of political life, areas in which the sovereign is entering into an ever more intimate symbiosis not only with the jurist but also with the doctor, the scientist, the expert, and the priest. . . . Certain events that are fundamental for the political history of modernity (such as the declaration of rights), as well as others that seem instead to represent an incomprehensible intrusion of bio-scientific principles into the political order (such as National Socialist eugenics and its elimination of "life that is unworthy of being lived," or the contemporary debate on normative determination of death criteria), acquire their true sense only if they are brought back to the common biopolitical (or thanatopolitical) context to which they belong. From this perspective, the camp as the pure, absolute, and impassable biopolitical space (insofar as it is founded solely on the state of exception)—will appear as the hidden paradigm of the political space of modernity, whose metamorphosis and disguise we will have to learn to recognize.[47]

It is this biopolitics produced in large part by the reduction of the sublime to the spectacle, I submit, so antithetical to the idea of being proffered by Melville's counter-mnemonic engagement with the ethos of American exceptionalism in texts like *Moby-Dick* and *Pierre* (among others), that Twain inadvertently espouses in rendering Hank Morgan—"the Yankee of the Yankees"—his sovereign exceptionalist spokesperson in *A Connecticut Yankee in King Arthur's Court*.

CODA

As my invocation of Giorgio Agamben's *Homo Sacer* suggests, the foregoing stark contrast between Herman Melville's and Mark Twain's interpretations of the filial relationship between the American exceptionalist ethos and the sublime is not simply an exercise in American literary historiography. Rather, it has been undertaken as a genealogy in Michel Foucault's Nietzschean sense of the word—that is, as "a history of [the American] present."[48] What is remarkable about the juxtaposition of these resonant Melville and Twain texts—and demanding of critical thought—is their uncannily precise prefiguration as early as the mid-nineteenth century of the essence of twenty-first century America. More specifically, each in his own way, Melville intentionally, Twain inadvertently, anticipates the globally oriented America of the era between the Vietnam War and the aftermath of September 11, 2001. They not only demonstrate the indissoluble relationship between American exceptionalism and the spectacle; they also, as we have seen, preenact its horrific consequences in the fraught global age in which we now precariously live. I am especially referring to the liminal America that, since the George W. Bush neoconservative administration's threshold declaration of the United States' unending War on Terror, has, like the captain of the Pequod and the Connecticut Yankee in their fictional contexts, harnessed the spectacle (the "shock and awe" apparatuses), the internationally illegal concept of "preemptive war," and the policy of "regime change" against what it unilaterally—which is to say, in a way that is reminiscent of the figure of the vigilante of the "Wild West"[49]—deems to be "rogue states" in the name of its redemptive errand in the world's wilderness. To put it alternatively—in a way that is anticipated by Ahab's spectacular sovereign announcement of his war against the white whale (in the name of all of humanity) that galvanizes the crew of the Pequod into an "unswerving"[50] "ship of state" in behalf of his fiery pursuit, and the Connecticut Yankee's spectacular proclamation transforming sixth-century England into a modern republic that mobilizes his band of ventriloquized British youth in behalf of his genocidal high-tech war against the evils of feudalism—I am referring to the Bush administration's sovereign decision, in the wake of 9/11, declaring the United States a national emergency ("homeland security") state that made the state of exception the rule or, in Agamben's terms, a state in which, in rendering the border between law and illegality indistinguishable, "everything is possible":

> Hannah Arendt once observed that in the camps, the principle that supports totalitarian rule and that common sense obstinately refuses to admit come fully to light: this is the principle according to which "everything is possible." Only because camps constitute a space of exception . . . —in which not only is law completely suspended but fact and law are completely confused—is everything in the camp truly possible. If this particular juridico-political structure of the camps—the task of which is precisely to create a stable exception—is not understood, the incredible things that happened there remain completely unintelligible. Whoever entered the camp moved in a zone of indistinction between outside and inside, exception and rule, licit and illicit, in which the very concepts of subjective right and juridical protection no longer made any sense. . . . Insofar as its inhabitants were stripped of every political status and wholly reduced to bare life, the camp was also the most absolute biopolitical space ever to have been realized, in which power confronts nothing but pure life, without any mediation. This is why the camp is the very paradigm of political space at the [liminal] point at which politics becomes biopolitical and *homo sacer* is virtually confused with citizen.

Addressing the self-righteousness of modern societies like the United States, which distinguish their "benign" democratic polities from that of "evil" totalitarian states, Agamben adds—in a gesture not incidentally reminiscent of Edward Said's contrapuntal reading:

> The correct question to pose concerning the horrors committed in the camps is, therefore, not the hypocritical one of how crimes of such atrocity could be committed against human beings. It would be more honest and, above all, more

useful to investigate carefully the juridical procedures and deployments of power by which human beings could be so completely deprived of their rights and prerogatives that no act committed against them could appear any longer a crime. (At this point, in fact, everything had truly become possible.) (HS, 170–71)

I have demonstrated elsewhere at some length the hitherto disavowed violent consequences of the liminal post–9/11 American global posture epitomized by the Bush administration's unleashing of its unending "War on [Islamic] Terror" and its establishment of the homeland security state as the norm.[51] Here, in the opening close of this introductory chapter on the appropriation of the sublime in American literature and art, it will suffice simply to point to a resonating and decisively telling parallel between Mark Twain's late and liminal ("Wild West"–style) fictional appropriation and spectacular repetition of the various aspects of the American errand in the sublime American wilderness in *A Connecticut Yankee* and the actual official American response (by the government, the media, and the experts) to al Qaeda's attacks on the World Trade Center and the Pentagon on 9/11. I rely for this latter reality on Susan Faludi's devastatingly acute and resonant witness to the liminal moment of this latest mimicking of the exceptionalist American errand:

> We reacted to our trauma, in other words, not by interrogating but by cocooning ourselves in the celluloid chrysalis of the baby boom's childhood. In the male version of that reverie, some nameless reflex had returned us to that 1950s' badland where conquest and triumph played and replayed in an infinite loop. . . . From deep within that dream world, our commander in chief issued remarks like "We'll smoke him out" and "Wanted Dead or Alive," our political candidates proved their double-barreled worthiness for post–9/11 office by brandishing guns on the campaign trail, our journalists cast city firefighters as tall-in-the-saddle cowboys patrolling a Wild West stage set, and our pundits proclaimed our nation's ability to vanquish "barbarians" in a faraway land they dubbed "Indian Country." The retreat into a fantasized yesteryear was pervasive, from the morning of the televised attack (ABC news anchor Peter Jennings called the national electronics enclave "the equivalent to a campfire in the days as the wagon trains were making their way westward") to the first post–9/11 supper at Camp David (the war cabinet was served a "Wild West menu of buffalo meat"), to our invasion of Iraq (which a tank crew from the Sixty-fourth Armored Regiment inaugurated with a "Seminole war dance") to our ongoing prosecution of the war on terror (which *Wall Street Journal* editor Max Boot equated with the small-scale "savage wars" waged in the republic's earlier days and which *Atlantic Monthly* correspondent Robert Kaplan hailed as "back to the days of fighting the Indians" and "really about taming the frontier").[52]

Taking my directive from Karl Marx's *Eighteenth Brumaire*, I need only add to Susan Faludi's potentializing counter-mnemonic witness that, at the liminal point of the obsessively recollective and excess-prone logic of the American exceptionalist ethos, the grimly tragic American past manifests itself as present farce. This untimely contemporary farcical liminality does not diminish one iota the horrific consequences of the recollective repetitive American errand. Rather, it discloses with a kind of opening finality its Achilles' heel: its very intrinsic excess gives us back the voice that the spectacle—the dumbfounding American sublime—has bereaved us of—if we have the courage to accept it.

CHAPTER 2

American Exceptionalism in the Post–9/11 Era

The Myth and the Reality

GOT HIM!

Vengeance at last!

US nails the bastard

—   Front page headline caption of a photo of Osama bin Laden,

New York Post, May 2, 2011

The spectacle presents itself as something enormously positive, indisputable, and inaccessible. It says nothing more than "that which appears is good, and that which is good appears." The attitude which it demands in principle is passive acceptance, which in fact it already obtained by its manner of appearance without reply, by its monopoly of appearance.

—Guy Debord, *The Society of the Spectacle*

I

The phrase "American exceptionialism" has become pervasive both in the discourse of the American political class (both of the Republican and Democratic political parties) and in the academic discourse called American studies since the bombing of the Twin Towers and the Pentagon by al Qaeda on September 11, 2001. As the sociologist Jerome Karabel has observed, the term became popular in American political circles during the Ronald Reagan administration and its Cold War against Soviet communism,

but what is new in recent years [since September 11, 2001] is that public expression—which had come to mean in popular parlance that the United States is not only different from, but superior to other countries—has become something of a required civic ritual of American politicians. This new definition of American exceptionalism has coincided with an extraordinary increase in public discussion of the term, with reference in print media increasing from two in 1880 to a stunning 2,580 this year [2011] through November. What might be called the "U.S. as Number One" version of "American exceptionalism" enjoys broad popular support among the public. According to a Gallup poll from December 2010, 80 percent of Americans agree that "because of the United States' history and the Constitution—the United States has a unique character that makes it the greatest country in the world." Support for this proportion varied somewhat along party lines, but not by much: 91 percent of Republicans agreed, but so, too, did 73 percent of Democrats.[1]

What is missing in Karabel's accounting, however, besides a definition of American exceptionalism adequate to its importance as a contemporary American cultural symbol, is a dimension that renders these statistics deeply disturbing to anyone authentically interested in the political health of the peoples of the United States: the simultaneous emergence to prominence of a very significant and growing body of academic writing in the United States—now, thanks to its decisive impact on American literary and cultural studies, called "The New Americanist studies"—that is genealogical in intent and has as its purpose to disclose the invisible underside that the American exceptionalism ethos has systematically disavowed from its beginnings. I am referring to the history of violence against America's "others" inaugurated by the American Puritans in the name of their belief, modeled on the Old Testament Israelite exodus from captivity to the Promised Land, in their "election" by God and their divinely sanctioned "vocation"—their "errand in the [New World] wilderness," continued through the period of westward expansion under the aegis of "Manifest Destiny" to the Cold War (including the devastating ten-year hot war in Vietnam); and, most recently, the United States' War on [Islamic] Terror in the wake of the bombing of the World Trade Center and the Pentagon by al Qaeda on September 11, 2001.

These disturbing statistics—and the *astonishing absence of reference in the speeches and in the media's reportage* to the quite visible emergence in academia of a genealogical transnational discourse whose purpose is, minimally, to modify the exorbitant celebratory claims of the myth of American exceptionalism and, maximally, to disclose the systematic violence that is intrinsic to its logic and practice in behalf of envisioning a more humane global polity—were dramatically manifest in both the spectacle-oriented

Republican and Democratic national conventions that nominated Mitt Romney and Barack Obama as presidential candidates in the election of 2012. What could not possibly be missed by the American public was not only the pervasive—indeed, systematic and ideologically determining—use of the term "American exceptionalism" by both Republican and Democratic speakers throughout the conventions, but also, suggesting the underlying sameness of the avowedly different political discourses of both parties as they pertain to the status of the United States in the now global-ized context,. the purely—that is, excessive—celebratory nature of these references. Indeed, in keeping with the statistics (and the spectacular repre-sentational excess intrinsic to the exceptionalist logic of American excep-tionalism), it was as if both the Republican and Democratic spokespersons in behalf of their party's right to rule over the next four years were vying over which party was more exceptionalist than the other. For the sake of convenience and brevity, however, I will restrict the following critical com-mentary on the American political class's staged use of the term "American exceptionalism" throughout the Republican and Democratic presidential conventions of 2012 to the exemplary speeches of two spokespersons from each party: Republican Senators John McCain of Arizona and Marco Rubio from Florida, on the one hand, and Democratic Senator John Kerry of Massachusetts (now secretary of state) and President Barack Obama, on the other. But before undertaking such a critical commentary, it will be necessary, if all too briefly, to render present and visible that which is spec-trally absent in the speeches defining America of the contemporary Ameri-can political class; I mean the long and sustained history of violence, theoretical and practical, against human life that the emergent genealogical New Americanist studies, by way of what Edward Said proleptically called a "contrapuntal reading," have disclosed to have been perennially closed off and disavowed by the celebratory discourse of American exceptionalism.

2

As Donald Pease has shown, the phrase "American exceptionalism" was, ironically, first used by Joseph Stalin during the 1920s to identify an American communist group, called "the Lovestoneites," as heretical to the international agenda of communism:

> American exceptionalism has been retroactively assigned to the origins of America. But the term did not in fact emerge into common usage until the late

1920s when Joseph Stalin invented it to accuse the Lovestoneite faction of the American Communist Party of a heretical deviation from party orthodoxies. Stalin's usage of the term as a "heresy" is helpful in explaining why exceptionalism was reappropriated as the core tenet of belief within cold war orthodoxy. Since Stalin had excommunicated the Lovestoneite sect for having described the United States as exempt from the laws of historical motion, to which Europe was subject, cold war ideologues transposed American exceptionalism into the revelation of the truth about its nature that explained *why* the United States was exempt not merely from Marxian incursions but from the historical laws Marx had codified. As the placeholder of a communist heresy, American exceptionalism named the limit to the political provenance of the Soviet Empire. As the manifestation of economic and political processes that negated communism at its core, the "heresy" constituted the primary means whereby U.S. citizens could imagine the nullification of communism. [2]

Pease's ironic genealogy is accurate, but his emphasis on its Cold War provenance of the term "American exceptionalism" should not obscure the historical reality (to which Pease also adheres) that the polyvalent onto-political ethos to which the term refers has its origins much earlier in the American Puritans' complex self-understanding of their exodus from the Old World to the "Promised Land" of the New World.[3] I mean, more specifically, their Calvinist *providential* view of history, which, bending the exegetical directives of orthodox—"typological" or "figural"—Christian interpretation of the Old Testament and the New Testament to their purposes, enabled them to read their seventeenth-century historical condition and their Protestant vocation as the ultimate fulfillment of the Old Testament Israelites' divinely ordained exodus from Egypt, the land of "fleshpots," to the Promised Land of Canaan. To put it succinctly, the American Puritans, following the directives of their figural biblical exegesis, viewed themselves as exceptional—as a youthful people elected by God to undertake his "errand in the [New World] wilderness" to fulfill the rationalizing work abandoned by the Old World, a world that, in forsaking the Word in favor of the World, had become old, decadent, and tyrannical—that is, "over-civilized."

This understanding of American exceptionalism is, no doubt, the historical source of the simple meaning implied by the contemporary American political class (and the American public) when it invokes the term to refer to the United States' moral superiority over the other nations of the world. But, as the New Americanist scholarship makes clear, this understanding is an immense oversimplification that obscures the dark underside of its positive assertions. As Sacvan Bercovitch, a proto–New Americanist scholar, points out in his groundbreaking *American Jeremiad* (1978), the fundamental problem of the American Puritans was the problem of recidivism or backsliding: how to maintain the absolutely necessary covenantal community and, at the same time, the youthful energy that was the imperative of their calling or vocation. For the "errand in the wilderness," as such, was a civilizing vocation, which is to say, a labor the fruits of which made life in the wilderness easier, more comfortable, less strenuous. This was the essential ontological and cultural paradox that the exceptionalism of the founding Puritans faced and, according to Bercovitch, overcame in their behalf and in behalf of the future of the American national identity, by way of the ritualization of the "American jeremiad":

> The American Puritan jeremiad was the ritual of a culture on an errand—which is to say, a culture based on a faith in process. Substituting teleology for hierarchy, it discarded the Old World ideal of stasis for a New World vision of the future. *Its function was to create a climate of anxiety that helped to release the restless "progressivist" energies required for the success of the venture.* The European jeremiad also thrived on anxiety, of course. Like all "traditionalist" forms of ritual, it used fear and trembling to teach acceptance of fixed forms. *But the American Puritan jeremiad went much farther. It made anxiety its end as well as its means. Crisis was the social norm it sought to inculcate. The very concept of errand, after all, implied a state of unfulfillment. The future, though divinely assured, was never quite there, and New England's Jeremiahs set out to provide the sense of insecurity that would ensure the outcome.* Denouncing or affirming, their vision fed on the distance between promise and fact.[4]

Though Bercovitch does not use the term, his ontological insight into the origins of the American exceptionalist ethos was indeed groundbreaking. But, as I have shown elsewhere,[5] in arguing in behalf of the priority of the Puritan thesis on the origins of the American national identity against the then dominant frontier thesis inaugurated by the historian Frederick Jackson Turner at the time of the official closing of the frontier and institutionalized by the American myth and symbol school—Henry Nash Smith, F. O. Matthiessen, Leo Marx, and R. W. B. Lewis, among others—during the Cold War in the name of American exceptionalism, Bercovitch was blinded by his ontological insight to the political implications of the American exceptionalist ethos.

Indeed, Bercovitch's overdetermination of the ontological foundation of the Puritan "progressivist" vocation concealed to him the ideological *affiliation* between the Puritan thesis and the history-based frontier thesis.

For what is suggested by attending to the Puritan paradox—that the civilizational errand necessarily produces overcivilization—and to the jeremiadic solution—the instigation of perpetual rejuvenating anxiety-provoking crisis in the covenantal community—is that both these historical theses concerning the origins and hegemonic exceptionalist character of the American national identity have *America's intrinsic need for a perpetual "frontier" or "enemy" in common*: an Other—an alien/inferior entity on the other side of the always moving dividing line between good and evil, settlement and wilderness, civilization and savagery, that threatens the divinely ordained errand and must, therefore, according to the imperatives of this exceptionalist logic, be eradicated by violence in behalf of the errand. The separation of church and state enacted by the American Constitution in the eighteenth century changed nothing as far as this exceptionalist paradigm is concerned. In the post-Revolutionary period—the time of American expansionist history overdetermined by the myth and symbol school—the providential ontology of the Puritans was simply secularized. It became Manifest Destiny: God's Providence became History. Under its dispensation the alien native Americans who occupied the vast wilderness of the West were "doomed"—destined by History to extinction—just as the native Americans were who occupied the wilderness of the Massachusetts Bay Colony. In fact, Frederick Jackson Turner's "The Significance of the Frontier in American History" is a late nineteenth-century American jeremiad: in expressing anxiety over the official closing of the Western frontier, he was tacitly calling for the extension of the (imperial) frontier into the Pacific—the globalization of American exceptionalism that ended in the occupation of the Hawaiian Islands and the imperial Spanish-American War.

This pattern of American exceptionalist practice, aptly called "rejuvenation through violence" by the proto–New Americanist Richard Slotkin,[6] continued throughout the period of westward expansion to the present day. In the late nineteenth century, following the closing of the frontier, it was epitomized by Mark Twain's *A Connecticut Yankee in King Arthur's Court* (1889). In this quintessential American novel, Twain's protagonist, Hank Morgan, wakes from a blow to the head inflicted in a fight at the Colt Firearms Company in Hartford, Connecticut, where he works as a supervisor, to find himself in sixth-century feudal England, a world that, from his modern American (exceptionalist)—scientific-technological-industrial-republican—perspective, appears to him at first to be a lunatic asylum in its amalgam of tyranny and primitivism. Characterizing himself at the outset of his sojourn in the essential binarist language of American exceptional-ism—"I am an American . . . a Yankee of Yankees—and practical; yes, and nearly barren of sentiment, I suppose—or poetry in other words,"[7] he reads his transformed condition as the sign of his American calling—a history-ordained vocation (errand) committed to bringing the spectacular amelio-rative technoscientific and republican fruits of his self-reliant modern America to this benighted feudal world. In the process of technologizing and industrializing Arthurian England by way of his superior, because practically derived, "magic," however, Morgan's "Americanizing" project is met with resistance by the magician, Merlin, who, to the Connecticut Yankee, represents superstition—the obsolete Old World mode of knowl-edge intrinsic to primitive societies under the aegis of "the Established Church"—and the British knight errantry that relies on that church-authorized superstition for political power over the masses. Morgan, how-ever, remains unerring in the pursuit of his errand in the Old World wilderness. Like his antebellum predecessor, Captain Ahab, in his "fiery pursuit" of Moby Dick (though without the ironic awareness of the devas-tating consequences underscored by the author), he will not be "swerved" from his rationalizing errand. Ahab is so certain of the truth of his Ameri-can exceptionalist ethos that he will pursue its logic to his limits:

> Swerve me? Ye cannot swerve me, else ye swerve yourselves! Man has ye there. Swerve me? The path to my fixed purpose is laid with iron rails, whereon my soul is grooved to run. Over unsounded gorges, through the rifled hearts of mountains, under torrents' beds, unerringly I rush! Naught's an obstacle, naught's an angle to the iron way.[8]

This practical fulfillment of the American exceptionalist logic of the "Yankee of Yankees" is consummated at the "Battle of the Sand Belt," after Morgan has proclaimed a regime change that turned feudal England into an American-style republic. Beleaguered by the massed forces of the resistant British knighthood, Morgan (supported by his ventriloquized native aide, Clarence), predictably resorts to the spectacular—mind- or language-numbing—"magic" of his practical American technoscientific knowledge to achieve his preordained exceptionalist and "redemptive" end. Combining the efficient mass-killing firepower of the high-tech Gatling guns he has assembled at the mouth of the cave and the equally efficient lethal potential of modern electrical science, which takes the form of a system of electrically wired fences, he unleashes—*stages*, from his perspective—a spectacular—or, to anticipate, a "shock and awe"—display of violence that terminates in the extermination of his enemy immediately and en masse. I requote the passage cited in Chapter 1 to underscore the continuity of spectacular violence unleashed by "the Yankee of Yankees" not only with the American past but also with the American future:

> I sent a current through the third fence, now; and almost immediately through the fourth and fifth, so quickly were the gaps filled up. I believed the time was come, now, for my climax; I believed that that whole army was in our trap. Anyway, it was high time to find out. So I touched a button and set fifty electric suns aflame on the top of our precipice.
>
> Land, what a sight! We were enclosed in three walls of dead men! All the other fences were pretty nearly filled with the living, who were stealthily working their way forward through the wires. The sudden glare paralyzed this host, petrified them, you may say, with astonishment; there was just one instant for the enemy to utilize their immobility in, and I didn't lose the chance. You see, in another instant they would have recovered their faculties, then they'd have burst into a cheer and made a rush, and my wires would have gone down before it; but that lost instant lost them their opportunity forever; while even that slight fragment of time was still unspent, I shot the current through all the fences and struck the whole host dead in their tracks. *There* was a groan you could *hear*! It voiced the death-pang of eleven thousand men. It swelled out on the night with awful pathos.
>
> A glance showed that the rest of the enemy—perhaps ten thousand strong— were between us and the encircling ditch, and pressing forward to assault. Consequently we had them *all*! And had them past help. Time for the last act of the tragedy. I fired the three appointed revolver shots—which meant:
>
> "Turn on the water!"
>
> There was a sudden rush and roar, and in a minute the mountain brook was raging through the big ditch and creating a river a hundred feet wide and twenty-five deep.
>
> "Stand to your guns, men! Open fire!"
>
> The thirteen gatling guns began to vomit death into the fated ten thousand. They halted, they stood their ground a moment against that withering deluge of fire, then they broke, faced about and swept toward the ditch like chaff before a gale. A full part of their force never reached the top of the lofty embankment; the three-fourths reached it and plunged over—to death by drowning.
>
> Within ten short minutes after we had opened fire, armed resistance was totally annihilated, the campaign was ended, we fifty-four were masters of England! Twenty-five thousand men lay dead around us. (CY, 254–55)

What is especially significant about Mark Twain's *A Connecticut Yankee* is that it is remarkably proleptic of the historical itinerary of the American exceptionalist ethos in the twentieth and, particularly, the twenty-first century. In locating his story's mis en scène at the liminal point of the American exceptionalist logic's trajectory, it inadvertently—as the insistent uneasiness of the myth and symbol school's response to the Battle of the Sand Belt testifies[9]—anticipates the *problematization* of the American exceptionalist ethos at the end of the twentieth century (the Vietnam War) and the beginning of the twenty-first (the post–9/11 War on [Islamic] Terror). (It is no accident that it was during this liminal period that the term "American exceptionalism" emerged in the national rhetoric to characterize the hitherto silent pervasiveness of America's sense of superiority over the Old World.) In overdetermining the liminal point of the perennial logic of American exceptionalism, in other words, Twain's novel inadvertently anticipates the self-de-struction of the American exceptionalist ethos—the disclosure at the point of its fulfillment that its (hegemonic) truth is, in fact, an ideology—in the next century, when the dominant culture, in the name of "the American Century," pursued its benign logical imperatives to its devastating practical historical limit.

For example, Twain's novel, particularly the Connecticut Yankee's mass slaughter of the British knight errantry at the Battle of the Sand Belt, prefigured the practical consequences of the use to which the American exceptionalist ethos was put during the Vietnam War—the "hot war" of the Cold War—epitomized by Michael Herr's account of the United States' response to the Tet Offensive, which, for him, was a synecdoche of the United States' destruction of Vietnam in the name of "saving it for the free world"—and in natural reaction to the Viet Cong's strategic refusal (Bartleby-style) to conduct its resistance according to the unerring (Ahabian) terms dictated by the United States' traditional Western—frontal and forwarding—concept of war:

> We took a huge collective nervous breakdown, it was the compression and heat of heavy contact generated out until every American in Vietnam got a taste. Vietnam was a dark room full of deadly objects, the VC were everywhere all at once like a spider cancer, and instead of losing the war in little pieces over years we lost it fast in under a week. After that, we were like the character in the pop grunt mythology, dead but too dumb to lie down. Our worst dread of yellow peril became realized; we saw them now dying by the thousands all over the country, yet they didn't seem depleted, let alone exhausted, as the Mission was claiming by the first day. We took space back quickly, expensively, with total panic and close to maximum brutality. Our machine was devastating. And versatile. It could do everything but stop. As one American major said, in a

successful attempt at attaining history, "We had to destroy Ben Tre in order to save it." That's how most of the country came back under what we called control, and how it remained essentially occupied by the Viet Cong and the North until the day years later when there were none of us left there.[10]

But it is the American exceptionalism of the period between the implosion of the Soviet Union, the kicking of the "Vietnam Syndrome" in the first Gulf War, and the aftermath of the bombing of the World Trade Center and the Pentagon by al Qaeda that Twain's novel most fully anticipates: the period culminating in the War on [Islamic] Terror initiated by the George W. Bush administration as the calling of the American people of the twenty-first century[11] and in the name of American exceptionalism. I mean that liminal moment of American history that bore witness to the *fulfillment* of the logic of American exceptionalism and disclosed its ethos to be an ideological agent that not only disavowed the violence intrinsic to its logic, but also, in so doing, exposed the complex but polyvalent mechanism, intrinsic to the "exceptionalism" of American exceptionalism, that justified that violence: the rejuvenating, anxiety-provoking jeremiad—the spectacle-producing ritual that, in justifying preemptive war, unilateral regime change (and the imposition of a ventriloquized polity), and shock-and-awe tactics, became the means of turning anything or anyone that was an obstacle to the achievement of its errand into exterminatable enemies—or, in Giorgio Agamben's apt terms, *homo sacer*: bare life, life that can be killed without the killing being called murder.[12]

That my analysis of this liminal moment in the historical itinerary of American exceptionalism is not at all an exaggeration is borne witness to by Samuel P. Huntington, one of the most prestigious and influential intellectual deputies of the George W. Bush administration—the popularizer of the phrase "the clash of civilization," not incidentally[13]—in his post–9/11 book aptly titled *Who Are We?: Challenges to America's National Identity* (2004). In this book, as we have seen in Chapter 1, Huntington not only answers the question of the subtitle by overtly invoking the Puritan myth of America's origins:

They took the lead in defining their settlement based on "a Covenant with God" to create "a city on a hill" as a model for all the world, and people of the Protestant faiths soon also came to see themselves and America in a similar way. In the seventeenth and eighteenth centuries, Americans defined their mission in the New World in biblical terms. They were a "chosen people," on an "errand

in the wilderness," creating "the new Israel" or the "new Jerusalem" in what was
clearly "the promised land." America was the site of "a new Heaven and new
earth, the home of justice," God's country. . . . This sense of holy mission was
easily expanded into millenarian themes of America as "the redeemer nation"
and "the visionary republic."[14]

As the title of his post–9/11 nationalist book suggests, Huntington's *Who
Are We?* is also patently a contemporary American jeremiad, which,
attuned to the flagging public commitment to the War on Terror incumbent on what he calls "the deconstruction of America" (the emergence of
"subnational identities" that challenged the "Anglo-Protestant core culture," and the stalling of the United States' preemptive mission in the
Iraq wilderness, is intended to induce the national anxiety that has perennially rejuvenated the energy and solidarity of the covenantal people.
What is especially telling about Huntington's American exceptionalist
jeremiad is his *overt* identification of the traditional American Jeremiahs'
appeal to a perpetual rejuvenating frontier with the more ideological need
for a perpetual enemy.

Huntington's jeremiad thus does not restrict its historical parameters
to the post–9/11 occasion. Rather, he constellates it into the Cold War
context—particularly its coming to its end with the implosion of the
Soviet Union. Like his predecessor Jeremiahs, whose American exceptionalist logic compelled them to think the consequences of peace—and,
not incidentally, echoing the friend/foe theory of politics of the German
National Socialist political theorist Carl Schmitt—Huntington is compelled by his jeremiad to read the end of the Cold War as a threat to the
exceptionalism that America has always invoked to distinguish itself
from the decadent Old World:

> At the end of the twentieth century, democracy was left without a significant
> secular ideological rival, and the United States was left without a peer competi-
> tor. Among foreign policy elites, the result was euphoria, pride, arrogance [the
> reference is to Francis Fukuyama's 1992 book *The End of History and the Last
> Man*]—and uncertainty. The absence of an ideological threat produced an
> absence of purpose. "Nations need enemies," Charles Krauthammer [a presti-
> gious neoconservative policy expert] commented as the Cold War ends. "Take
> away one, and they find another." The ideal enemy for America would be ideo-
> logically hostile, racially and culturally different, and militarily strong enough
> to pose a credible threat to Americana security. The foreign policy debates of the
> 1990s were already over who might be such an enemy. (WAW, 263)

It is at this liminal point in his jeremiad, which, as I have suggested—and Huntington's rhetorical anxiety in the last sentence confirms—is a spectacle-producing instrument by which Huntington dramatically brings the bombings of the World Trade Center and the Pentagon, which he has strategically marginalized, to center stage. In a chapter blatantly entitled "America's Search for an Enemy," he briefly summarizes the anxious debates by American policy experts concerning the qualifications of possible candidates for this bizarre status. Then, in a secular rhetoric reminiscent of the Puritans' reading of their providential calling—one implying that History, not policy makers, has identified America's new rejuvenating enemy—he brings his narrative to its spectacular—dumbstriking—close by invoking the 9/11 al Qaeda (Islamic terrorist) bombings on American soil:

> The cultural gap between Islam and America's Christianity and Anglo-Protestantism reinforces Islam's enemy qualifications. And on September 11, 2001, Osama bin Laden ended America's search. The attacks on New York and Washington followed by the wars with Afghanistan and Iraq and the more diffuse "war on terrorism," make militant Islam America's first enemy of the twenty-first century. (WAW, 264–65)

I will return to the spectral figure of Osama bin Laden, whom Huntington, significantly, in typical American exceptionalist fashion, renders a personification of his understanding of Islam, in the second part of this essay, which analyzes the uses to which the term "American exceptionalism" was put during the Republican and Democratic national conventions of 2012, where his name is invoked again and again in a similar ritualistic manner. Here, I want to underscore the remarkable parallel between Huntington's late, overt jeremiadic representation of the practical imperatives for America of the al Qaeda bombings and the George W. Bush administration's late American exceptionalist practice in the "global wilderness" allegedly produced by militant Islam. In unerringly pursuing the logic of American exceptionalism to its limits, Huntington's not only justifies the relay of violent practices intrinsic to it—"preemptive war," the spectacular military tactics of "shock and awe," unilateral "regime change" that establishes ventriloquized governments—that was determinative of the George W. Bush administration's spectacular War on Terror in the aftermath of September 11, 2001.[15] In overtly naming the "wilderness" or the "frontier" that hitherto occluded the violence accompanying

its rationalization and fructification as perpetual enemy, his exceptionalism also justifies the Bush administration's establishment of the (global)
homeland security state, in which the (exceptional) state of emergency
becomes the norm. Indeed, in the end, as Abu Ghraib, Guantánamo, and
the detention camps established by the United States in foreign states to
enable the illegal violence against human suspects it euphemistically calls
"extraordinary rendition" bear witness, Huntington's American exceptionalist logic becomes exemplary of that momentum of modern democratic societies diagnosed by Giorgio Agamben, which, under the aegis of
biopolitics, reduces human life (*bios*) to "bare life" (*zoé*), life that can be
killed with impunity, and of which the political paradigm is the concentration camp:

> Hannah Arendt once observed that in the camps, the principle that supports
> totalitarian rule and that common sense obstinately refuses to admit comes fully
> to light: this is the principle according to which "everything is possible." Only
> because the camps constitute a space of exception . . . in which not only is law
> completely suspended but fact and law are completely confused—is everything
> in the camp truly possible. If this particular juridico-political structure of the
> camps—the task of which is precisely to create a stable exception—is not under-
> stood, the incredible things that happened there remain completely unintelli-
> gible. Whoever entered the camp moved in a zone of indistinction between
> outside and inside, exception and rule, licit and illicit, in which the very concept
> of subjective right and juridical protection no longer made any sense. . . . Insofar
> as its inhabitants were stripped of every political status and wholly reduced to
> bare life, the camp was also the most absolute biopolitical space ever to have
> been realized, in which power confronts nothing but pure life, without media-
> tion. That is why the camp is the very paradigm of political space at the point of
> which politics becomes biopolitics and *homo sacer* is virtually confused with the
> citizen. The correct question to pose concerning the horrors committed in the
> camp is, therefore, not the hypocritical one of how crimes of such atrocity could
> be committed against humans. It would be more honest and, above all, more
> useful to investigate carefully the juridical procedures and deployments of
> power by which human beings could be so completely deprived of their right
> and prerogatives that no act committed against them could appear any longer as
> a crime. (HS, 171–72)

3

This all too briefly summarized counter-history of American exceptionalist history is what has been retrieved by the emergent New Americanist

scholarship. Taking its novel research directives from the transnationalist demands of the globalization of the planet and acknowledging the urgent need to "see" American exceptionalism from the point of view of the disavowed victims of its representational and global practice (contrapuntally, as it were), this new scholarship has been enabled to render visible the contradictions disclosed by the fulfillment in practice (the War on Terror) of the logical imperatives of the American exceptionalist ethos. It is this retrieved history that—remarkably—is virtually absent in the discourse of the contemporary—post–9/11 or "post–ground zero"— American political class, even after the fall of George W. Bush and his neoconservative administration. And it is because of this remarkable absence, I suggest, that this counter-history must be reasserted and underscored. As I noted at the outset, this disturbing absence is borne synecdochic witness to not only by the pervasiveness of the term "American exceptionalism"—more or less nonexistent in the previous rhetoric of American politicians and the media—in the speeches of both Republicans and Democrats at the national presidential conventions of 2012, but also, and above all, by the uniformly celebratory tenor of these ubiquitous references. In what follows, I will examine in some detail the speeches of two highly visible Republican speakers, Senator John McCain of Arizona and Senator Marco Rubio of Florida, and two equally influential Democratic speakers, Senator John Kerry of Massachusetts and President Barack Obama, in the estranging light of this New Americanist scholarship. Following the directives of this counter-mnemonic contrapuntal scholarship, my purpose will be to show not only how incredibly remote the celebratory discourses about the American national identity of these contemporary American politicians are from historical reality (or, at any rate, from the way the vast victimized populations of America's Others view its spectacular exceptionalist global representations and practices); it will also be to show how their particular representations of American exceptionalism contribute insidiously and collectively, however inadvertently, to the incremental reduction of the democratic exceptionalist state to a state in which the state of exception (and its biopolitics) becomes the rule and the camp its political paradigm.

Senator John McCain's speech endorsing the nomination of Mitt Romney as the Republican candidate for the presidency of the United States at the 2012 Republican national convention in Tampa, Florida, not only invokes the term "American exceptionalism" twice in his speech; he invokes it in such a way as to make it clear that it is, against the Democratic Party's recidivism, what is essentially at stake in this "historic" election. Recalling his audience to America's vocation to a "sacred cause," McCain goes on not only to identify these origins with the Puritan founders of the American exceptionalist national identity, but also to show that this divinely ordained vocation *to lead,* embodied in John Winthrop's characterization of the Massachusetts Bay Colony as a "city on the hill"—a beacon for the rest of mankind—is what essentially has characterized America's history:

> At our best [as opposed to the Obama administration's errancy], America has led. We have led by our example as a shining city on a hill, we have led in the directions of patriots from both parties. We have led shoulder to shoulder with steadfast friends and allies. We have led by giving voice to the voiceless, insisting that every human life has dignity, and aiding those brave souls who risk everything to secure the inalienable rights that are endowed to all by our creator. (APPLAUSE) We have led with generous hearts, moved by an abiding love of justice, to help others eradicate disease, lift themselves from poverty, live under laws of their own making, and determine their own destinies.
>
> We have led when necessary with the armed might of freedom's defenders, and always we have led from the front, never from behind. (APPLAUSE)
>
> This is what makes America an exceptionalist nation. It is not only who we are, it is the record of what we have done.[16]

McCain's summary record of exceptionalist America's domestic foreign practice patently flies in the face of historical reality. In the domain of foreign policy to which McCain refers, for example, the New Americanist scholars, as we have seen, have persuasively shown that the United States, whatever its rhetorical justifications, has, in fact, perennially harnessed its exceptionalist ethos—and its spectacular "might" to aggrandizing its power: not to give voice to the voiceless but, on the contrary, as in the case of the Bush administration's typical practice of "regime change," to ventriloquize these voices, to interpellate them, to render them subjected subjects. And in the domain of domestic policy, to which he also refers, McCain's record does not remotely accord with historical reality. As Scott Shane, one of the very few mainstream journalists attuned to the New Americanist scholarship, writes about American leadership under the thrall of what he calls "the opiate of exceptionalism" in the *New York Times* in the wake of the presidential national conventions:

> Imagine a presidential candidate who spoke bluntly about American problems, dwelling on measures to which the United States lags its economic peers. What

might a mythical candidate talk about on the stump? He might vow to turn around the dismal statistics on child poverty, declaring it an outrage that of the 35 most economically advanced countries, *the United States ranks 34th*, edging out only Romania. He might take on educational achievement, noting that this country comes in only *28th in the percentage of 4-year-olds* enrolled in preschool, and at the other end of the scale, 14th in the percentage of 25- to 34-year-olds with a higher education. He might hammer on infant mortality, where the United States ranks worse than 48 other countries and territories, or point out that, contrary to fervent popular belief, that United States trails most of Europe, Australia, and Canada in *social mobility*.

The candidate might try to stir up his audience by flipping a familiar campaign trope: America is indeed No. 1, he might declare—*in locking its citizens up*, with an incarceration rate far higher than that of the likes of Russia, Cuba, Iran, or China; *in obesity*, easily outweighing second-place Mexico and with nearly 10 times the rate of Japan; *in energy use* per person, with double the consumption of prosperous Germany.[17]

Equally telling as his invocation of the term "American exceptionalism" to exalt the United States is McCain's enframement of his argument against the Democratic Party and the incumbent Barack Obama's administration in the form of the American jeremiad, that ritual of rejuvenation that, as we have seen, in the historical process transformed the American's psyche's need for a perpetual wilderness to the need of a perpetual threatening enemy. Immediately following his orchestrated annunciation of the term "American exceptionalism," McCain tells his covenantal audience:

We are now being tested by an array of threats that are more complex, more numerous, and just as deep and deadly as I can recall in my lifetime. We face a consequential choice, and make no mistake, it is a choice. We can choose to follow a declining path toward a future that is dimmer and more dangerous than our past. Or we can choose to reform our failing government, revitalize our ailing economy, and renew the foundations of our power and leadership in the world.

That is what is at stake in this election. (APPLAUSE) Unfortunately, for four years [under Obama's errant presidential aegis], we have drifted away from our proudest traditions of global leadership. Traditions that are truly bipartisan. We've let the challenges we face at home and abroad become much harder to solve. We can't afford to stay on that course any longer. We can't afford to cause our friends and allies, from Latin America to Europe to Asia to the Middle East, and especially in Israel, a nation under existential threat, to doubt America's leadership.

I will return to the issue of the defense of Israel's very existence against the Arab world later in this chapter. Here, I want to highlight not only the traditional Puritan theme of recidivism (the "backsliding" that haunted the Puritans' sense of community) in McCain's American jeremiad, but also and above all, its ritualized rejuvenating function: in Bercovitch's words, the creation of "a climate of anxiety" in the covenantal community by way of spectacularizing the threat to its existence posed by an implied barbarous enemy that would ensure the solidarity and the vocational energy of its covenantal members.

What necessarily follows, then, is an extended ritualized list of President Obama's betrayals of the leadership and American exceptionalist promise—and, by way of the astonishing claim that the oppressed peoples of the contemporary world, particularly in the Middle East and North Africa, look to America at this time of crisis for redemption, the reaffirmation, seemingly abandoned by the Democrats, of the perennial belief in America's election by History as redeemer nation:

> They're liberating themselves from oppressive rulers and they want America's support. They want America's assistance as they struggle to live in peace and security, to expand opportunities for themselves and their children, to replace the injustices of despots with the institutions of democracy and freedom. America must be on the right side of history.

Having represented Obama's presidential administration in terms of his loss of faith in America's chosenness and the betrayal of the world's peoples' dreams of redemption by America and America's homeland security, McCain concludes his jeremiad by expressing his trust in Mitt Romney as the contemporary American in whom the American exceptionalist ethos continues to burn like a gemlike flame:

> I—I trust him to affirm our nation's exceptionalist character and responsibilities. I trust him to know that our security and economic interests are inextricably tied to the progress of our values. I trust him to know that if America doesn't lead, our adversaries will and the world will go darker, and poorer and much more dangerous.
>
> I trust him to know that an American president always, always, always stands up for the rights and freedoms and justice of all peoples. (APPLAUSE)
>
> I trust Mitt Romney to know that good can triumph over evil, that justice can vanquish tyranny, that love can conquer hate, that the desire for freedom is eternal and universal and that America is still the best hope of mankind.

Whereas Senator John McCain's speech celebrating the nomination of Mitt Romney to the presidency of the United States focused on America's exceptionalism vis à vis its relationship to the peoples of the rest of the world, Senator Marco Rubio's speech introducing Romney focused almost entirely on America's domestic exceptionalism. Senator Rubio, a second-generation Cuban American, begins (and ends) his speech introducing Romney and celebrating the American exceptionalist ethos by rendering his personal life story exemplary of its promise:

> I watched my first convention in 1980 with my grandfather. My grandfather was born to a farming family in rural Cuba. Childhood polio left him permanently disabled. He was the only one in his family that knew how to read. He was a huge influence on the growing up [*sic*]. As a boy I sat on the porch of my house and listened to his stories about his history and politics and baseball, as he would talk on one of three daily (*inaudible*) cigars. Now I don't remember all the things he talked to me about. But the one thing I remember is the one thing he wanted me never to forget. That the dreams he had when he was young became impossible to achieve. But there was no limit to how far I could go, because I was an American. (APPLAUSE)
>
> Now for those of us—here is why I say that—here's why I say that. Because for those of us who were born and raised in this country, sometimes it becomes easy to forget how special America is. But my grandfather understood how different America was from the rest of the world because he knew life outside America.
>
> Tonight you will hear from another man who understands what makes America exceptional.[18]

Senator Rubio goes on to characterize his version of the American (exceptionalist) dream by predictably focusing on the "uncontestable" capitalist versions of self-reliance, practicality, and suspicion of governmental interference, those early American personal values so much more productive of material progress than the overcivilized values of the Old World that rendered the United States the richest nation in the world: "Mitt Romney knows America's prosperity did not happen because our government simply spent money. It happened because our people use their own money to open a business. And when they succeed, they hire more people, who invest or spend their money in the economy, helping others start a business or create jobs." In the process, he, like Senator McCain, blatantly disavows the contradictory domestic statistics disclosed by the New Americanists. But what is more significant for Senator

Rubio about his personal optimistic version of American exceptionalism—
and, more telling in its articulation, about its ideological implications—
is his forced identification of American exceptionalism with America's
perennial Other. His repeated romanticized reference to his promise/
fulfillment story as a Cuban immigrant whose childhood dream came true
testifies to this:

> Yes, we live in troubled times, but the story of those who came before us reminds
> us that America has always been about new beginnings, and Mitt Romney is
> running for president because he knows, if we are willing to do for our children
> what our parents did for us, life in America can be better than it has ever been.
> (APPLAUSE)
>
> . . .
>
> My Dad was a bartender. My mom was a cashier, a hotel maid, a stock clerk
> at Kmart. They never made it big. They were never rich, and yet they were suc-
> cessful, because just a few decades removed from hopelessness, they made pos-
> sible for us all the things that have been impossible for them.
>
> Many nights growing up I would hear my father's keys at the door as he came
> home after another 16-hour day. Many mornings, I woke up just as my mother
> got home from the overnight shift at Kmart. When you're young and in a hurry,
> the meaning of moments like this escapes you. Now, as my children get older I
> understand it better. My dad used to tell us—(SPEAKING IN SPANISH)—in this
> country you'll be able to accomplish all the things we never could.
>
> A few years ago, I noticed a bartender behind the portable bar in the back of
> the ballroom. I remembered my father, who worked as many years as a banquet
> bartender [*sic*]. He was grateful for the work he had, but that's not like he wanted
> for us. You see, he stood behind the bar all those years so that one day I could
> stand behind a podium, in the front of the room.

In his retrospective telling, Senator Rubio's triumphant personal "journey, from behind the bar to behind this podium, goes to the essence of the
American miracle—that we're exceptional, not because we have more rich
people here. We are special because dreams that are impossible anywhere
else, they come true here." When, however, this American exceptionalist
promise/fulfillment narrative is read in the light of the contrapuntal history retrieved by the New Americanist studies by way of reading its structure against the grain, it undergoes a remarkable sea change. From this
estranged perspective Senator Rubio's narrative is seen not only to disavow
the long history of the life-damaging discrimination and abuse inflicted
by Americans in the benign name of American exceptionalism on its multiple Others—native Americans, blacks, women, ethnic minorities in its

past, and immigrants—not least Hispanic immigrants—in Senator Rubio's very visible present; equally, and possibly more damaging, this contrapuntal history suggests that the very self of Senator Rubio's story (and its vocation), like that of so many other immigrants,[19] is itself, in Louis Althusser's apt term, the consequence of its interpellation by the American Subject—the hailing that renders the subject a "subjected subject"—or, in the more immediate language of American exceptionalism, its ventriloquizing by the American exceptionalist calling.

4

Tellingly, the use of the term "American exceptionalism" was even more prominent, both as referent and as emphasis, in the speeches celebrating the incumbent president and his American domestic and foreign agenda by Democratic speakers at the Democratic National Convention in Charlotte, North Carolina. This emphasis was, no doubt, partly because the Democratic leadership was strategically intent on co-opting the Republicans' insistent prior jeremiadic claim that the Obama administration, particularly in its foreign policy, was betraying the imperative of world leadership intrinsic to the American exceptionalist ethos. Whatever the motives of the Democratic speakers' disavowal of recidivism and their consequent overdetermination of the use of the term, however, the fact remains that they, like their Republican counterparts, were *overtly and systematically* identifying the first four years of the Obama administration with America's traditional self-understanding as a chosen nation with a transcendentally ordained redemptive errand in the post–9/11 global wilderness. Indeed, it seemed as if the Democratic speakers were vying against the Republicans to represent the Democratic Party under the aegis of Barack Obama as more exceptionalist than their opponents. This was certainly true in the case of Senator John Kerry of Massachusetts in his speech mocking the exceptionalist qualifications of the Republican nominee and celebrating the accomplishments of the Obama presidency, particularly in the domain of global politics, and President Obama's speech accepting the presidential nomination for a second term, which, though the term is muted, is saturated with the American exceptionalist ethos. The senator repeatedly invoked the term "American exceptionalism" and the president its exceptionalist meaning centrally to make clear to the American public that its promissory redemptive domestic and global agenda was President Obama's throughout his first term in office and to assure doubters that it would continue to be in his second term.

In typical American jeremiadic fashion, Senator Kerry opened his short but forceful speech by predictably invoking the "crisis" that threatens the covenantal American community—thus representing the long-standing American aggression in the Middle East as defense—and by reminding his audience of Democrats (and the American public at large) that the resolution of this threatening crisis depended on the right choice of presidents:

> In this campaign, we have a fundamental choice. Will we protect our country and our allies, advance our interests and ideals, do battle where we must and make peace where we can? Or will we entrust our place in the world to someone who just hasn't learned the lessons of the last decade? We've all learned Mitt Romney doesn't know much about foreign policy. But he has these "neocon advisors" who know all the wrong things about foreign policy. [The reference is to the neoconservative authors of "Project for the New American Century" (PNAC), which became the touchstone of President George W. Bush's exceptionalist imperialist policy in Iraq and Afghanistan long before September 11, 2001.][20] He would rely on them—after all, he's the great outsourcer. But I say to you: This is not the time to outsource the job of commander in chief. Our opponents like to talk about "American exceptionalism" but all they do is talk. They forget that we are exceptional not because we say we are, but because we do exceptionalist things. We break out of the Great Depression, win two world wars, save lives fighting AIDS, pull people out of poverty, defend freedom, go to the moon—and produce exceptionalist people who even give their lives for civil rights and human rights.[21]

Following up on the inaugural traditional American distinction he makes between doing and saying, Kerry went on to contrast the Republican Party's (recidivist) lip service to American exceptionalism with the Democratic Party's authentic practice of its progressive and redemptive values, a contrast echoing Senator McCain that culminates in the identification of the idea of leading inherent in the exceptionalist ethos and its representation of the frontier experience[22] with that of the active leadership of President Obama:

> Despite what you heard in Tampa, an exceptional country does care about the rise of oceans and the future of the planet. That is a responsibility from the Scriptures—and that too is a responsibility of the leader of the free world. The only thing exceptional about today's Republicans is that—almost without exception—they oppose everything that has made American exceptional in the

first place. An exceptional nation demands the leadership of an exceptional president. And, my fellow Americans, that president is Barack Obama.

In typical and predictable jeremiadic fashion, Kerry, focusing on America's involvement in the Middle East, then summarized the George W. Bush administration's betrayal of the American exceptionalist ethos during his eight-year presidential regime. He recalled "the disarray and disaster [President Obama] inherited" from the Bush era: "A war of choice in Iraq had become a war without end, and a war of necessity in Afghanistan had become a war of neglect. Our alliances were shredded. Our moral authority was in tatters. America was isolated in the world. Our military was stretched to the breaking point. Iran was marching unchecked toward a nuclear weapon. And Osama bin Laden was still plotting."

I will return (as Kerry does) to the senator's pointed, indeed, *dramatically staged*, reference to the continuing threat posed by Osama bin Laden to the security of the United States. Here, in keeping with his identification of Obama with the active leadership endemic to the American exceptionalist ethos, I want to underscore Senator Kerry's representation of the president, in opposition to his Republican predecessor's unexceptionalist legacy of a "quagmire" reminiscent of Vietnam and the recidivist rhetorical evasions of his opponent, as the epitome of the American exceptionalist leader (of the "free world") who *enacts* the imperative of the exceptionalist "promise":

> And President Obama kept his promises. He promised to end the war in Iraq—and he has—and our heroes have come back home. He promised to end the war in Afghanistan responsibly—and he is—and our heroes there are coming home. He promised to focus like a laser on al Qaeda—and he has—our forces have eliminated more of its leadership in the last three years than in the eight years that came before. And after more than ten years without justice for the thousands of Americans murdered on 9/11, after Mitt Romney said it would be "naïve" to go into Pakistan to pursue the terrorists, it took President Obama, against the advice of many, to give that order to finally rid this earth of Osama bin Laden. Ask Osama bin Laden if he is better off now than he was four years ago.

Senator Kerry went on to itemize other promises the president had fulfilled in the name of the American exceptionalist ethos—"stand[ing] with Israel to tighten sanctions on Iran," "working with Russia to reduce the threat of nuclear weapons," and "enlisting our allies" to rid Libya of the tyrant Moammar Gadhafi and bring freedom to the Libyan people.

What is deeply disturbing about this litany of alleged fulfilled promises (besides the factual unfulfillment of some of them) is not simply the
patent similarity of these claims about American exceptionalism of a prestigious Democratic speaker (now secretary of state) with those expected
exceptionalist claims of the Republican speakers. Equally disturbing is its
disavowal of—its apparent blindness to—the perennial aggressive violence
against its recalcitrant Middle Eastern others that, as the New American
studies have borne massive witness, has systematically accompanied these
fulfillments of the American exceptionalist promise. (Senator Kerry's
underscoring of President Obama's undeviating commitment to defend-
ing Israel, a militantly apartheid state, and his astonishing appeal to its
racist and extreme right-wing prime minister, Benjamin Netanyahu, to
setting "the record straight" over Mitt Romney's charge that President
Obama was abandoning its perennial commitment to the security of
Israel, bear synecdochical witness to this shameful disavowal.) To put it
all too briefly, Kerry's speech celebrating the Obama administration's
American exceptionalism, no less than those of his Republican counterparts, utterly obliterated the sustained violent history of the United States'
offensive intervention in the Middle East during the period of the Cold
War, which bore witness to its massive and decisive contribution to the
destabilization of that critical geopolitical region in the name of the
United States' exceptionalist errand in the world's global wilderness—
and the establishment of the homeland security state that prepared the
way for the insidious normalization of the state of exception.

But it is not only the similarity between Senator Kerry's and his
Republican counterparts' exceptionalist disavowals that needs to be registered. It is also, and perhaps above all, the similarity between the most
positive—and therefore exemplary—evidence he offers as testimony to
the Obama administration's fulfillment of the "promises" of the American exceptionalist ethos with that of his Republican opponents. I am
referring to the senator's staged climactic invocation of the spectacle of
the unerringly—"surgically executed"—Navy Seals' "search and destroy
mission" (to use the still current memorandum language of the United
States' failed war in Vietnam) that, once and for all, "rid this earth of
Osama bin Laden." "Ask Osama bin Laden if he is better off now than he
was four years ago," he said triumphantly in response to his Republican
opponents, thus implying, in its "mission accomplished" tenor (massively
exploited by the mainstream media, as the first epigraph of this chapter
testifies), that, with Osama bin Laden's spectacular assassination, insti-

gated in the name of the exceptionalist logic of American exceptionalism, the anxiety-provoking "problem" allegedly haunting the security of the American homeland and the world at large had been solved, if not yet practically annulled.

What is especially remarkable about this dramatic search-and-destroy narrative and its spectacular conclusion celebrated as a promise President Obama fulfilled by the prestigious left-of-center Democrat John Kerry is that it precisely echoes the unerring narrative announced and focalized as a spectacle by George W. Bush in his incremental post–9/11 identification (reduction) of the enormous complexities of the Middle Eastern Arab world—*complexities, as the New Americanist scholars have persuasively shown, produced in very large part, initially, by the depredations of Western colonialist exceptionalism and, then, since the globalizing Cold War, by the United States' exceptionalist errand in the Arab "wilderness"*: "No matter how long it takes, America will find you [Osama bin Laden], and will bring you to justice," he said decisively in his fifth-anniversary speech to the U.S. Congress commemorating September 11, 2001. The only difference is that Bush's Republican administration failed in its effort to hunt down Obama bin Laden, whereas the Democratic administration under the "exceptionalist" leadership of Barack Obama did.[23]

However, it is not simply the remarkable continuity between the neo-conservative Republican Bush and the Democratic Obama administration's reductive exceptionalist invocation and spectacularization of Osama bin Laden that needs registering here. More importantly, I want to point to and underscore the perennial onto-psychological mechanism, *intrinsic to the exceptionalist logic of American exceptionalism from the Puritans to the present*, that lies deeply embedded in this triumphalist reduction at its liminal point: that willful reification or objectification by violence of the anxiety-provoking differential dynamics of historicity that brings "composure" (*Pax*: peace) in the aftermath of its bloodletting.

But because it seems that Kerry's speech, particularly his spectacularization of the "surgically executed" killing of Osama bin Laden,[24] was strategically orchestrated to anticipate and highlight President Obama's own climactic reference to this highly visible fulfilled promise, it will be necessary, first, to briefly address the latter's speech accepting his nomination for a second term. As I have noted, Obama, unlike Senator Kerry, did not overtly invoke the term "American exceptionalism" in his speech,[25] but the idea was everywhere patently manifest in his rhetoric, which clearly echoed—and tacitly responded to—the Republicans' sustained charge, made highly visible by the media, that his ambiguous comments in Strasburg in 2009—"I believe in American exceptionalism, just as I suspect the Brits believe in British exceptionalism and the Greeks believed in Greek exceptionalism"—were a manifestation of his recidivist antiexceptionalism. Unlike the Republican speakers' assumptions about the meaning of the American exceptionalist ethos, which were purely celebratory of capitalist America, Obama's was nuanced, incorporating in a way that his opponents do not the primacy of the citizen—people—in the American polity at the domestic site and acknowledging the obstacles in the way of accomplishing the errand in the world's wilderness. And, in keeping with the immediate main concern of the American public, he emphasized the economy rather than the United States' global policy. But nothing in his speech calls into question the idea of America as redeemer nation. On the contrary, as his rousing conclusion testifies, it reiterates in the very language of the Puritan founders the transcendental source of America's chosenness (its calling) and its redemptive vocation:

> America, I never said this journey would be easy, and I won't promise that now. Yes, our pain is harder—but it leads to a better place. Yes, our road is longer— but we travel it together. We don't turn back. We leave no one behind. We pull each other up. We draw strength from our victories, and we learn from our mistakes, but we keep our eyes fixed on the distant horizon, knowing that Providence is with us, and that we are surely blessed to be citizens of the greatest nation on earth.

And, like his Republican opponents, therefore, he tacitly obliterates from the American cultural memory the predatory historical role that American exceptionalism has, in fact, perennially and systematically played at home and globally in the process of fulfilling its redemptive errand.

As I have observed, however, it is not only these contradictory political disavowals that need to be registered for the purpose of understanding the subtly complex operations of the exceptionalist logic of American exceptionalism. Equally, if not more, important is the onto-psychological mechanism that resides, *as its deepest structure*, at the core of Obama's and America's exceptionalist ethos. I mean, as I previously noted in underscoring the precise similarity of Senator Kerry's spectacularization of the execution of Osama bin Laden and George W. Bush's own spectacularization ten years earlier in the wake of 9/11, that exceptionalism—*the imperative to excess inhering in the word*—in the pursuit of the potential of its unerring logic to its limits. For Obama, too, like Senator Kerry (and

President Bush) not only singled out the spectacular execution of Osama bin Laden to underscore his exceptional leadership and commitment to the "promise" and charged this symbolic reference with the aura of the spectacle (it received the longest and most boisterous ovation of his speech from his audience). Like Kerry and Bush before him, the president also invoked the spectacular assassination of bin Laden to activate the heroic frontier narrative endemic to the exceptionalism of the American cultural memory, which, whatever the particular historical occasion (and aftermath), invariably ends with the decisively triumphant "mission accomplished."[26]

> In a world of new threats and new challenges, we can choose leadership that has been tested and proven. Four year ago, I promised to end the war in Iraq. We did. I promised to refocus on the terrorists who actually attacked us on 9/11. We have. We've blunted the Taliban's momentum in Afghanistan, and in 2014 our longest war will be over. A new tower rises above the New York skyline, al Qaeda is on the path to defeat, and Osama bin Laden is dead.

Read against the grain, as the New Americanists have done (and Walter Benjamin asserts is the global task of the "historical materialist"),[27] however, this American frontier narrative invariably ends in the reification of a complex historical reality—one invariably produced by the barbarous civilizing "errand"—and the annihilation of the threat this reification allegedly embodies. But we need not invoke the historical materialism of Benjamin or the witness of the New Americanists for the purpose of disclosing this ultimate disavowal inhering in the American exceptionalist narrative. What comes more immediately to hand for this task of exposure—especially if we recall the spectacular rhetoric Senator Kerry uses to characterize President Obama's pursuit of Osama bin Laden ("he promised to focus like a laser on al-Qaeda")—are two apocalyptic—but neglected—troubling moments from two texts of the American literary tradition itself, counter-mnemonic texts written by Herman Melville that, in the middle of the century of westward expansion, revealed the Puritan origins of the American exceptionalist ethos and its cumulative hegemonic power and, in so doing, proleptically disclosed the violent underside of its alleged benignity at the liminal point of its unerring logic. The first, which is at the absent center of *Moby-Dick*, characterizes the *onto-psychological ground* of Captain Ahab's "fiery pursuit" of what Ishmael, the narrator, pointedly refers to as the "White Whale." Though I have quoted this passage in Chapter 1, I cite it again at this critical juncture to underscore the uncanny sameness (but radical difference in meaning) between Melville's representation of the consequences of this exceptionalist onto-psychological drive and those of President Bush, Senator Kerry, and President Obama:

> And then it was, that suddenly sweeping his sickle-shaped lower jaw beneath him, Moby Dick had reaped away Ahab's leg, as a mower a blade of grass in the field. . . . The White Whale swam before him as the *monomaniac incarnation of all those malicious agencies* which some deep men feel eating in them, till they are left living on with half a heart and half a lung. That intangible malignity which has been from the beginning; to whose dominion even the modern Christians ascribe one-half of the worlds; which the ancient Ophites of the east reverenced in their statue devil;—Ahab did not fall down and worship it like them; but deliriously transferring its idea to the abhorred white whale, he pitted himself, all mutilated, against it. *All* that most maddens and torments; *all* that stirs up the lee of things; all truth with malice in it; *all* that cracks the sinews and cakes the brain; *all* the subtle demonisms of life and thought; *all* evil, to crazy Ahab, *were visibly personified, and made practically assailable in Moby Dick.* He piled upon the whale's white hump the sum of *all the general rage and hate felt by his whole race from Adam down; and then, as if his chest had been a mortar, he burst his hot heart's shell upon it.*[28]

Indissolubly related to this first apocalyptic moment, the second—which is at the absent center of those chapters, still to be fully understood, of *The Confidence-Man: His Masquerade* that articulate "the metaphysics of Indian-hating"—characterizes the *practical worldly* imperatives of the onto-psychic logic of American exceptionalism:

> The Indian-hater *par excellence* the judge defined to be one "who, having with his mother's milk drank in small love for red men, in youth or early manhood, ere the sensibilities become osseous, received at their hand some signal outrage, or, which in effect is much the same, some of his kin have, or some friend. Now, nature all around him by her solitudes wooing or bidding him muse upon the matter, he accordingly does so, till the thought develops such attraction, that much as straggling vapors troop from all sides to a storm-cloud, so straggling thoughts of other outrages troop to the nucleus thought, assimilate with it, and swell it. At last, taking counsel with the elements, he comes to his resolution. An intenser Hannibal, he make a vow, *the hate of which is a vortex from whose suction scarce the remotest chip of the guilty race may reasonably feel secure.* Next, he declares himself and settles his temporal affairs. With the solemnity of a Spaniard turned monk, he takes leave of his kin; or rather, these leave-takings have something of the still more impressive finality of death-bed adieus. Last, he commits himself to the forest primeval; there, so long as life shall be his, to act

upon a calm, cloistered scheme of strategical, implacable, and lonesome vengeance. Ever on the noiseless trail; cool, collected, patient; less seen than felt; snuffing, smelling—*a Leather-stocking Nemesis.* In the settlements he will not be seen again; in eyes of old companions tears may start at some chance thing that speaks of him; but they never look for him, nor call; they know he will not come. Suns and seasons fleet; the tiger-lily blows and falls; babes are born and leap in their mothers' arms; but the Indian-hater is good as gone to his long home, *and "Terror" is his epitaph.*[29]

In both these complementary liminal passages Melville not only discloses the "monomaniacal" worldly violence that is endemic to but disavowed by the binary logic of the benign American exceptionalist errand. Equally, if not more importantly, he discloses, by way of locating his interrogation of the unerring paranoid logic of American exceptionalism at its liminal point, the deep onto-psychological structure that justifies this contradictory worldly violence: the will to power, authorized, indeed, commanded, as a *calling* by a transcendental signified (or *logos*) that ruthlessly reduces the "threatening" differential many to a spectacular objectified (or personified) One to render "*it,*" in the uncannily proleptic terms Melville uses to epitomize the culmination of Ahab's monomaniacal "fiery pursuit" of the ultimately unpredictable White Whale, "*practically* assailable." In thus bearing witness to the contradiction that lies at the determining center of American exceptionalist practice in the middle of the nineteenth century, Melville also anticipates the contemporary American political class's spectacular violent paranoid reduction of the haunting "problem" of the volatile Middle East to "Osama bin Laden"—"Got Him!" And, by focusing the spectacular violence enabled by this reduction—and its ultimate futility, it should be underscored—he proleptically bears witness to the self-de-struction [30] (not the negation but the decolonization of its structure) of the American exceptionalism ethos.[31] This is what I mean by underscoring the extraordinary incommensurability between the myth and the reality of American exceptionalism in the subtitle of this chapter about the discourse of political class in the United States.

5

Finally, though not least, as I have insinuated all along in my rhetoric, there is the question of the relationship between the spectacle and the exceptionalist logic of American exceptionalism. By "spectacle," I mean, with Guy Debord, that extreme, visually oriented, and calculative mode of representation, fundamental to the West but consummated in the democratic capitalism of the modern age, that, in substituting the simulacral image for temporal worldly reality, has as its essential purpose to "strike [the spectator] dumb":

> Where the real world changes into simple images, the simple images become real beings and effective motivations *of hypnotic behavior* [my emphasis]. The spectacle, as a tendency to *make one see* the world by means of various specialized mediations (it can no longer be grasped directly) *naturally finds vision to be the privileged human sense which the sense of touch was for other epochs* [my emphasis]; the most abstract, the most mystifiable sense corresponds to the generalized abstraction of present-day society. But the spectacle is not identifiable with mere gazing, even combined with hearing. It is that which escapes the activity of men, that which escapes reconsideration and correction by their work. *It is the opposite of dialogue.* Wherever there is independent representation, the spectacle reconstitutes itself.[32]

Or, more precisely with Giorgio Agamben, who, as I have shown in Chapter 1, has appropriated Debord's revolutionary insight into the hypnotic effect of the spectacle for the contemporary global political occasion:

> It is evident, after all, that the spectacle is language, the very communicativity and linguistic being of humans. This means that an integrated Marxian analysis should take into consideration the fact that capitalism . . . not only aims at the expropriation of productive activity, but also, and above all, at the alienation of language itself, of the linguistic and communicative nature of human beings, of that *logos* in which Heraclitus identifies the Commons.[33]

As I have observed, the spectacle is intrinsic to the very idea of American exceptionalism in that it proffers extremity as a positive value. In pursuing the practical imperatives of the visualist logic of exceptionalism to their limits in Afghanistan and Iraq, for example, the George W. Bush administration invoked—and endowed mythic status to—the (now ubiquitous) term "shock and awe" to characterize its staged spectacular high-tech military campaign in behalf of its exceptionalist policy of unilateral "regime change" in the Middle East. The Bush administration's appropriation of the spectacle for its neo-imperial project was no accident. As I have shown in Chapter 1, the genealogy of these "exceptionalist" tactics of conquest had its origins at the outset of the European colonization of America, when, for example, from the beginning of his imperial expedition in the New World, Cortés "organized veritable *son et lumière* [sound and light] spectacles with his horses and cannons" as his essential means of stupefying the "savage" natives into submission.[34]

From this liminal perspective afforded by the New Americanists' counter-mnemonic genealogy of the American national identity we are enabled to perceive the dark disavowed to which we have been hitherto blinded by the benign discourse of American exceptionalism. From this estranged perspective, more specifically, we not only see that both the Republican and Democratic national conventions, the mis en scène itself of this meditation on the use of the term "American exceptionalism," are *staged spectacles* in Debord's and, particularly, in Agamben's sense of the term. We also see—and, more decisively—that the resonant specific precipitate of these general spectacles—the spectacularization of the surgically executed assassination of Osama bin Laden by the U.S. Navy Seals team, for example—are intended, like the "shock and awe" tactics that, in fact, inaugurated the unending wars in Afghanistan and Iraq (not to say the normalization of the state of exception and the reduction of human life to bare life), to reduce their audiences to spectators—and their voices to awed silence—which is to say, in Hannah Arendt's enabling term—if we refuse to forget that nothing has changed in the Middle East since this symbolic execution, that the war rages on—*to deny a people who identify their exceptionalism with the dialogics of democracy, a "polity."*[35] But it is not simply the *futile* violence concealed by the celebratory exceptional discourse of the American political class that is disclosed by America's fulfillment of the practical imperatives of its logic in the Middle East. In pursuing these imperatives to their liminal point, as I have observed, the nationalist discourse of American exceptionalism has *self-de-structed*. This not only means that the spectacular regime of truth it embodies was delegitimated; more importantly, it means that the "degraded" and "threatening" historicity—language or, better, word*s*, (*not The Word*), in the last instance—that the exceptionalist *logos* that had reified or spatialized and spectacularized was liberated from the bondage of *structure*—decolonized, as it were—and rendered open to its positive possibilities. If human being and language (word*s*) are one—if *anthropos* is *"a zoon logon* [words] *echon"*—as the self-de-struction of the American exceptionalist ethos reveals, then this self-de-struction also points to a coming community, which in retrieving word*s*—"the linguistic and communicative nature of human beings," as Agamben, following Hannah Arendt, puts it—restores a *polity* to the Commons. What, it will be

recalled from Chapter 1, follows the passage on the spectacularity of the
spectacle from Agamben's globally oriented meditation on Guy Debord's
legacy, quoted previously, is this:

> The extreme form of the expropriation of the Common is the spectacle, in other
> words, the politics in which we live. But this also means that what we encounter
> in the spectacle is our very linguistic nature inverted. For this reason (precisely
> because what is being expropriated is the possibility itself of a common good),
> the spectacle's violence is so destructive; but, for the same reason, the spectacle
> still contains something like a positive possibility—and it is our task to use this
> possibility against it. (MN, 81–82)[36]

As a polity whose essence is word*s*, that which the spectacle annuls, the
coming community becomes an "unhomed homeland," one in which
the friend/foe binary intrinsic to the *polis* of the modern nation-state
is rendered "inoperative": the binaries remain identities, but now they
become productive: a loving strife. In Agamben's terms, "The space [of
this polity] would coincide neither with any of the homogeneous national
territories nor with their topographical sum, but would rather act on
them by articulating and perforating them topologically as in the Klein
bottle or in the Möbius strip, *where exterior and interior in-determine
each other.*"[37]

Agamben is not necessarily addressing contemporary America—and
American exceptionalism—in pointing to the Achilles' heel of the society of the spectacle that exposes itself at the liminal point of its spectacular logic or suggesting the positive possibilities concerning the
coming *polis*. But clearly, his globally oriented analysis of this liminal
condition is uncannily à propos of the post–9/11 American occasion. By
this I not only mean the United States' loss of global hegemony in the
wake of its unleashing of its War on Terror; its unilateral commitment
to "preemptive wars," to "regime change," and the installation of ventriloquized "democratic" governments; its employment of the tactics of
shock and awe in Afghanistan and Iraq; and its tacit normalization of
the state of exception—all in the name of American exceptionalism. I
also mean the emergence, with this loss of global hegemony, of a global
consciousness in all those Others of America that America hitherto
spoke for. Seen in the light of this interregnum—and the continuing
exceptionalism of the American political class—the imperative for
Americanist scholarship becomes remarkably manifest—and urgent. In
keeping with the emergent New Americanists' dialogic global initiative,

it calls for the abandonment of the historically delegitimated American exceptionalist ethos and the strident nationalist (and imperialist) perspective it apotheosizes in favor of a transnational perspective that, in a rhetoric remarkably similar to Agamben's, the late Edward W. Said envisioned the coming *polis* as " 'the complete concert dancing together' contrapuntally."

CHAPTER 3

"The Center Will Not Hold"

The Widening Gyre of the New, New Americanist Studies

It is no exaggeration to say that liberation as an intellectual mission, born in the resistance and opposition to the confinements and ravages of imperialism, has shifted from the settled, established, and domesticated dynamics of culture to its unhoused, decentered and exilic energies, energies whose incarnation today is the migrant, and whose consciousness is the intellectual and artist in exile, the political figure between domains, between forms, between homes, and between languages.

—Edward W. Said, *Culture and Imperialism*

So, floating on the margin of the ensuing scene, in full sight of it, when the half-spent suction of the sunk ship reached me, I was then, but slowly, drawn towards the closing vortex. When I reached it, it had subsided to a creamy pool. Round and round, then, and ever contracting towards the button-like black bubble at the axis of that slowly wheeling circle, like another Ixion I did revolve. Till, gaining that vital center, the black bubble upward burst; and now, liberated by reason of its cunning spring, and, owing to its great buoyancy, rising with great force, the coffin life-buoy shot lengthwise from the sea, fell over, and floated by my side. Buoyed up by that coffin, for almost one whole day and night, I floated on a soft and dirge-like main. The unharming sharks, they glided by as if with padlocks on their mouths; the savage sea-hawks sailed with sheathed beaks. On the second day, a sail drew near, nearer, and picked me up at last. It was the devious-cruising Rachel, that in her retracing search after her missing children, only found another orphan.

—Herman Melville, *Moby-Dick*

I

In the summer of 2000, shortly before the epochal bombing of the World Trade Center and the Pentagon by al Qaeda on September 11, 2001, and President George W. Bush's spectacular annunciation of the United States' War on Terror, I delivered a paper entitled "American Studies in 'the Age of the World Picture: Thinking the Question of Language,'" at the Humanities Institute at Dartmouth College (published after 9/11 in 2002) in Donald E. Pease and Robyn Wiegman's inaugural volume, *The Futures of American Studies*.[1] In that contribution to the New Americanist project, I criticized the promising counter-mnemonic initiative of the "New Americanists" for remaining too local in an age that had irreversibly become global. It was my view then that these New Americanists remained vestigially bound to the American exceptionalist ethos in a global age, dominated by the United States, that has brought the spatializing logic of Western metaphysical thinking (thinking *meta ta physica*: from after or above things-as-they-are) to its fulfillment (and theoretical demise) by way of the final reduction of temporality to a "world picture" (and the disclosure of the nothing [*das Nichts*] it cannot finally contain). More specifically, I argued that, for all their interrogation of the celebratory discourse of American exceptionalism (the American Adam of the myth and symbol school that inaugurated American studies in the World War II period), these New Americanists, with a few exceptions, were not global enough. By this I meant that they had not yet achieved the inside-outside (decentered or exilic) perspective that would have (1) enabled them to perceive exceptionalist America from the eyes of its victimized "others" and (2) that, in thus remaining vestigially *inside* the metaphysical ontology of American exceptionalism, they were unwittingly compelled to fulfill the prophetic dictates of Francis Fukuyama's (de Tocquevillean/Hegelian) annunciation of the "end of History" in the wake of the triumph of American democracy over Soviet communism—and the absolute vindication of the "truth" of the American exceptionalist:

> What is emerging victorious is not so much liberal practice, as the liberal *idea*. That is to say for a very large part of the world, there is now no ideology with pretension to universality that is in a position to challenge liberal democracy, and no universal principle of legitimacy other than the sovereignty of the people. *Even non-democrats will have to speak the language of democracy in order to justify their deviation from the single universal standard.*[2]

Commenting on this prophetic American exceptionalist annunciation of the end of History, I wrote:

> The universalist-instrumentalist discourse that frames the triumphalist American vision of the brave new post–Cold War world rings hollow in the wake of its self-destruction during the Vietnam War and of the postmodern thinking that has tacitly theorized the violence inherent in its saying. Nevertheless, New Americanists continue unthinkingly to use this language even when it opposes the violence of its practices, thus becoming unwitting accomplices of the very regime of truth it would delegitimate. This complicity, for example, is manifest, as Paul Bové has decisively shown, in [Sacvan] Bercovitch's "reformist" mode of dealing with problems confronting the Americanist seeking for alternatives to the consensus-producing imperatives of the American jeremiadic discourse, specifically, his disabling delimitation of critical options to those made available by that discourse: "the option [for American critics] is not multiplicity or consensus. It is whether to make use of the categories of the culture or to be used by them."[3]

My frame of reference at that time was not simply the Vietnam War—the self-destruction, at this liminal point, of the long forwarding historical itinerary of America's "errand in [the world's] wilderness," of the American exceptionalist ethos by way of the American war machine's unerring destruction of Vietnam in the name of "saving" it for democracy. As this obscene paradox suggests, it was also the disclosure of the banality of the evil that the American exceptionalist language wrought on that "new frontier" with the leaking of the Pentagon Papers by Daniel Ellsberg. Michael Herr, it will be recalled, put this dreadful reality in an unforgettable synecdochical way in his account of the Tet Offensive:

> Our worst dread of yellow peril became realized; we now saw them dying by the thousands all over the country, yet they didn't seem depleted, let alone exhausted, as the Mission was claiming by the fourth day. We took space back quickly, expensively, with total panic and close to maximum brutality. Our machine was devastating. And versatile. It could do everything but stop. As one American major said, in a successful attempt of attaining history, "We had to destroy Ben Tre in order to save it." That's how most of the country came back under what we called control, and how it remained essentially occupied by the Viet Cong and the North until the day years later when there were none of us left there.[4]

The national forgetting of the apocalyptic violence inherent in the redemptive logic of American exceptionalism disclosed by the United States' brutal conduct of the war in Vietnam became the paranoid purpose of the American political class (Republican and Democrat) and the culture industry in the aftermath of that catastrophic war. It took the form of representing the protest movement in the United States against the war as a national paranoia—"the Vietnam Syndrome." And this sustained, massive ideological initiative of forgetting, aided and abetted by Saddam Hussein, a former client of the United States in the Middle East, was successfully accomplished during the first George Bush's administration with what was then represented by the American government and the media as the spectacular "surgical" victory of the American army in the first Gulf War (August 2, 1990–February 28, 1991), an accomplishment epitomized by the president's exclamation to a reporter, "Thank God, we've kicked the Vietnam syndrome at last."[5] What the finality of this exclamation of relief meant ideologically was that the "healing" of the Vietnam syndrome was the healing of the wounded American exceptionalist ethos—and, as the euphoria of the political class and the media made spectacularly clear, the redemption of America's exceptionalist errand in the world's wilderness. It established, before 9/11, the ideological justification for the second Bush administration's War on Terror in the name of America's redemptive global mission. It is this recuperative initiative—this rejuvenation of the American exceptionalist ethos and the realization of the myth—that, I will suggest, the new, post–9/11 generation of New Americanists has not adequately registered in its effort to transcend the limitations of its predecessors by way of the "transnationalization" of American studies.

2

Since the al Qaeda attacks on American soil on September 11, 2001, and the United States' annunciation, under the aegis of the George W. Bush administration, of the United States' interminable global War on Terror, the blindness of the New Americanist studies to the global context I had pointed to at Dartmouth College in the summer of 2000 have been overcome. In the decade or so following 9/11, a remarkably large archive of New Americanist scholarship and criticism addressing American studies according to the urgent imperatives of the waning of the nation-state system and the globalization of the planet has been produced. Edited volumes such as Wai Chee Dimock and Lawrence Buell's *Shades of the Planet: American Literature as World Literature* (2007); Janice Radway, Kevin Gaines, Barry Shank, and Penny von Eschen's *American Studies:*

An Anthology (2009);[6] Russ Castronovo and Susan Gillman's *States of Emergency: The Object of American Studies* (2009); Brian T. Edwards and Dilip Parameshwar Gaonkar's *Globalizing American Studies* (2010); and Donald E. Pease, Winfried Fluck, and John Carlos Rowe's *Re-Framing the Transnational Turn in American Studies* (2011),[7] among others, which include the essays of a wide range of prestigious and neophyte New Americanist scholars and books such as Paul Giles's *Virtual America: Transnational Fictions and the Transatlantic Imaginary* (2002)[8] and *The Global Re-Mapping of American Literature* (2011); Donald Pease's *The New American Exceptionalism* (2009); and Paul Jay's *Global Matters: The Transnational Turn in Literary Studies* (2010),[9] among others, bear witness to this radical transformation of American studies. Despite the great diversity of perspectives, most leave behind the founding Puritan school of Americanist studies associated with Perry Miller and Sacvan Bercovitch and the nation-oriented myth and symbol field imaginary associated with Henry Nash Smith (*The Virgin Land*); Leo Marx (*The Machine in the Garden*); and R. W. B. Lewis (*The American Adam*), among others. Instead, as a number of the subtitles attest, this new generation of New Americanists takes its point of departure in the *trans*national turn compelled by the rapid globalization of the planet in the wake of World War II, which is to say, the self-destruction of the Western imperial project, the rise of the postcolonial consciousness, and the neo-liberal globalization of the "free market." The consequence of this transnational turn, as virtually all these post–9/11 New Americanist texts testify, has been the supersession of the emphasis of study on the national by the postnational or transnational, or, to anticipate, the *overdetermination* of the global over the local.[10] I am, of course, in some significant degree in solidarity with this turn in New Americanist studies, not least because (1) it has enabled the silenced peoples of the world—the multitudes who have hitherto been *spoken for* by the West—to *speak for themselves* or, in Dipesh Chakrabarty's resonant terms, to "provincialize Europe"—that is, to avow the violence against them that the hegemonic (exceptionalist) Western interpretation of history has always disavowed[11]; and (2), in so doing, this perspectival turn reveals the unexceptionalist essence of American exceptionalism. But, I submit, in overdetermining the transnational—in collapsing borders and boundaries—the trinity of "state, nation, territory" that underlies the modern nation-state system in favor of the "global" or the postnational[12]—this promising "new" Americanist initiative has gone too far in the direction I was calling for in 2000 in "American Studies in the Age of the World Picture." That is, as richly diverse as the transnationalizing of American studies seems to be, the one aspect that this diversity has surprisingly—unfortunately—in common is its marginalization of the hegemonic American exceptionalist ethos in the name of its "anti-exceptionalism." Despite its remarkable resurrection after 9/11 (now overtly, as the prolific use of the literal term by the American political class testifies) and the government of the United States' declaration of its exceptionalist War on Terror and on the rogue states that harbor them,[13] the new New Americanist transnational initiative views the manifestations of post–9/11 American exceptionalism, when it addresses it at all, as merely one of many, often unrelated, global projects—weather, gender, race, education, information, migration, the Americas, domestic politics, ecology, neo-liberal capitalism—rather than, as global history from the Vietnam War to the War on Terror patently bears witness, the locus that determines the structural feature of all these others.

Let me amplify what I mean by this paradigm shift from the local to the global enacted by these new New Americanists in the last decade by way of invoking the spatial metaphor that has informed not only the history of the West's representation of being (metaphysics), as Jacques Derrida has shown,[14] but also its political logic of belonging (the concept of the nation-state) and its comportment toward its Others (imperialism). I am referring to the centered circle, or, more precisely, the *exceptionalist* center/origin and the ever-expanding circumference or periphery that is intrinsic to the imperial logic (the "will to power" over difference) of thinking *meta ta physica* (from after or above or beyond things-as-they-are). The Achilles' heel of the sovereign logic of this exceptionalist/imperial metaphor lies in its inexorable imperative to expand its circumference, to incorporate and tether everything in space and every event in time to its commanding center. This is because the farther away from the center the circumference recedes, the weaker the tether that binds it to the sovereign center becomes. At a certain point in the centrifugal process the periphery eventually disintegrates, which is to say, it annuls the (power) of the exceptionalist center. To quote W. B. Yeats's "Second Coming" (without adhering to his conservative nostalgic judgment):

> Turning and turning in the widening gyre
> The falcon cannot hear the falconer;
> Things fall apart; the centre cannot hold;
> Mere anarchy is loosed upon the world,

The blood-dimmed tide is loosed, and everywhere
The ceremony of innocence is drowned;
The best lack all conviction, while the worst
Are full of passionate intensity.[15]

Taking my directives from this centrifugal temporal dynamics of the center/periphery, I am suggesting that the new New Americanists to whom I am referring all too prematurely assume that the globalization of the planet and the demise of the nation-state (the emergence of the global and the annulment of the local) have been historically accomplished. Though they take their theoretical point of departure from the decentering of the metaphysical center, it is, paradoxically, the panoptic perspective enabled by the "center elsewhere" that, like that of the traditional Americanists they oppose, determines their representation of the contemporary historical occasion. In thus positioning themselves outside of— and in opposition to—the local, not incidentally, they tacitly circumscribe the "exilic consciousness"—the in-between, the outside-inside condition that Edward Said posited as the most efficacious agency of resistance to contemporary power relations. For all their insistence on attending to history, they seem blinded by the oversight of their global problematic to its local historical actualities.[16] Indeed, this New Americanist oversight for all practical purposes annuls the local of the local-global dyad, or, more specifically, the role that the nation-state, particularly the United States, continues to play in the world at large. Despite the continuing identification of their scholarly discipline with America, they, like the exponents of world literature (*Weltliteratur*)—Pascale Casanova, David Damrosch, Franco Moretti, and John Pizer, among many others,[17] and the exponents of cosmopolitanism (Martha Nussbaum and Bruce Robins, among others), who have clearly influenced their global vision, their historical perspective is so broad that it effaces the culturally and politically fraught post–9/11 occasion and the urgent need to resist the form of globalism it is taking by way of the harnessing of the American state to the dynamics of the global free market.[18] To put it generally, what this panoptic global perspective overlooks in its all too easy, sometimes euphoric representation of the contemporary historical occasion as "deterritorialized"[19] is that global humanity, in fact, lives in an *interregnum*, in between the local (or national) and the global, a world-system (the nation-state) that is dying (but is not in fact dead) and a decentered world struggling to be born.

It is true that, on the one hand, the American exceptionalist myth self-de-structed *theoretically* during the course of the Vietnam War ("We had to destroy Ben Tre in order to save it") and then again, even more decisively, with George W. Bush's declaration of the United States' unending global War on Terror and the rogue states, like Iraq and Afghanistan, that harbored terrorists in the aftermath of September 11, 2001, and, on the other, that the multiplication of contrapuntal postcolonial voices have challenged the American version of the exceptionalist Western narrative of modern global history. But this theoretical self-de-struction has not manifested itself in the destruction of American exceptionalist praxis. Despite its theoretical disintegration, the American exceptionalist ethos continues, after the fall of the Bush administration, to remain intact as a hegemonic "truth." The tentative speech-bereaving spectacle of American high-tech war-making, the "domino theory," the creation of puppet regimes, and the establishment of torture camps inaugurated by the United States in the name of America's exceptionalist errand on the "New [Southeast Asian] Frontier" were brought to their liminal (and revelatory) point of development by the George W. Bush administration after 9/11 when it identified the United States as a homeland security state:

> The security environment confronting the United States today is radically different from what we have faced before. Yet the first duty of the United States government remains what it always has been: to protect the American people and American interests. It is an enduring American principle that this duty obligates the government to anticipate and counter threats, using all elements of national power, before the threats can do grave damage. The greater the threat, the greater the risk of inaction—and the more compelling the case for taking anticipatory action to defend ourselves, even if uncertainty remains as to the time and place of the enemy's attack. There are few greater threats than a terrorist attack with WMD [Weapons of Mass Destruction].
>
> To forestall or prevent such hostile acts by our adversaries, the United States will, if necessary, act preemptively in exercising our inherent right of self-defense. The United States will not resort to force in all cases to preempt emerging threats. Our preference is that nonmilitary actions succeed. And no country should ever use preemption as a pretext for aggression.[20]

I am referring specifically to the Bush administration's illegal doctrine of preemptive war (the invasion of Afghanistan and Iraq); the "shock and awe" military tactics that were intended to strike these Third World peoples dumb; the systematic institutionalization of concentration camps

(Abu Ghraib and Guantánamo); the practice of detention and torture without legal recourse obscenely called "extraordinary rendition" by its apologists; the tethering (however contradictorily) of the American state to the neoliberal global free market, indeed, as Robert Marzec has forcefully shown, the militarization of the global ecos in the name of national security;[21] and, not least, the declaration of a global state of emergency in the name of homeland security (The Homeland Security Act), all enacted in the name of the redemptive American exceptionalist ethos and the *Pax Americana.*[22] In short, what was tentatively inaugurated in the period of the Vietnam War in the name of the "exceptionalist American state" became under the aegis of the sovereign Bush administration the global normalization of the state of exception: the biopoliticization of human life, which is to say, with Giorgio Agamben's identification of modern democratic (particularly American) political practice and Nazi biopolitics in mind, the reduction of *bios* to *zoé*, bare life (*nuda vida*), life that can be killed without the killing being called homicide.

> The wish to lend a sacrificial aura to the extermination of Jews by means of the term "Holocaust" was . . . an irresponsible historiographical blindness. The Jew living under Nazism is the privileged negative referent of the new biopolitical sovereignty and is, as such, a flagrant case of *homo sacer* in the sense of a life that may be killed but not sacrificed. His killing therefore constitutes . . . neither capital punishment nor a sacrifice, but simply the actualization of a mere "capacity to be killed" inherent in the condition of the Jew as such. The truth—which is difficult for the victims to face, but which we must have the courage not to cover with sacrificial veils—is that the Jews were exterminated not in a mad and giant holocaust but exactly as Hitler had announced, "as lice." Which is to say, as bare life. The dimension in which these exterminations took place is neither religion nor law, but biopolitics.
>
> If it is true that the figure proposed by our age is that of unsacrificeable life that has nevertheless become capable of being killed to an unprecedented degree, then the bare life of *homo sacer* concerns us in a special way. Sacredness is a line of flight still present in contemporary politics. A line that is as such moving into zones increasingly vast and dark, to the point of ultimately coinciding with the biological life itself of citizens. If today there is no longer any one clear figure of the sacred man, it is perhaps because we are all virtually *homines sacri.*[23]

3

Nothing substantial has changed since the fall of the Bush administration and the election of Barack Obama. To be sure, the cultural rhetoric of this Democratic administration, playing as it does to both political constituencies, has become less strident and aggressively exceptionalist than that of the Bush administration. But it continues to represent itself and the Americana people fundamentally in terms of the American exceptionalist ethos and its redemptive global mission. More importantly, its domestic and global practice remains basically the same as that of the Bush administration. The Bush doctrines of preemptive war and regime change; its tactics of staging the spectacle; and its harnessing of the power of the state to the global free market have not been explicitly renounced; the War on Terror continues; Guantánamo and the lawless detention camps in political indeterminate zones remain open and operative; the torture of Arabs suspected of terrorism (euphemistically called "enhanced interrogation techniques") and the targeting of terrorist suspects by CIA hit squads (now drones) go on. In sum, the Bush administration's establishment of the homeland security state in the wake of the al Qaeda bombing of the World Trade Center and the Pentagon and enacted by Congress as The Homeland Security Act of 2002[24]—the sovereign executive decision that rendered the state of exception the global rule—remains the determining "law" of American domestic and global practice.[25] Equally importantly, it is the American exceptionalist ethos—the perennial belief that History has ordained America as the redeemer nation—that continues to inform this law.

That this national condition remains the case in the wake of the election of a Democratic president is borne witness to by the sudden adoption and massive take-off of the celebratory use of the term "American exceptionalism" by the American political class (Republican and Democrat) and the culture industry in the aftermath of 9/11 as a jeremiadic strategy for covenantal rejuvenation. As the sociologist Jerome Karabel has observed about the remarkable popularization of the term since its emergence during the Reagan administration's Cold War against the Soviet Union: "According to a Gallup poll from December 2010, 80 percent of Americans agree that 'because of the United States' history and the Constitution—the United States has a unique character that makes it the greatest country in the world.' Support for this proposition varied somewhat along party lines, but not by much: 91 percent of Republicans agreed, but so, too, did 73 percent of Democrats."[26] Indeed, these telling statistics were dramatically corroborated during the national presidential election conventions of 2012, during which the Democratic Party speakers in behalf of Obama (including Obama himself) vied with the Republican speakers in behalf of Mitt Romney over which candidate (and party) was more faithful in its practice to the redemptive imperatives of the American exceptionalist ethos. In Chapter 2, I analyzed in some detail a number of these speeches by the American political class to show the continuing hegemonic power of the term. Here, for the specific purpose of this chapter, I will restrict my commentary to a brief rehearsal of the spectacular use (in the Debordian sense) to which Senator John Kerry (now secretary of state in the Obama administration) put the term in behalf of persuading the American public, against earlier and persistent jeremiadic accusations of betrayal by Republican spokespersons, that President Obama's administration was continuing America's perennial exceptionalist errand in the world's wilderness.[27] I am referring to his staging (for effect) of his encomium to the president's American exceptionalism by way of his triumphant (but equivocal) climactic assertion that Obama's "promise" to fulfill the redemptive (symbolic) goal of America's global mission in the wake of 9/11 culminated in what the previous Republican administration had not achieved: the spectacular—"surgically executed"—assassination of Osama bin Laden, the living symbol of the threat posed by jihadist Islam to the security of the American people:

> And President Obama kept his promise. He promised to end the war in Iraq—and he has—and our heroes have come home. He promised to end the war in Afghanistan responsibly—and he is—and our heroes there are coming home. He promised to focus like a laser on al Qaeda—and he has—our forces have eliminated more of its leadership in the last three years than in all the eight years that came before. And after more than ten years without justice for thousands of Americans murdered on 9/11, after Mitt Romney said it would be "naïve" to go into Pakistan to pursue the terrorist, it took President Obama, against the advice of many, to give that order to finally rid this earth of Osama bin Laden. Ask Osama bin Laden if he is better off now than he was four years ago. [INORDINATE APPLAUSE][28]

In thus identifying American exceptionalism as the determining agent of the spectacular assassination of Osama bin Laden, Senator Kerry not only brings to fulfillment the conservative Republican George W. Bush's Texan-inflected Ahabism—his exceptionalist and monomaniac promise to hunt down Osama bin Laden—but, in so doing, he also brings to its liminal point the essential—massively destructive (and finally self-defeating)—*exceptional* (onto)logic, or, rather, the (onto)logic of exceptionalism—of the American exceptional ethos: the objectification of the complexities of history (produced in large part by Western and American colonialism) to render them, as Melville proleptically observed of Captain Ahab's monomaniacal exceptionalism, *"practically assailable."*[29] Despite the growing counter-mnemonic scholarship of the New Americanists pointing to a quite different evaluation of American exceptionalism, what seems to be astonishing about this discourse of the contemporary post–9/11 American political class is its obliviousness to its findings.

My purpose in thus retrieving this recent American history is, in sum, to underscore two affiliated urgent points, which, despite their patent visibility, have been strangely marginalized if not entirely overlooked by the new New Americanist globalized discourses. The first is that the American exceptionalist ethos continues at the present historical conjuncture to determine America's mission in the world. Despite its theoretical self-destruction (the disclosure of the violence it always disavows during the Vietnam War and again during the global War on Terror), it has not, as yet, become, in the Gramscian sense of the word, a (conscious and articulate) *ideology*; it remains, that is, a *hegemonic* discourse (what I have been calling, after Jacques Rancière, an "ethos")[30]: a polyvalent ideology that is taken by the American political class and the vast majority of the interpellated ("called") American public to be reality: "common sense," "the way things are." At the risk of rehearsing the obvious, I quote at length Raymond Williams's precise and resonant rendition of Antonio Gramsci's enabling and indispensable, yet curiously marginalized, distinction between "ideology" and "hegemony," which, in determining the difference between—and the sameness of—modern totalitarian and democratic/capitalist societies, remarkably epitomizes the American exceptionalist ethos:

> The concept of hegemony often, in practice, resembles the definitions [of "ideology" as a *consciously* held world view of both the dominant and subordinate classes], but it is distinct in its refusal to equate consciousness with the articulate formal system which can be and ordinarily is abstracted as "ideology." It of course does not exclude the articulate and formal meanings, values, and beliefs which a dominant class develops and propagates. But it does not equate these with consciousness, or rather it does not reduce consciousness to them. Instead it sees the relations of domination and subordination, in their forms as practical consciousness, as in effect a saturation of the whole process of living—not only of political and economic activity, nor only of manifest social activity, but of the whole substance of lived identities and relationships, to such a depth that the

pressures and limits of what can ultimately be seen as a specific economic, political, and cultural system seem to most of us the pressures and limits of simple experience and common sense. Hegemony is then not only the articulate upper level of "ideology," nor are its forms of control only those ordinarily seen as "manipulation" or "indoctrination." It is a whole body of practices and expectations, over the whole of living: our senses and assignments of energy, our shaping perceptions of ourselves and our world. It is a lived system of meanings and values—constitutive and constituting—which as they are experienced as practices appear as reciprocally confirming. It thus constitutes a sense of reality for most people in the society, a sense of absolute because experienced reality beyond which it is very difficult for most members of society to move, in most areas of their lives. It is, that is to say, in the strongest sense a "culture," but a culture which has also to be seen as the lived dominance and subordination of particular classes.[31]

4

The second point I want to underscore in thus recalling the dominant role that American exceptionalism continues to play in the contemporary world, despite the volatile dynamic of globalization, is that our contemporary occasion is not the end of an era, whether of History or the American Century. It is rather *the occasion of the interregnum*. By this term I not only mean the "now time" between a centered world (the nation-state and its intrinsic exceptionalism) that is dying *but, in the form of the United States, is willfully, desperately, and dangerously trying to remain alive*, and a decentered world struggling to be born. I also mean "the now time" of the exilic consciousness, that damaged but thus estranging and illuminating local/global perspective of, in Edward Said's still compelling words, "the intellectual and artist in exile, the political figure between domains, between forms, between homes, and between languages," who is the consciousness of the ubiquitous deracinated "migrant," that incarnation of the "unhoused, decentered, and exilic energies" that, "today," in the wake of the implosion of the Western imperial project and the replacement of "the settled, established, and domesticated dynamics of culture," has become the new agent of liberation from oppression.[32] That is to say, to return to the metaphor of the centered circle (the local and the global), the interregnum compels the authentic intellectual to be both inside and outside the "world," at home and not at home, at once (a-part). From this estranged and estranging perspective—this profane alienating time of the now—as Said empoweringly observes, "all things are indeed counter, original, spare, strange": *potential* as such.[33] To put this imperative of the profane time of the now of the interregnum in Giorgio Agamben's alternative terms, in the interregnum the exilic intellectual's vocation becomes the "revocation of all vocations"[34]—the rendering inoperative of the interpellating ethos—in this case, American exceptionalism—that renders the individual human being a subjected subject, the willing *servant* of a higher (transcendental) cause, which is to say, the liberation of humanity from the bondage of a logic of belonging that serves the mystified few to a logic that returns the commons to the common. From the exilic perspective of this in-between time, too, one is enabled to envision a coming *polis* of the commons untethered to the sovereign and totalitarian center elsewhere, or, in Said's paradoxical and resonantly heuristic phrase, "'the complete consort dancing together' contrapuntally."

Given the continuing, if contested, authority of the polyvalent American exceptionalist ethos in the discourse and practice of the American political class throughout the post–9/11 era, it comes as a surprise to find that, in "remapping" American studies, the great majority of New Americanist texts published in the last decade either marginalize "America" (interrogate the validity of the term "American studies"), minimize America's exceptionalism, or virtually erase it in the process of overdetermining the site of the global or, rather, the plural aspects of the global. Of course, the tacit purpose of this overdetermination of the global (when it is not simply a matter of academic fashion) is, more or less, in keeping with the dictates of the global perspective, to diminish the imperial authority of the United States and, more generally, the concept of the nation-state. But the result of this outside Archimedean perspective, as I have been arguing, has been to distort the historical reality of the post–9/11 occasion. This distortion is evident in some significant degree in all the New American texts I have referred to. A remarkable example of this effacement of the visible local can be found in Wei Chee Dimock's "Planet America: Set and Subset," the introduction surveying the influential volume of New Americanist essays she edited with Lawrence Buell entitled *Shades of the Planet: American Literature as World Literature* (2007), which makes no significant reference to the primary role the perennial American exceptionalist ethos has played on a global scale since the Bush administration's declaration of America's War on Terror. It is true that Dimock refers in passing to 9/11 as a turning point in the history of American studies:

After the World Trade Center, and after Katrina, few of us are under the illusion that the Unites States is sovereign in any absolute sense. The nation seems to have come literally "unbundled" before our eyes, its fabric of life torn apart by extremist militant groups, and, by physical forces of even greater scope, wrought by climate change and the intensification of hurricane cycles. Territorial sovereignty, we suddenly realize, is no more than a legal fiction, a man-made fiction.[35]

But, it is not, in fact, America's unending exceptionalist War on Terror and the massive "collateral damage" it is inflicting that she overdetermines in introducing the topic of the globalizing of American literary studies and the essays that follow.[36] Indeed, the War on Terror and the "redemptive" exceptionalism of its origins are marginalized in the sequel (and in the following essays). It is, rather, as the emphasis in the above passage anticipates, "Katrina," the ecological disaster that befell New Orleans as a result of the United States' indifference to global warming that, she claims, has precipitated the planetization of American studies:

What Katrina dramatizes . . . is a form of "globalization" different from either scenarios [the emergence of a "global civil society" in the wake of the decline of the nation-state envisioned by such theorists as Jürgen Habermas and Michael Walzer, on the one hand, and the global free market under the aegis of the United States warned against by theorists such as Fredric Jameson, on the other]. Not benign, it is at the same time not predicated on the primacy of any nation. Long accustomed to seeing itself as the de facto center of the world—a military superpower, the largest economy, and the moral arbiter to boot—the United States suddenly finds itself downgraded to something considerably less. "It's like being in a Third World country," Mitch Handler, a manager in Louisiana's biggest public hospital, said to the Associated Press about the plight of hurricane victims. The Third-Worlding of a superpower came with a shock not only to Louisiana and Mississippi but to unbelieving eyes everywhere. Not the actor but the acted upon, the United States is simply the spot where catastrophe hits, the place on the map where large-scale forces, unleashed elsewhere, come home to roost. What does it mean for the United States to be on the receiving end of things? . . . Scale enlargement has stripped from this nation any dream of unchallenged primacy. If Europe has already been "provincialized"—has been revealed to be a smaller player in world history than previously imagined, as Dipesh Chakrabarty argues—the United States seems poised to follow. . . .

In this context, it seems important to rethink the adequacy of a nation-based paradigm [of American literary studies]. Is "American" an adjective that can stand on its own, uninflected, unentangled, and unconstrained? Can an autonomous field be built on its chronology and geography, equal to the task of phenomenal description and causal explanation? Janice Radway, in her presidential address to the American Studies Association of 1998, answers with a resounding "no," and proposes a name change for the association for just that reason. (PA, 2)

Dimock is, of course, justified in calling into question the sovereignty of the nation-state, "America," and the exceptionalism it implies. But her identification of the ground of this identification with Katrina *as such*—without pointing to the negative effects on the domestic site (in this case the ecologically vulnerable city New Orleans and its black population) of the United States' War on Terror—not only flies in the face of contemporary history. In deflecting attention from the unending, massively destructive global War on Terror being perpetrated by the United States in the name of its assumed redemptive global errand, it also defuses the urgency of naming this unerring exceptionalist justification as the normalization of the state of exception on both the local and global scale—a normalization, not incidentally, that includes the United States' right to militarize the ecos in the name of national security[37]—and, thus, of resisting not only its drive to reduce human life to life that can be killed with impunity, but also, in the end, to destroy the planet.

The deflection of critical attention to exceptionalist America endemic to this overdetermined global perspective of Wei Chee Dimock (and the majority of essays in the volume) is also plainly evident in various degrees in the other recent anthologies of New Americanist studies. But its disabling effect is most visible in the introduction to (and contents of) the volume entitled *The Globalization of American Studies*, edited by Brian T. Edwards and Dilip Parameshwar Gaonkar, a compilation of the best essays presented at the ongoing conferences of the "Global American Studies" project (GLAS) at Northwestern University. And this is because, unlike the editors of the other anthologies, who overdetermine the global at the expense of the local, these take the point of departure of their global perspective (and their summary of the essays in the volume) by invoking the myth of American exceptionalism (which, following Henry Luce, they refer to as "the American Century") only to dismiss it, along with the United States' exceptionalist post–9/11 War on Terror and its rendering of the state of exception the rule, as having run its historical course. That is to say, they begin from the vantage point of the "historical" coming-to-its-end of the myth of American exceptionalism, the dissolution, as it were, of the center intrinsic to the widening gyre. Thus, their introduction begins with an extended (and rather labored) commentary on the essay inaugurating the volume, Donald E. Pease's "American

Studies after American Exceptionalism?: Toward a Comparative Analysis of Imperial State Exceptionalism," the purpose of which is to challenge its thesis concerning the viability of American exceptionalism in the era of globalization:

> The question is whether American exceptionalism has always already been implicated in some sort of imperial formation, as Pease argues, with the American Century serving as the most recent incarnation of that imperial strand. This historical question, which Pease argues with considerable precision and force, need not, however, be the starting point for this introduction. If American exceptionalism was always implicated in American imperialism, so long as American imperialism does not come to an end, neither will some versions of American exceptionalism invoked to sustain that imperialism come to an end. In this we agree with Pease, but the question we ask is the following: What happens to American studies when the American Century—which can be variously described, including as an imperial formation, but which always refers to a particular logic of the circulation of capital, signs, texts, and (cultural) goods—comes to an end or enters its *longue durée*? If the American Century in the Lucean sense is coming or has come to an end, then we expect that the particular link between American exceptionalism and American studies is bound to change, if it has not already changed.[38]

Edwards and Gaonkar thus modify, if they do not entirely reject, Pease's thesis about the continuing existence of American exceptionalism by way of assuming, against historical reality, that the American Century has for all practical purposes come to its end. Admittedly they express ambiguousness about this end:

> The American Century cannot be critiqued out of existence, even if it renews itself in the guise of a decentered empire, as Michael Hardt and Antonio Negri would have us believe. Instead, it can only come to an end. We need to come to that time when American exceptionalism has to stand alone, in the multilateral world of the global. Indeed, we believe that we have come to that time, *or nearly so*. Therefore we suggest that the closing of the so-called American Century, less as unit of time than a decided shift in global conditions, signals the weakening of the long-and-enduring myth of American exceptionalism. American studies, as a result, must yield to a context within which such a formation—of America's special place and role in the world—requires the bracketing of fictions that can no longer be sustained. (GAS, 50; my emphasis)

This qualification is a telling one, but, as the content of the essay testifies, it has no importance to the editors' argument (and to that of most of the essays in the volume) about the "closing of the American Century."[39]

Indeed, the ambiguity strikes one as a specter of the historical reality of the interregnum—the exceptionalism that continues to inform America's global practice—that haunts Edward's and Gaonkar's overdetermined global thesis. Like the other texts to which I have referred thus far, Edwards's and Gaonkar's bear spectral witness to the new New Americanist betrayal of the critical imperatives of the interregnum.

5

The small anthology edited by Russ Castronovo and Susan Gillman entitled *States of Emergency: The Object of American Studies* is, in this respect, more adequate than the Dimock and Buell volume, because, as the title suggests, it identifies the issue at stake for New Americanists as the rendering of the state of exception (emergency) as the global rule. In their "Introduction: The Study of the American Problems," however, the editors' global (as opposed to local) orientation renders their analysis finally inadequate to the critical imperatives of the interregnum, in which local and global belong together. Symptomatic of this inadequacy is the labored way the editors attempt to relate the global issues referred to in the essays—weather, slavery, neo-liberal capital, homosexuality, torture. Their overdetermination of the global perspective, that is, blinds them to the fact that it is the (local) American exceptionalist state, understood at its liminal point, as in the case of the Vietnam War and especially the post–9/11 War on Terror, that has precipitated the ominous normalization of the state of exception and thus constitutes the hidden paradigm that informs all the global topics to which the essay refers.

Two essays in this volume constitute exceptions to this general marginalization of the destructive role the United States continues to play on the global scene: Anne McClintock's "Paranoid Empire: Specters from Guantánamo and Abu Ghraib" and Ian Baucom's "Cicero's Ghost: The Atlantic, the Enemy, and the Laws of War." The first distinguishes itself by way of its brilliantly corrosive analysis of the notorious Abu Ghraib photographs depicting American soldiers torturing Arabs suspected of being terrorists, which, against the official representation that identifies the agents as exceptions to America's redemptive global mission ("bad apples"), demonstrates decisively that they were manifestations of an official paranoia that is the result of an imperial society's coherence around "contradictory cultural narratives, self-mythologies, practices and identities that oscillate between delusions of inherent superiority and omnipotence and phantasms of threat and engulfment."[40] The second distinguishes itself by way of its illuminating genealogy of the West's concept of the "unjust enemy" that has enabled its perennial colonizing project.

McClintock's focus on the "superior" (exceptionalist) imperial society's need for a perpetual enemy constitutes a major contribution to the understanding of both the strength and weakness of the Western imperial project. But in universalizing the paranoia informing the practice of torture at Abu Ghraib, it diverts attention from the specifically *American* version of this paranoia and its long history. Thus, for example, in introducing the theme of what she calls "the enemy deficit" that is intrinsic to imperial power, McClintock invokes the famous last lines of the modern Greek poet Constantine Cavafy's "Waiting for the Barbarians": "And now what shall become of us [the Romans] without any barbarians?/ Those people were a kind of solution." Commenting on these lines, she writes:

> C. P. Cavafy wrote "Waiting for the Barbarians" in 1927. But the poem haunts the aftermath of 9/11 with the force of an uncanny and prescient *déjà vu*. To what dilemma are the "barbarians a kind of solution"? Every modern empire faces an abiding crisis of legitimacy in that it flings its power over territories and peoples who have not consented to that power. Cavafy's insight is that an imperial state claims legitimacy only by evoking the threat of the barbarians. It is only the threat of the barbarians that constitutes the silhouette of the empire's borders in the first place. On the other hand, the hallucination of the barbarians disturbs the empire with perpetual nightmares of impending attack. The enemy is the abject of empire: the rejected from which we cannot part. And without the barbarians the legitimacy of empire vanishes like a disappearing phantom. These people were a kind of solution. (PE, 92)

McClintock then goes on to illustrate Cavafy's thesis by recalling, first, the dominant American culture's deep anxiety—she quotes General Peter Schoomaker, head of the U.S Army; Dick Cheney; Colin Powell; George W. Bush; and the neo-cons of the Project for the New American Century—over the loss of such an enemy with the end of the Cold War with the Soviet Union and, then, in Cavafy's language, their relief, if not euphoria, in the wake of al Qaeda's bombing of the World Trade Center and the Pentagon:

> The 9/11 attacks came as a dazzling solution to both the enemy deficit and the problem of legitimacy. General Schoomaker saw the attacks as an immense boon: "There is a huge silver lining in this cloud. . . . War is a tremendous focus.

Now we have this focusing opportunity, and we have the fact that (terrorists) have actually attacked our homeland, which gives it some oomph." After the 2001 invasion of Afghanistan, Powell noted, "America will have a continuing interest and presence in Central Asia of a kind we could not have dreamed of before." Charles Krauthammer called for a declaration of total war. "We no longer have to search for a name for the post–Cold War era," he declared, "It will henceforth be known as the age of terrorism." (PE, 93)

McClintock's Cavafian focus on the anxiety-provoking "enemy deficit" constitutes a significant contribution to our understanding of the paranoid dynamics of the imperial imagination. But her overdetermined universalizing global perspective blinds her to the more immediate origins of the American version of the paranoid imperial syndrome. That is to say, her recurrent reference to the American political class's vacillation between "delirium of grandeur" and "nightmare of perpetual threat" and thus of the paranoid need for a perpetual rejuvenating enemy can be more accurately—and, from the point of view of resistance, more productively—understood as having its genealogical origins in the American jeremiad. I mean that long and abiding ritualized (hegemonized) American cultural tradition, coeval with the origins of American exceptionalism, that, as I have shown in Chapter 1, had its origins, according to Sacvan Bercovitch, in the American Puritans' effort to combat recidivism—the very cultural backsliding that its errand in the New World wilderness was intended to transcend—by way of the instigation of anxiety—the threat of a perpetual enemy on the other side of a perpetual frontier. I requote from Bercovitch's *American Jeremiad* not only to suggest the remarkable parallel with McClintock's Cavafy but also to underscore the *difference* of this same between the process-oriented New World and the static Old World vocations and the hegemonic nature of the American jeremiad: the perennial national ritual that has ensured the rejuvenation (through violence) of the American covenantal people[41]:

> The American Puritan jeremiad was the ritual of culture on an errand—which is to say, a culture based on a faith in process. Substituting teleology for hierarchy, it discarded the Old World ideal of stasis for a New World vision of the future. Its function was to create a climate of anxiety that helped release the restless "progressive" energies required for the success of the venture. The European jeremiads also thrived on anxiety, of course. Like all traditional forms of ritual, it used fear and trembling to teach acceptance of fixed social norms. *But the American Puritan jeremiad went much further. It made anxiety its end as well as its means. Crisis was the social norm it sought to inculcate.* The very concept of

errand, after all, implied a state of *un*fulfillment. The future, though divinely assured, was never quite there, and New England's Jeremiads set out to provide the sense of insecurity that would ensure the outcome. Denouncing or affirming, their vision fed on the distance between promise and fact.[42]

Similarly, Ian Baucom, in "Cicero's Ghost: The Atlantic, the Enemy, the Laws of War," locates the genealogical origins of the Bush administration's representation of the terrorist suspects incarcerated and tortured in indeterminate juridical zones such as Abu Ghraib and Guantánamo as "unlawful combatants" back to European origins: the discourse and practice of modern Western nation-states, which identified the "unjust (nomadic) enemy" as one that was not organized into a national polity, thus violating "the law of nature" and justifying its destruction by sovereign (sedentary and civilized) states with impunity.[43] The difference between the two is a matter of degree of historical specificity. Whereas McClintock, via Cavafy's poem, locates the origins of contemporary America's "unjust enemy"—the barbarian Arab who can be tortured without the torture being subject to punishment—in the general imperial Roman distinction between civilization and barbarism, Baucom locates it in the early modern tradition of European jurisprudential discourse on war and the commonwealth instigated by the question of Black Atlantic slavery and going back from Immanuel Kant (*The Metaphysics of Morals*) to Thomas Hobbes (*Leviathan*), Hugo Grotius (*The Rights of War and Peace*), and Alberico Gentili (*De Jure Belli Libri*), who, in turn, find their source in Cicero's *Philippics* (against "'the bandit,'" Mark Antony, and his "'villainous band of brigands.'")[44] Taking his point of departure from the commentary justifying America's war against Iraq ("The Pentagon's New Map") of American policy expert Thomas P. M. Barnett, former director of "the New Rules Set Project, a collaborative project sponsored by the Naval War College and the investment consulting firm Cantor Fitzgerald," Baucom succinctly summarizes his globalized version of this genealogical history of America's version of the unjust enemy as follows:

> The key argument central to the mid-seventeenth-century law of war (and central again, in overtly Hobbesian terms, to Kant's own theory of international and cosmopolitan right) thus returns as key to Barnett's new map of capital, law, and war. In response to the appearance of a "predatory" people living in a putatively real state of nature on the boundaries and beyond the outposts of stable nation-states and the circulating flow of capital—people living in that "lawless condition in which man is a wolf to man" (*homo homini lupus* [Hobbes]), the condition of human life one of a perpetual war of all against all, and the pursuit

of commerce impossible in the absence of an overawing law-and-contract-securing power—sovereign power can again extend itself as a law-constituting power of violence and, in so extending law and violence, extend the flow of capital. And it is not at all an accident that at precisely the moment in which this Hobbesian-Kantian map of war should re-emerge, or that at the very frontier of its Gulf War testing ground, so too should the figure of the *inimicus* return to the law-suspending center of the law of war: now in the form of the "unlawful enemy combatant" identified in President Bush's October 2001 order of War and subsequently written into U.S. law by the Military Commissions Act of 2006—a figure, once again, distinguishable from the "lawful enemies" of the imperial state by the failure to "belong to a State party": a figure, once again inimical, rightless, legally exceptional, and languishing indefinitely, but by law, within yet another of the Atlantic's legally free and empty zones; a melancholy successor figure in the long line of "Capman," "Hottentots," "brigands," "*inimici,*" and "unjust enemies," against whom the imperial state has held its own "rights" to be "unlimited." (CG, 138)

As in the case of McClintock's genealogical focus on America's perennial "enemy deficit," Baucom's remarkably similar, but more historically specific, genealogical focus on its perennial reliance on "the unjust enemy" sheds new and welcomed light not only on the United States' justification of its War on Terror and its use of torture against "terrorist suspects" at Abu Ghraib, Guantánamo, and other indefinite zones of detention, but also on the United States' post–9/11 American imaginary. This is especially true of Baucom's resonant implication, by way of his identification of America's understanding of the "unlawful combatant" with that of the Western tradition at large—the "unjust enemy," the "*inimicus,*" "*the homo homini lupus*"—that the pervasive American discourse and practice pertaining to an always threatening enemy (or frontier) is *ultimately* no different, in reality, from "the unjust enemy" of all the other Old World imperial nation-states from which it distinguishes itself. (Tellingly, however, Baucom, like McClintock, does not overtly articulate this parallel.) As in the case of McClintock's genealogy, however, Baucom overdetermines the global perspective at the expense of the local. And, in thus violating the imperatives of the historical interregnum, he marginalizes, if he does not entirely efface, the particular—and, crucially, the historically *differentiating*—origins of America's perennial representation of "the unjust enemy" and the violence it inflicts on their minds and bodies. In short, his distance from the center, like McClintock's, blinds him to the fundamental role that the American jeremiad has played in the formation of the American national identity as an exceptionalist and redemptive identity from America's Puritan origins, through the era of the removal of the Native Americans to reservations (camps) and their eventual extermination (including the reduction of Africans to slaves, which is Baucom's primary example of the continuity between President Bush's "unlawful combatant" and the Old World's "unjust enemy") to the present 9/11 occasion. I mean, to repeat, the instigation of anxiety in the covenantal people by way of identifying the alien Other beyond the frontier between civilization and wilderness as a threatening enemy in behalf of *always already* rejuvenating (by violence) its communal energies in the face of the backsliding that is endemic to the very civilizing process of its errand.

Had McClintock and Baucom been more attentive to American history in tracing the genealogy of official America's post–9/11 American representation of its global itinerary, epitomized by Abu Ghraib Guantánamo, they, no doubt, would have been directed by their focus on "the unjust enemy" to the prestigious neoconservative Samuel P. Huntington's very visible justificatory defense of George W. Bush's War on Terror in the face of what he refers to as "the deconstruction of America." I am referring to *Who Are We: The Challenges to America's National Identity* (2004),[45] which, as we have seen in Chapter 1, traces the American national identity (the "Protestant core culture") that the Bush administration would secure against "militant Islam" back to the Puritan "errand in the wilderness":

> The settling of America was, of course, a result of economic and other motives, as well as religious ones. Yet religion still was central. . . . Religious intensity was undoubtedly greatest among the Puritans, especially in Massachusetts. They took the lead in defining their settlement based on "a Covenant with God" to create "a city on a hill" as a model for all the world, and people of the Protestant faiths soon also came to see themselves and America in a similar way. In the seventeenth and eighteenth centuries, Americans defined their mission in the New World in biblical terms. They were a "chosen people," on an "errand in the wilderness," creating "the new Israel," or the "new Jerusalem" in what was clearly "the promised land." America was the site of a "new Heaven and a new earth, the home of justice," God's country. The settlement of America was vested, as Sacvan Bercovitch put it, "with all the emotional, spiritual, and intellectual appeal of a religious quest." This sense of holy mission was easily expanded into millenarian themes of America as "the redeemer nation" and "the visionary republic." (WAW 64)

and, as the title itself and Huntington's reference to Sacvan Bercovitch make patently clear, is consciously written in the American jeremiadic vein.

Huntington's jeremiadic ideological itinerary, in fact, culminates in a disquisition on America's perennial need for an enemy that is remarkably similar, though ideologically antithetical, to Anne McClintock's characterization of what she calls the Bush administration's paranoid "enemy deficit." Unlike his neoconservative predecessor, Francis Fukuyama, who represented the end of America's Cold War against Soviet communism euphorically as the triumph of American democracy and "end of History,"[46] Huntington, in this culminating chapter tellingly entitled "In Search of an Enemy," dwells, paradoxically it would seem to most, on the negative consequence of this triumphant "end." Like the previous American Jeremiads—John Winthrop, Jonathan Edwards, Francis Parkman, Daniel Webster, Frederick Jackson Turner, Mark Twain, William Lederer, and Eugene Burdick, among many others—he overdetermines America's loss of the anxiety-provoking enemy:

> At the end of the century, Democracy was left without a significant secular ideological rival, and the United States was left without a peer competitor. Among American foreign policy elites, the results were euphoria, pride, arrogance—and uncertainty. The absence of an ideological threat produced an absence of purpose. "Nations need enemies," Charles Krauthammer commented as the Cold War ends. "Take away one, and they find another." The ideal enemy for America would be ideologically hostile, racially and culturally different, and militantly strong enough to pose a credible threat to American security. The foreign policy debates of the 1990s were already over who might be such an enemy. (WAW, 262)

It is at this point in Huntington's jeremiad, as I have observed elsewhere, that "the attacks on the World Trade Center and the Pentagon on 9/11 come from the margins, where they have been lying in wait from the beginning, to center stage."[47] In a rhetoric worthy of Mark Twain's signature American exceptionalist technique of staging for effect—or more to the point, of Guy Debord's corrosive analysis of Western modernity's use of the spectacle to bereave its human objects of speech; that is, a polity—Huntington goes on calculatively to orchestrate a spectacular end of his narrative of exceptionalist America's anxious "search for an enemy." Beginning with a rapid but suspense-inducing survey of the possible candidates for the status of America's post–Cold War enemy—Serbia, China, Iran, Iraq, Pakistan—he concludes with a resonant—and, to invoke McClintock language, paranoid finality:

> The cultural gap between Islam and America's Christianity and Anglo-Protestantism reinforces Islam's enemy qualifications. And on September 11,

2001, Osama bin Laden ended America's search. The attacks on New York and Washington followed by the wars with Afghanistan and Iraq and the more diffuse "war on terrorism" make militant Islam America's first enemy of the twenty-first century. (WAW, 264–65)

6

I conclude this chapter with a brief critical commentary on Paul Giles's influential *The Re-Mapping of Americana Literature* (2011), which, it seems to me, epitomizes what is most problematic, if not entirely disabling, about this New Americanist tendency to overdetermine the global at the expense of the local, the American exceptionalism that has informed America's national identity and its practice from the Puritans' genocidal war against the Pequots to George W. Bush's administration's post–9/11 "war on [Islamic] terror." Giles's revisionary "re-mapping" of American literature brings numerous "subversive" texts hitherto marginalized by the exceptionalist tradition to visibility. Furthermore, in reading canonical American texts against the nationalist grain, it sheds productive light on the American literary tradition—that is, his intervention complicates the narrative of American literature canonized by the celebratory myth and symbol school of Americanist studies and is thus welcomed. But the spectacle of his erudite invocation of forgotten American texts and his disorienting globalized readings of canonical national texts should not awe us into acquiescing to his revisionary thesis. In fact, they distract attention from its otherwise patent vulnerability. In what follows I will identify this hidden vulnerability by way of making five brief but indissolubly related points pertaining to Giles's global "re-mapping" model to suggest what is troubling—and perhaps even disabling—about his revisionary thesis on American literature.

My first point has to do with the presiding metaphor of mapping (or remapping) itself, since it has become increasingly prominent in New Americanist studies. Giles's inaugural and determining invocation of Deleuze's and Guattari's concept of "de-territorializing" to characterize the history of American literature hidden by the thesis that posits American exceptionalism as the founding and abiding origin of the Americana national identity is confusing if not contradictory. The concept of cartography he uses to articulate this deterritorialization derives from Mercator's, which is to say, the very *spatializing* concept that, in replacing the old existential and *temporally oriented* "periplus" by the projection of parallel and longitude coordinates, enabled a panoptic view of the "unknown" from within. I mean, more specifically, that version of the spatialized "*tableaux vivant*," born in the period of the Enlightenment, as Foucault has shown, that, in privileging the distanced panoptic eye, enables the observer to spatialize and domesticate the mysterious *terra incognita*, thus becoming the primary apparatus of the exploration and colonization of the New World, the territorialization of its wilderness. Giles, of course, uses the metaphor of cartography against itself. But in thus privileging the panoptic eye and its distancing/spatializing perspective, his project becomes an apparatus of capture complicit with the mapping intrinsic to the territorializing dynamics of imperialism. Ironically, critique of this panoptic modern cartography in the name of experiencing the phenomena of being immediately—that is, existentially, was made by two recent American poets, Ezra Pound and Charles Olson, who were critical of the imperialism inherent in the cartographic mentality of American modernity. Thus Pound's recurrent appeal to the Phoenician sailor Hanno's periplus:

> not as land seen on a map
> but sea bord seen by men sailing[48]

Thus also Charles Olson's similar appeal to Juan de la Cosa, Columbus's shipboard mapmaker:

> Behaim—and nothing Insular Azores to
> Cipangu (Candyn)
> Somewhere also there where spices
>
> And yes, in the Atlantic,
> one floating island: de
> Sant Brand
>   and. . . .
>   But before La Cosa, nobody
>   could have a mappemunde[49]

My second point is that Giles's overdetermined (panoptic) global perspective compels him to minimize, if not entirely erase, the Puritan thesis, inaugurated by Perry Miller and especially Sacvan Bercovitch, about the origins of the American national identity. This is especially evident in his misrepresentation of Bercovitch's scholarship, particularly by way of not directly addressing *American Jeremiad*, most evident in his "heretical" reading of Cotton Mather's *Magnalia Christi Americana*:

There is a certain heretical quality to such an approach [reconsidering Cotton Mather's major work "along a geographic axis" and reading "it within a transatlantic context, as an example of Restoration style being creatively reconfigured within an American context"] not only because it goes against the Bercovitch line of New England as a protected space bound into an apocalyptic rhetoric of "New England promise" but also because it cuts across the premise that the organizing principle of the *Magnalia* is "generational" [*Puritan Origins*, 75, 130] with Mather seeking to bind New England in a diachronic continuum across time. There is clearly a filiopietist strand to the *Magnalia*, with Mather paying homage to his father Increase, to John Winthrop, and many others as he seeks to canonize New England history and to institutionalize its legacy. But if the content of the text is filiopietistic, the form, I would argue, is primarily Augustan, owing less to Increase Mather than to John Dryden, the arch enemy of the Puritans. (GR, 46)

In representing the "Bercovitch line" as identifying Puritan "New England as a protected space," Giles travesties both the concepts of history and language that inform *American Jeremiad*. In focusing on the Puritans' figural (or typological) mode of interpreting historical events and their related need for a perpetual rejuvenating enemy, Bercovitch demonstrates that the Puritan errand in the New World was not only intrinsically "global" and transtemporal in its perspective but also imperial in practice. Thus, contrary to the implications of Giles's representation, he can be seen as a precursor of the New Americanist counter-memory. All this is borne witness to by Bercovitch's brief but decisive commentary on Mather's *Magnalia Christi Americana*, which, as he notes earlier in his text, epitomizes the historical itinerary of America "from visible saint to American patriot, sacred errand to manifest destiny, from colony to republic to imperial power" (AJ, 92):

> Mather's millenarianism at this time is worth special emphasis because the *Magnalia* has often been read as a cry of despair. . . . The significance of those deliverances are [*sic*] indicated by the title of the last section of the last book, "Arma Virosque Cano," a title that recalls the Virgilian invocation with which Mather opens the History (as well as the numerous echoes of Virgil thereafter), and so suggest the epic proportions of his narrative. For Mather, of course, New England's story not only parallels but supersedes that of the founding of Rome [by a saving remnant], as his literary "assistance" from Christ excels the inspiration of Virgil's muse, as the "exemplary heroes" he celebrates resemble but outshine the men of Aeneas' band—not only as Christians but as seafarers and conquerors of hostile pagan tribes. Undoubtedly the proper title for Mather's

work is the exultant one he gave it: *Magnalia Christi Americana*, The Great Acts of Christ in America. (AJ, 87)

My third point, related to the second, is that Giles's marginalization of the Puritan thesis about the origins of the American national identity in favor of his overdetermined global thesis also tacitly marginalizes the patent continuity between the American jeremiad—the Puritan need for a perpetual rejuvenating enemy—and the frontier thesis inaugurated by Frederick Jackson Turner at the time of the official closing of the American frontier and incorporated by the myth and symbol school of Americanists in behalf of America's Cold War against Soviet communism.[50]

My fourth point focuses on the linguistic aspect of the Puritan providential concept of history. In identifying Mather's literary style (in the above passage) with the "Augustan" style of the Old World English poet John Dryden, Giles, in keeping with his minimization of the Puritan/frontier thesis, obscures the difference between Mather's Puritan *figural* poesis and Dryden's "allegorical" style:

> One of the dominant strains in the *Magnalia* is the tension between history and allegory, the stresses involved in the struggle to bring temporal events into alignment with a providential pattern. This precisely links Mather again with Dryden, whose historical satire "Absalom and Achitophel" and other works play with both the analogies and the disjunctions between contemporary monarchs and mythological or biblical archetypes. The whole idea of parallelisms is highly significant tropologically for Mather in the *Magnalia*, something evident at both a microcosmic level . . . and also a macrocosmic level. . . . Throughout the *Magnalia*, indeed, the search for parallels becomes self-conscious, even compulsive. (GR, 48)

In thus identifying Mather's with Dryden's style, Giles collapses the very essential distinction, implicit in Bercovitch but explicit in Eric Auerbach, between the figural interpretation of the Puritans, which understands the parallels it draws between disparate particular images as fundamentally *historical* and the allegorical interpretation of those "Augustans" like Dryden, who view the parallel images as imaginative and ahistorical abstractions:

> Figural interpretation establishes a connection between two events or persons, the first of which signifies not only itself but also the second, while the second encompasses or fulfills the first. The two poles of the figure are separated in time, *but both being real events or figures, are within time, within the stream of*

historical life. Only the understanding of the two persons or events is a spiritual act, but this spiritual act deals with concrete events whether past, present, or future and not with concepts or abstractions; these are not secondary, since promise and fulfillment are real historical events, which have either happened in the incarnation of the Word, or will happen with the second coming. . . . Since in figural interpretation one thing stands for another, since one thing represents and signifies the other, figural interpretation is "allegorical" in the widest sense. But it differs from most of the allegorical forms known to us by the historicity both of the sign and what it signifies.[51]

Of course, as Giles points out, Mather "is always pondering self-critically the question of how far parallels of any kind might legitimately be pursued" (GR, 48). But this self-critical pondering is not the result of questioning Puritan providential history and the figural method of historical exegesis. It is rather the natural consequence of the human problem of trying to incorporate every detail in space and every moment in historical time (the "fall of a sparrow" or Virgil's *Aeneid*, for example) into a total design. In the conclusion of his commentary on the *Magnalia*, Giles, defining Mather's literary accomplishment as the making of "an American Augustan style," writes, "Drawing deliberately upon classical myth and Virgil's conception of epic, Mather crosses [the 'baroque' elements that other revisionary commentators on the text have identified with writers like Melville, Borges, and Faulkner] with Christian piety and scientific rationalism to create a work whose tortuous energy derives from its manifold rhetoric of self-contradiction" (GR, 54). If, however, the structure and rhetorical style of the *Magnalia* is seen in the light of this crucial distinction between Puritan figural exegesis and allegory, it then can also be seen that its "tortuous energy"—and, I would add, its engaging power in behalf of the Puritan redemptive mission—resides, not in its Drydenesque "Augustan" (Old World) style, but in its Puritan New World vocation.[52]

My last, but not least point is that, in thus effacing the Puritan thesis about the origins of the American national identity, which, as I have observed, tacitly effaces the frontier thesis extending from Turner and the myth and symbol school of Americanists, through the intellectual deputies of the presidencies of the Vietnam War era to George W. Bush's administration's post–9/11 War on Terror, Giles's overdetermined deterritorializing global perspective minimizes the historical reality of American exceptionalism and the violence it has always disavowed: not least its perpetual exceptionalist appeal to the state of emergency that justifies the establishment of the state of exception (the homeland security state) as the norm. In so doing, he suggests, if he does not literally state, like so many of the new New Americanists, that America, in keeping with its self-representation as a New World, has always been plural, multicultural, hybrid, transnational, global. It is, of course, true that American exceptionalism is a myth. But, to recall Gramsci, it is also true that this myth has produced *reality*, as the history of Indian removal in the nineteenth century, the Vietnam War, and, most recently, the unending War on Terror bear stark witness. It should not be forgotten—it is the decisive lesson bequeathed to us by poststructuralist theory from Nietzsche to Althusser—that when a fiction (ideology) becomes hegemonic, "a representation of the imagined relationship of individuals to their real conditions of existence," it also becomes history. In short, we might say, adapting a vernacular commonplace to Yeats's lines about the widening gyre from "The Second Coming" quoted in my title, that Giles's "heretical" readings of American literature, particularly those early texts such as Cotton Mather's *Magnalia Christi Americana* and Timothy Dwight's *The Conquest of Canaan* that were hitherto identified as founding works of the American exceptionalist tradition, are "far out."

*

What I have said in this chapter about the new New Americanist studies is not intended to disparage its globalizing or transnationalizing initiative. As I have observed, globalizing the national contributes to the disclosure of the dark side of the nation-state and, in so doing, facilitates thinking an alternative—decentered and nonidentitarian—communal *polis*. As such, it is a welcomed initiative. Furthermore, as I have noted, its implied collapsing of the distinction between American exceptionalism and the exceptionalism of the Old World nation-states—the disclosure that there is no ultimate difference between the exceptionalism that defines their national identities—contributes significantly to the task of resisting America's errand in the global "wilderness." My intention, undertaken in the spirit of dialogue, is, rather, to show that this new New Americanist counter-mnemonic initiative's overdetermination of the global perspective—its perception of the world from the vantage point of the expanding gyre, where the center no longer holds—obliterates the actual history of our contemporary post–9/11 occasion, which is bearing witness to an uneven struggle between a reactionary United

States, armed by its exceptionalist ethos and the most powerful—and spectacular—weapons of mass destruction in the world, and a multitude of deracinated people, unhomed by the depredations of exceptionalist nation-state imperialism, who are symptomatically clamoring for a new, alternative global polity. As "New Americanists," therefore, it is from this interregnum—this in-between, estranged world, that we must take our critical—counter-mnemonic—directives in addressing our globalizing occasion.

CHAPTER 4

American Exceptionalism and the Calling

A Genealogy of the Vocational Ethic

I shall call an apparatus literally anything that has in some way the capacity to capture, orient, determine, intercept, model, control, or secure the gestures, behaviors, opinions or discourses of living human beings.

—Giorgio Agamben, "What Is an Apparatus?"

There are no hierarchies, no infinite, no such many as mass, there are only
eyes in all heads,
to be looked out of . . .

—Charles Olson, "Letter 5," *The Maximus Poems*

I

On January 29, 2002, in the wake of the United States' inauguration of its War on Terror (the invasion of Afghanistan), George W. Bush, in his State of the Union Address, told his American audience:

States like these ["rogue states" such as North Korea, Iraq, and Iran] and their allies constitute an axis of evil, arming to threaten the peace of the world. By seeking weapons of mass destruction, these regimes pose a grave and growing danger. They could provide these arms to terrorists, giving them the means to match their hatred. They could attack our allies or attempt to blackmail the United States. In any of these cases, the price of indifference would be catastrophic.

We will work closely with our coalition to deny terrorists and their state sponsors the materials, technology, and expertise to make and deliver weapons of mass destruction. We will develop and deploy effective missile defenses to protect America and our allies from sudden attack. (APPLAUSE) And all nations should know: America will do what is necessary to ensure our nation's security.

We'll be deliberate, yet time is not on our side. I will not wait on events, while dangers gather. I will not stand by, as peril draws closer and closer. The United States of America will not permit the world's most dangerous regimes to threaten us with the world's most destructive weapons. (APPLAUSE)

Our war on terror is well begun, but it is only begun. This campaign may not be finished on our watch—yet it must be and will be waged on our watch.

We can't stop short. If we stop now—leaving terror camps intact and terror states unchecked—our sense of security would be false and temporary. *History has called America and our allies to action, and it is both our responsibility and our privilege to fight freedom's fight.*[1]

Much can be said about Bush's speech (and many others during his time "on watch," as he often put his presidency) to show how central the American exceptionalism ethos was to his vision of America's global role in the post–9/11 world: the perception of an impending catastrophe enacted by an enemy as a positive and promising event, the unerringly certain attitude of the redeemer nation, the language of the frontier, the unilaterality of the intended global action, the assumption of the impending *Pax Americana*, and so on. For the purpose of this final chapter—and because it subsumes all the other aspects of the American exceptionalist ethos—however, I will focus on President Bush's typically American—that is, historically resonant—reference to the American "vocation." I mean, more specifically, his invocation of a transcendental signified (a higher cause, as it were), in this case, History (the secularized version of the Word of God), that, in the face of an alleged "axis of evil" fanatically committed to reducing the civilized world to wilderness, calls America to the task of preventing this impending global catastrophe. And this is because, in the face of the emergence of a recent body of New Americanist studies that has marginalized, if not effaced, the Puritan thesis about the origins of the America national identity as devoid of an adequate foundation in history, I want, by way of a genealogy of President Bush's invocation of the "call of History," to suggest, that, on the contrary, the Puritan thesis, in its secularized and hegemonized form, particularly that central, polyvalent, and enabling ethical core of its multifaceted exceptionalist character referred to as "the calling," persists, however beleaguered, into the present post–9/11 occasion and thus urgently demands far more scholarly and critical attention than it is receiving from the new, globally oriented New Americanist studies.[2]

In keeping with the transnational turn in American studies, though without abandoning the local or national (that is, the imperatives of the historical reality of the interregnum) as the new New Americanists tend to do in overdetermining the global, I will undertake this genealogy by way of invoking the powerful witness of three Continental theorists of Western modernity—Max Weber (the Protestant work ethic), Louis Althusser (the concept of interpellation), and Giorgio Agamben (the "means/end" ethics of the vocation), all of whom, both in direct and indirect ways, have had the occasion to think the negative consequences of the celebrated Puritan calling for modern democratic capitalist societies, particularly the United States. But before undertaking particular analyses of these Continental thinkers' critique of Western/American (democratic/capitalist) modernity, it will be necessary, in the face of a tendency on the part of New Americanist genealogists to discount (or remain oblivious to) the ontological site of the continuum of being, to emphasize that the point of departure of each of these critics of modernity is their recognition of the continuity (within difference) of Western history—that is, their acknowledgment of this history as, in Martin Heidegger's term, an "onto-theo-logical tradition." I mean the interpretation of the be-*ing* of being (its radical temporality) in all its practical manifestations *meta–ta- physica:* from after or above or beyond things-as-they-are—that is, teleologically. That is to say, each of these theorists perceives Western modernity (this is, of course, a tautology), not as a radical break with the Christian tradition (particularly its Protestant version) as it is usually assumed, but as a naturalization of the supernatural, a secularization of this theological interpretation of being, the substitution of the *Anthropo-logos* for the *Theo-logos* or, more specifically, the idea of History (Manifest Destiny) for Providence.

2

Thus the essential point of departure of Max Weber's analysis of the Puritans' calling and its indissoluble relationality with the "spirit of capitalism" is the Puritan (Calvinist) notion of providence or providential history, which for them consisted of two indissolubly related aspects: the doctrine of predestination, according to which an absolutely inscrutable God endows grace on some of the community ("the elect") and denies it to others (the "preterite" or "passed over"); and the idea of history as providential, or teleological: predetermined, with a beginning, middle, and end, in which the end (*telos*) is present in the temporal process from the beginning. I will return to the second aspect of providential history later. Here, in relation to the significance of the Puritan calling, I will focus on the first: predetermination.

The Calvinist idea that the inscrutable God chooses some for salvation and damns others is, according to Weber, at the heart of the Puritan calling (*Beruf*, in German)—and its secularized development into the modern "spirit of capitalism." Because the purposes of their Calvinist God were inscrutable, "the consequence for the life of a generation which surrendered to [the 'magnificent consistency of this doctrine'] was a feeling of unprecedented inner loneliness of the single individual."[3] To underscore the crucial intensity of this internalization and individualization of life, Weber goes on to contrast it point by point with the Catholic tradition that offered its members the comforts of collectivity:

> In what was for the man of the age of the Reformation the most important thing in his life, his eternal salvation, he was forced to follow his path alone to meet his destiny which had been decreed for him for eternity. No one could help him. No priest, for the chosen one can understand the word of God only in his own heart. No sacraments, for though the sacraments had been ordained by God for the increase of His glory, and must hence be scrupulously observed, they are not a means to the attainment of grace, but only the subjective *externa subsidia* of faith. No Church, for though it was held that *extra ecclesiam nulla salus* in the sense that whoever kept away from the true Church could never belong to God's chosen band, nevertheless the membership of the external Church included the doomed. They should belong to it and be subjected to its discipline, not in order thus to attain salvation, that is impossible, but because, for the glory of God, they too must be forced to obey His commandment. Finally, even no God. For even Christ had died only for the elect, for whose benefit God had decreed His martyrdom from eternity. (PE, 104)

The consequence of this epochal subjectivization of the collective self, however, was not confusion as such, since for the individual Puritan election was a given (the questioning of his/her election would be an admission of lack of faith). Taking his/her directives from the broader Calvinist doctrine that interpreted the task of humanity at large as the rationalizing of the earth not for personal gain, but for the glory of God (*in majorem gloriam Dei*), this internalized Puritan came to rely on methodical good works or, more specifically, the *success* of methodical good works, in a worldly calling as the means of affirming the certitude of election. This, according to Weber, produced the fundamental paradox of the Puritan work ethic, which eventually led to the spirit of capitalism: "worldly asceticism"; or, as Perry Miller, following Weber, succinctly puts it in his commentary on the American Puritan John Cotton's "Christian Calling," "the phrase to describe this ['razor's edge'] attitude soon became: loving the world with weaned affections."[4]

This is the resonant way that Weber puts this evental paradox, by way of his reading of Richard Baxter and Benjamin Franklin, at the point of his analysis of the Puritan calling when Protestant theology begins to become secularized as the emergent "spirit of capitalism":

> It is our next task to follow out the results of the Puritan idea of the calling in the business world, now that the above sketch has attempted to show its religious foundations. With all the differences of detail and emphasis which these different ascetic movements [Calvinism, Pietism, and Methodism] show in the aspects with which we have been concerned, much of these same characteristics are present and important in them. But for our purposes the decisive point was, to recapitulate, the conception of the state of religious grace, common to all the denominations, as a status which marks off its possessors from the degradation of the flesh, from the world.
>
> On the other hand, though the means by which it was attained differed for different doctrines, it could not be guaranteed by any magical sacraments, by relief in the confession, nor by individual good works. That was only possible by proof in a specific type of conduct unmistakably different from the way of life of the natural man. From that followed for the individual an incentive methodically to supervise his own state of grace in his own conduct, and thus to penetrate it with asceticism. *But . . . this ascetic conduct meant a rational planning of the whole of one's life in accordance with God's will. And this asceticism was no longer an* opus supererogationis, *but something which could be required of everyone who would be certain of salvation.* The religious life of the saints, as distinguished for the natural life, was—the most important point—no longer lived outside the world in monastic communities, but within the world and in institutions. The rationalization of conduct, within this world, but for the sake of the world beyond, was the consequence of the concept of calling of ascetic Protestantism. (PE, 153–54)

The great strength of Weber's genealogy is its decisive identification of the Puritan calling, the Protestant work ethic, and the spirit of capitalism, by which I mean living an ideology as if it were the truth, the way things are. Not least, Weber's genealogy shows indirectly that the American Puritan calling is not, ultimately, exceptional but a continuation in the New World of an evental transformation of Western humanity's comportment toward the world and that, contrary to the new New Americanist initiative that would deny it, the Puritan ethos, however secularized, continues to influence the American national psyche. Despite his invocation of crucial American texts, such as Benjamin Franklin's *Autobiography* (1771–89), that bridge the religious and secular moment of American history, however, Weber overdetermines the European historical context rather than the American in his genealogical analysis of the Protestant calling. He thus misses or minimizes the ideological import of at least two crucial and indissolubly related aspects of the Puritan calling—aspects that are pertinent to our contemporary post–9/11 occasion when the American exceptionalist ethos surfaces as an ideology—that a more sustained attention to the American historical tradition would undoubtedly reveal: (1) the enabling importance of the rhetoric of service and servitude that saturates the American Puritan discourse and, thus, (2) the assumption, intrinsic to the calling, particularly in its American avatar, that it is a chosenness (by God, a higher cause) that renders the chosen exceptional but at the same time the willing an undeviating servant of the chooser. As the American Puritan John Cotton puts this ethics of the "warrantable calling":

> First: faith draws the heart of a Christian to live in some warrantable calling. As soon as ever a man begins to look towards God and the ways of His grace, he will not rest till he find out some warrantable calling and employment. An instance you have in the prodigal son, that after he had received and spent his portion in vanity, and when he being pinched, he came home to himself, and coming home to his father, the very next thing after confession and repentance of his sin, the very next petition he makes is: *"Make me one of thy hired servants."* Next after desire of pardon of sin, then "put me into some calling," *though it be but of an hired servant, wherein he may bring in God any service.* A Christian would no sooner have his sin pardoned than his estate to be settled in some good calling: though not as a mercenary slave, but he would offer it up to God as a free-will offering; he would have his condition and heart settled in God's peace, but his life settled in a good calling, *though it be but of a day laborer—"yet make me as one that may do Thee some service."* (AP 173)[5]

3

It is at this point that my second transnational witness to the disavowed consequences of the American Puritan calling (election to exceptional status) that Weber minimized, if he did not entirely efface, comes in: the Marxist Louis Althusser. I am referring specifically to his well-known, yet still to be adequately understood, concept of "interpellation" (from the

Latin "*inter*" [between] and "*appellare*" [to hail or to call]), which he brilliantly and resonantly explicates in "Ideology and Ideological State Apparatuses: Notes towards an Investigation" by way of the Old Testament story of Moses's hailing by God (Exod. 3–7), so crucial to the prefigural exegetical practice of the Massachusetts Bay Puritans.

Weber, it is true, as I have suggested, distinguishes between a consciously held ideology (Catholic religion) and a lived ethos (the Puritan work ethic) to suggest what is unique (exceptional)—and powerfully persuasive—about "the spirit of capitalism," producing, as it does in the end, the "iron cage" (PE, 181) in which modern humanity is captured. But because his distinction, however suggestive, remains inchoate, a consequence, I suggest, of overdetermining the European Protestant context, it overlooks the indissoluble affiliation between the calling—the hailing of the human subject by a transcendental signified (a higher cause)—as a gesture granting him/her recognition—that is, exceptionalist status among the many (*oi poloi*)—and thus the consequent (willing) servitude to the higher One who calls him/her. In the wake of the calling, to anticipate, the human becomes a "subjected subject." It is precisely this insidious irony and its life-damaging consequences that Althusser underscores in his decisive critique of modern democratic capitalist societies. Armed by Antonio Gramsci's far more sophisticated version of this revelatory distinction (enunciated in his revolutionary analysis of the affiliative relationship between the apparently distinct "public" [or "political"] realm, where coercion rules, and "private" [or "civil"] realm, where the discourse of hegemony rules)[6] Althusser's purpose in "Ideology and Ideological State Apparatuses," as the title suggests, is to show not only that these democratic capitalist societies that celebrate the individual and his/her freedom against the tyranny of collectivity in totalitarian societies are no less coercive than their totalitarian opponents, but also, precisely by endowing its citizens with exceptionalist status, are far more difficult to resist.

Nor, as I have suggested, is it an accident that, like Weber (if not with Weber in mind), Althusser, in his genealogy of secular Western modernity, invokes the Old Testament—the calling of Moses by God to lead the Israelites out of captivity into the Promised Land (Exodus)—the foundation of Protestant, particularly American Puritan, theology—as the origin and exemplary model of the unique power relations of modern democratic capitalist societies. I quote at length to show both the parallel with Weber and the crucial difference. Designating the unique and absolutely other

God as the "Subject" and the humans he hails as "subjects," Althusser writes:

> It then emerges that the interpellation of individuals as subjects presupposes the "existence" of a Unique and central Other Subject, in whose Name the religious ideology interpellates all individuals as subjects. All this is clearly written in what is rightly called the Scriptures. "And it came to pass at the time that God the Lord (Yahweh) spoke to Moses in the cloud. And the Lord cried to Moses, 'Moses!' and Moses replied 'It is (really) I! I am Moses thy servant, speak and I shall listen!' And the Lord spoke to Moses and said to him, '*I am that I am.*'"
>
> God thus defines himself as the Subject *par excellence*, he who is through himself and for himself ("I am that I am") and he who interpellates his subject, the individual subjected to him by his very interpellation, i.e., the individual named Moses. And Moses, interpellated—called by his Name, having recognized that it "really" was he who was called by God, recognizes that he is a subject, a subject *of* God, a subject subjected to God, *a subject through the Subject and subjected to the Subject.* The proof: he obeys him, and makes his people obey God's Commandments.[7]

And this is how Althusser deciphers his counter-reading of the originating metaphysical/panoptic theological model of the calling that produces subjected subjects for a contemporary Western secular audience, particularly American, that lives the polyvalent imperatives—focused on "work," be it noted—of a democratic capitalist exceptionalism, both domestic and foreign, as if they were "the way things (really) are":

> Let me summarize what we have discovered about ideology in general.
>
> The duplicate mirror-structure of ideology ensures simultaneously:
>
> 1. The interpellation of "individuals" as subjects; their subjection to the Subject;
>
> 2. The mutual recognition of subjects and Subject, the subjects' recognition of each other, and finally the subject's recognition of himself;
>
> 3. The absolute guarantee that everything really is so, and that on condition that the subjects recognize what they are and behave accordingly, everything will be all right: Amen—"*So be it.*"
>
> Result: caught in this quadruple system of interpellation as subjects, of subjection to the Subject, of universal recognition and of absolute guarantee, the subjects "work"; they "work by themselves" in the vast majority of cases, with the exception of the "bad subjects" who on occasion provoke the intervention of one of the detachments of the (repressive) State Apparatus.[8] But the vast majority of (good) subjects work all right "all by themselves," i.e., by ideology (whose concrete forms are realized in the Ideological State Apparatuses). They are inserted into practices governed by the rituals of the ISAs. They "recognize" the existing

state of affairs (*das Bestehende*), that "it really is true that it is so and not other-wise," and that they must be obedient to God, to conscience, to the priest, to de Gaulle, to the boss, to the engineers, that thou shalt "love thy neighbor as thy-self," etc. Their concrete, material behaviour is simply the inscription in life of the admirable words of the prayer: *Amen—So be it.* (IISA, 180–81)

Admittedly, Althusser does not refer specifically to the American exceptionalist cultural tradition, to say nothing about its Puritan founda-tions. On the other hand, however, it is difficult not to believe that he was not indirectly relying on, and deepening, Weber's inaugural insight into the affiliative relationship between the Puritan calling—the *work* ethic—and "the spirit of capitalism." This possibility becomes especially evident when one attends to the remarkably similar focus of their genealogical projects on, for them, the inevitable transition in modernity of the West from a theological to a secular world in which the supernatural becomes naturalized and the Christian calling becomes an *ethics*, which is to say, with Raymond Williams's gloss on Gramsci's concept of "hegemony" and Althusser's "Ideological State Apparatuses," a "*lived* system of mean-ings and values—constitutive and constituting—which as they are expe-rienced as practices appear" to be "reciprocally confirming," thus constituting "a sense of reality for most people in the society, a sense of absolute because experienced reality beyond which it is very difficult for most members of the society to move, in most areas of their lives . . . that is . . . , in the strongest sense a 'culture,' but a culture that has also to be seen as the lived domination and subordination of particular classes."[9] In any case, this brief juxtaposition of Weber's and Althusser's genealogies of modern democratic capitalist societies not only bears witness to the persistence of the Puritan calling, understood as simultaneously a subjectivization (individualizing) and as the subjection of the human subject. It also goes far to illuminate the complex polyvalent ideological implications disavowed by the American exceptionalist ethos and heretofore not identified.

4

My third, but not least, transnational witness to the complex genealogy of the American exceptionalist ethos is the Italian philosopher Giorgio Agamben, one of whose central purposes as a critic of Western modernity has been to render the polyvalent binarist aspects of the modern demo-cratic capitalist work ethic "*inoperative*" (Italian, *inoperisita*), a project derived immediately from the French by way of Georges Bataille and

Jean-Luc Nancy's *désoeuvrement* (rendering unworkable) and behind that from Heidegger's destructive hermeneutics (*Destruktion*: the release [for thought] of the temporality colonized by its structuration by metaphysical thinking), but ultimately, as we shall see, from St. Paul's ubiquitous "*katargeō*," "a compound of *argeō*, which in turn derives from the adjective *argos*, meaning 'inoperative, not-at-work (*a-ergos*), inactive.' The compound therefore comes to mean, 'I make inoperative, I deactivate, I suspend the efficacy.'" [10] Like Althusser, Agamben does not refer overtly to the American Puritan calling, but like him and Max Weber (to whom he does refer), he centrally invokes that sect of Christianity, in his case, that was founded on the Apostle Paul, whose Epistles, particularly the Letter to the Corinthians 1 and Letter to the Romans, constitute one of the primary sources of the American Puritans' understanding of their election/calling.

What is especially useful about Agamben's invocation of St. Paul's Letter to the Romans is his revolutionary interpretation of Paul's *klēsis* (from the New Testament Greek *kaleō*: I call)—his "calling" by Christ—on the road to Damascus. This is because it renders inoperative the received meaning of the calling (Agamben's preferred word is "vocation" because it more clearly incorporates the idea of calling both in the sense of "address" and of "work") and thus not only discloses, contrapuntally, as it were, the hitherto disavowed aspects of the calling that rendered the Massachusetts Bay Colony Puritans and their secular American heirs exceptional—not least that their election to exceptionalist status was a tacit normalization of the state of exception (and the security state)[11]—but also, as we shall see, a radically different understanding of the calling/choosing that transforms the servitude that is intrinsic to the subjectifying "Protestant work ethic" and "the spirit of capitalism" into a vehicle of *potentiality as such*—that is, of radical (communal) democracy.

In the section pointedly entitled "Ethics" of *The Coming Community* (1993), which precedes *The Time that Remains*, his commentary on Paul's Letter to the Romans, by over a decade but suggests its continuity with his late meditations on *homo sacer*, Agamben underscores the presiding importance of the Western concept of vocation for his de-structive project, which renders the binary logic of its determining essentialism inoperative:

> The fact that must constitute the point of departure for any discourse on ethics is that there is no essence, no historical or spiritual vocation, no logical destiny that humans must enact or realize. This is the only reason why something like an ethics can exist, because it is clear that if humans were or had to be this or

that substance, this or that destiny, no ethical experience would be possible—there would be only tasks to be done.[12]

Agamben's radically subversive commentary on Paul's Epistle to the Romans constitutes, in many ways, a genealogy, remarkably similar to those of Weber and Althusser, of the modern, particularly American, democratic capitalist calling, as well as a subtle gloss on this enigmatic statement asserting the radical difference between an essentialist work ethic that conceals its reductive determinative coerciveness and an ethics that is grounded in radical freedom.

Agamben's critique of the modern Western ethics of vocation, particularly after the United States' declaration of its War on Terror—and its corollary normalization of the state of exception—in the wake of 9/11, has, as we shall see more fully, its origins in a radicalized version of Heidegger's de-struction of the "onto-theo-logical tradition." I mean by this ungainly locution the three epochs of the Western tradition that have interpreted being (*Sein*)—its radical temporality—from a transcendental or panoptic (meta-physical) perspective (a *logos*) that necessarily spatializes or reifies time to render "it" comprehensible, understood in terms of its etymological roots: the Latin—that is, Roman (not Greek), *cum*, "with," in the sense of "inclusiveness," and *prehendere*, "to take hold of," "to grasp," "to master." Put alternatively, to suggest the "ethical" imperatives of this reduction, this panoptic perspective on the be-*ing* of being, constitutes the transformation of the incomprehensible flow of time to a teleology determined by a *telos* or "higher cause"—God or History—that is, into an "appearance" that conceals a totalizing presence that *informs* time's apparent transience. Under this essentialist dispensation, humanity's "ethical" vocation is to work in time in behalf of fulfilling the imperatives of the *telos* or higher (transcendental) cause; or, as the discourse of Protestant Christianity has this "errand in the wilderness," "to labor [under the panoptic eye of God] in the vineyards of the Lord." And significantly, it is, if not the American Puritans as such, his commentary on Paul's Epistle to the Romans, appropriately entitled *The Time that Remains*, one of the foundational texts of the American Puritans' appeal to the calling, in which Agamben undertakes his fullest destructive genealogy of the modern democratic capitalist "ethics" of vocation.

In *The Time that Remains*, as I have noted, Agamben takes the point of departure of his complex dismantling of the Christian representation and institutionalization of St. Paul's messianism—and of the modern "ethics" of vocation—from the first line of the Epistle to the Romans, where he

refers to his calling "*kletos*" (Jerome's Latin translation: *vocatus*) by the
Messiah on the road to Damascus: "*Paulus doulos Christou Iesou, kletos
Apostolos aphorismenos eis euangelion Theou,*" which, to underscore Paul's
decisive identification of the called with lowliness or the passed over, he
literally glosses in the appendix as follows: "Paul slave of [the] Messiah
Jesus called emissary separated into [the] announcement of God." And in
his radically subversive analysis of Paul's extraordinarily important complex term, Agamben invokes centrally the apostle's Letter to the Corinthians (1 Cor. 7:17–22):

> But as God hath distributed to every man, as the Lord hath called everyone, so
> let him walk. And so ordain I in all communities [*ekklēsías*, another word from
> the same family as *kaleō*]. Is any man called being circumcised [a reference to the
> Jewish identity]? Let him not remove the mark of circumcision. Is any called
> with a foreskin [a reference to Greek identity]? Let him not be circumcised!
> Circumcision is nothing and foreskin is nothing. . . . Let every man abide in the
> same calling wherein he was called. Art thou called being a slave? Care not for
> it: but if thou mayest be made free, use it rather. For he that is called in the Lord,
> being a slave, is the Lord's freeman: likewise also he that is called, being free, is
> slave of the Messiah. (TR, 19)

In *The Protestant Ethic and the Spirit of Capitalism*, Max Weber,
according to Agamben, left the Protestant interpretation of the Pauline
calling more or less intact. Though his identification of the Protestant
work ethic with the spirit of capitalism was a momentous achievement,
his translation, despite his awareness of the ambiguities, of Paul's *klēsis* as
Beruf (vocation in the sense of a "worldly profession") was inadvertently
to continue the tradition inaugurated by Luther that reads Paul's revolutionary understanding of the *klēsis* as a call to wait for the *telos* to arrive
(postpone the imperatives of the time of the now), that is, to political
passivity (quietism). Paraphrasing Weber, Agamben writes:

> It is through the Lutheran version that the term originally signifying the voca-
> tion that only God or Messiah addresses to man acquires the modern sense of a
> "profession." Shortly after Luther, the Calvinists and the Puritans invested it
> with an entirely new ethical meaning. According to Weber, the Pauline text
> does not convey any positive valuation of world professions, but only an attitude
> of "eschatological indifference." This is a consequence of awaiting the imminent
> end of the first Christian communities. "Since everyone was waiting the coming
> of the Lord, then let everyone remain in the state [*Stand*] and the secular occu-
> pation [*Hantierung*] in which the call [*Ruf*] of the Lord has found him, and
> continue to labor as before." (TR, 20)

In response to Weber's interpretation of the Pauline calling "as an expression of 'eschatological indifference' toward worldly conditions" (22), Agamben, addressing the same passage from 1 Corinthians on the issue of the difference between the circumcised and uncircumcised, Jew and Greek, the law and rational knowledge, asserts, on the contrary, that the calling is profoundly worldly and "political":

> *Klēsis* indicates the particular transformation that every juridical and worldly condition undergoes because of, and only because of, its relation to the messianic event. It is therefore not a matter of eschatological indifference, *but of change, almost an internal shifting of each and every single worldly condition by virtue of being "called."* For Paul, *ekklesia* [another correlate of *klēsis*], the messianic community, is literally all *klēsis*, all messianic vocations. (TR, 22; my emphasis)

But the messianic politics of the calling is not the democratic capitalist politics bequeathed to modernity by the Puritans and epitomized by the work ethic articulated by Benjamin Franklin in his *Autobiography*. Returning to 1 Corinthians 7:29–32, Agamben reads Paul's revolutionary anti-identitarian assertion that "Circumcision is nothing, and foreskin is nothing," not as a rejection, but as a movement of nullification: "That which according to the law, made one man a Jew and the other a *goy*, one a slave and another a free man, is now annulled by the vocation." And to the question "why remain in this nothing?" Agamben responds with Weber's "eschatological indifference" in mind, "Once again, *meneto* ("remaining") does not convey indifference, it signifies the immobile and anaphoric gesture of the messianic calling, its being essentially and foremost a *calling of the calling*. For this reason, it may apply to any condition; but for this same reason, *it revokes a condition and radically puts it into question in the very act of adhering to it*" (TR, 23; second emphasis is mine). In short, according to Agamben—and echoing Althusser—"*The messianic vocation is the revocation of every vocation*":

> In this way, it defines what to me seems to be the only acceptable vocation. What is a vocation, but the revocation of each and every concrete factical vocation? This obviously does not entail substituting a less authentic vocation with a truer vocation. According to what norm would one be chosen over the other? No, the vocation calls the vocation itself, as though it were an urgency that works it from within and hollows it out, nullifying *it in the very gesture of maintaining and dwelling in it*. This, and nothing less than this, is what it means to have a vocation, what it means to live in messianic *klēsis*. (TR, 23–24; my emphasis)

Understood anaphorically as "the revocation of every vocation," the Pauline calling, that is to say, renders the transcendent (Mosaic) law inoperative. But, it is important to underscore, this does not mean an outright rejection of the law (its teleological or eschatological concept of time, its [exceptionalist] identitarian logic of belonging [Jew/Greek], and the work ethic intrinsic to it). These remain, but they no longer *work* in the life-damaging way they did under the dispensation of the vocation understood as service to a higher eschatological cause. This is because the dismantling of the eschatological time (which Agamben, following Gustave Guillaume, appropriately calls "operational time" [TR, 65]) incumbent on the Messianic calling precipitates the contemporaneous—what Paul refers to as *ho nyn kairos* (the time of the now) and Agamben reads as "the time that remains between time and its end" (TR, 62)—that is, *profane* time: the "disjointed" or "untimely" or "contemporaneous" time of *this* world[13]— by way of Walter Benjamin's *Jetztzeit*. And, in doing so, it releases potential as such from its traditional bondage (justified by the teleological interpretation of time) to the closing act. Under this new, "messianic" dispensation the division of law (and the ethical and political imperatives that stem from it) is divided to produce a remnant—"neither the all, nor a part of the all, but the impossibility for the part and the all to coincide with themselves or with each other." It is this refusal of universalisms, this situation of "every people" *"as a remnant, as not-all,"* that, according to Agamben, is the ultimate meaning of "apostle" (not prophet) Paul's "division of the divisions"—the rendering inoperative—of the law: "For him, the remnant no longer consists in a concept turned toward the future, as with the prophets; it concerns a present experience that defines the messianic 'now.' 'In the time of the now a remnant is produced [*gegonen*]'" (TR, 55). In other words, the concept of election, which produces the assumption of exceptionalism and a logic of belonging that pits humans against each other in a war to the end, is rendered inoperative. Under the messianic call everyone *in his/her singularity* is elected:

> If I had to mark out a political legacy in Paul's letters that was immediately traceable, I believe that the concept of the remnant would have to play a part. More specifically, it allows for a new perspective that dislodges our antiquated notions of a people and a democracy, however impossible it may be to completely renounce them. The people is neither the all nor the part, neither the majority nor the minority. Instead, it is that *which can never coincide with itself, as all or as part, that which infinitely remains or resists in each division, and, with*

all due respect to those who govern us, never allows us to be reduced to a majority or a minority. This remnant is the figure, or the substantiality assumed by a people in a decisive moment, and as such the only real political subject. (TR, 57; my emphasis)[14]

Given his relentless and devastating critique of the Christian/secular exegetical tradition that produced the Protestant work ethic and the spirit of capitalism, it should come as no surprise that Agamben (like a number of postmodern Continental theorists (Maurice Blanchot, Gilles Deleuze, Antonio Negri, among others),[15] invokes the American writer Herman Melville's heretical masterpiece "Bartleby, the Scrivener" as a prime exemplary witness both to disclose the violence that the benign democratic capitalist work ethic always disavows in the pursuit of its transcendentally ordained redemptive errand and to render its apparatuses of capture inoperative. I will return to Melville's anticipation of Agamben's dismantling of the modern vocational ethics later in this chapter. Here it will suffice for my present purpose to focus briefly on the ontological category—usually overlooked by "worldly critics"—on which the Protestant work ethic and the spirit of capitalism depend and that, according to Agamben, "Bartleby, the Scrivener: A Story of Wall Street" proleptically renders inoperative.[16] I am referring to the potentiality/act dyad (Aristotle's *dynamis*, which, as Agamben reminds us, "signifies power as much as it does possibility" [TR, 90]) and *energeia* (act), the founding principle of the means/end logic that informs the vocational ethics[17]—and the American Protestant capitalist exceptionalist ethos. This is the affiliative relation Agamben articulates in the brief but resonant chapter of *The Coming Community* entitled "Bartleby," which laconically postpones reference to Melville's strange and estranging protagonist until the last sentence. What Agamben strategically overdetermines in explaining the destabilizing figure of the ineffable scrivener is not the story; it is, rather, this perennial ontological potential/act category that has its ultimate origins in Aristotle. Aristotle's "De Anima," Agamben writes, with the means/end logic in mind, "articulates this theory in absolute terms with respect to the supreme theme of metaphysics. If thought were in fact only the potentiality to think this or that intelligibility, he argues, *it would always already have passed through to the act and would remain inferior to its own object. But thought in essence is pure potentiality; in other words, it is also the potential not to think.*" Agamben, then, to suggest the affiliation with

Bartleby, goes on to invoke Aristotle's comparison of this pure potentiality to "a writing tablet on which nothing is written" and concludes the chapter with the following resonant and liberating paradox, in which the weak— the impotent—becomes the strong (the potent):

> The perfect act of writing comes not from the power to write, but from an impotence that turns back on itself as a pure act (which Aristotle calls agent intellect). This is why in the Arab tradition [explicating Aristotle] agent intellect has the form of an angel whose name is Qalam, Pen, and its place is an unfathomable potentiality. Bartleby, a scribe who does not simply cease to write but "prefers not to," is the extreme image of this angel that writes nothing but its potentiality to not-write. (CC, 36.7)[18]

Following Aristotle's directive, implicit in his underscoring of the possibility not only to act but not to act (or not to write), Agamben's general purpose, in thus identifying Bartleby, the scrivener, who "prefers not to write," as the "extreme figure of this angel that writes nothing but the potentiality to not-write," is to liberate potentiality from its age-old servile dependence on the potent act, or, in words that are intended to recall the American Puritan ethic, to render inoperative the imperative of servitude to the higher (transcendental) cause. It is to retrieve the nothing that is ontologically prior to Being[19] and thus the open-ended, the question, the "means without end," the temporal, that is, the ethical imperatives of the disjointed or untimely time of contemporaneity, the profane time of the now *(ho nym kairos)* from the teleological structure—the apparatus of capture—in which it has been imprisoned under the aegis of Western civilization.

As the embodiment of this retrieval of potentiality as such from the bondage of the act, Bartleby, to put it in Agamben's alternative language, becomes the precursor of the "whatever being" of *The Coming Community*, which, in defying the modern nation-state's identitarian logic of belonging—being red, being French, being Muslim" (CC, 1)—confounds the power of its vocational ethics. Thus, as Agamben shows at the end of *The Coming Community*, where he invokes the evental demonstrations in Tiananmen Square (1989), Bartleby, as the epitome of the retrieval of potentiality as such of "whatever being," becomes a potent impotence. In rendering the means/end logic of the vocational structure of the modern state inoperative, he becomes the herald of a new means, more adequate than any other previous one, of resisting the apparatuses of capture that prevail in—and disfigure—capitalist modernity.[20]

5

I will return to these positive possibilities of the coming community opened up by the rendering inoperative of the vocational ethics intrinsic to the teleological time of American exceptionalism. Here, in order to show that my appeal to the three Continental witnesses, Max Weber, Louis Althusser, and Giorgio Agamben, has not been an imposition on American cultural history from the outside—and, at the same time to distinguish the American version of exceptionalism from the European— I will invoke the counter-mnemonic American tradition, which, though markedly in the minority, nevertheless has haunted the dominant American exceptionalism tradition, not only in a general way, but also in all its polyvalent specifics, not least, its vocational ethics. I am referring to the spectral tradition inaugurated by Herman Melville's interrogation of the American calling and retrieved by American postmodern writers, such as Charles Olson, Ralph Ellison, William Gaddis, Donald Barthelme, Robert Coover, Don DeLillo, Kathy Acker, Toni Morrison, and especially by Thomas Pynchon.[21] Though, as I have shown elsewhere, any of Melville's works from *Moby-Dick* on could be adduced for this purpose, I will restrict my remarks to brief commentaries on two of his texts after *Moby-Dick* that speak directly not only to the American exceptionalist calling but also to its origins in the Puritan doctrine of election and its covenantal "errand," the novella *Benito Cereno* (1855) and the short story "Bartleby, the Scrivener: A Story of Wall Street" (1853). I choose the first because it is a resonantly subversive portrait of the typical exceptionalist American—liberal, optimistic, tolerant, and conscientious in his vocation— who, having answered the American calling, becomes blinded by its transcendentally ordained redemptive vocational imperatives to the violence intrinsic to them. I choose the second, conversely, because, besides its enabling centrality in Agamben's subversive onto-political project, it is precisely a portrait of an American nobody (preterite: "passed over") who, unlike Captain Amasa Delano, refuses, in Gramsci's words, his "spontaneous consent" to the American calling and, in so doing, renders the entire political edifice (Wall Street) produced by the Protestant work ethic inoperative.[22]

The setting of "Benito Cereno," to be more specific, is pointedly an encounter by an American merchant vessel with a Spanish—that is, "Old World" slave ship, the *San Dominick*,[23] seemingly in distress, but in reality taken over by the slave cargo being transported from Africa to the

South American colonies. The captain of this American vessel is Amasa Delano, a New Englander with, as his name suggests, Puritan roots. Guided unerringly in his ameliorative errand by his redemptive exceptionalist ethos, he interprets (and reinterprets, when contradictory details manifest themselves) this scene of extreme distress staged for the intruding American "visitors" by the revolting slaves as the reality produced by nature. To use Louis Althusser's uncannily appropriate language, Captain Delano is an interpellated subject. In responding to the American calling he becomes a "subject"—a "free individual"—subjected to the hailing "Subject"—who, in the service of the errand he has been called to perform, can only see the picture that the higher cause has preordained him to see. Everything else—every unique detail in time and space that would give lie to this picture—is invisible to him. His American exceptionalist ethos, as it were, *sees for him*. And, as a result, his benign errand, Melville's counter-mnemonic story compels us to see, ends in disaster.

Captain Delano, that is to say, is by no means a stupid man. On the contrary, Melville goes all out to show that he is remarkably intelligent, acutely observant, sensitive to nuance, and capable of rationalizing the details he observed in the process of fulfilling the demands of his naval vocation. Indeed, Melville, I suggest, represents the New Englander as the epitome of the ideal American man of mid-century America—the figure who combines the attributes of the Puritan, the frontiersman, and the empirical scientist (or detective). However, Melville's purpose, in characterizing Delano as such an observant and intelligent man, is subversive. It is to underscore the dehumanizing blindness of his exceptionalist oversight. Despite his intelligence—and his typical American genial good will (tolerance)—to be more specific, it is Delano's deeply inscribed—and disavowed—New World prejudice against the "decadent" Old World Spanish captain, Benito Cereno, and, above all, the racism intrinsic to his redemptive vocation that in every instant prevents this "good man" from perceiving what is manifestly, from beginning to end, everywhere in front of his observant eyes.

This persistent blindness of the American "visitor's"[24] exceptionalism—and its spectral consequences—is epitomized in the exquisite scene, staged by Babo, the acutely intelligent mastermind of the plot the revolting slaves are enacting, in which, feigning before Captain Delano to be shaving his master, the slave is, in fact, threatening him into silence. As Babo hovers menacingly over Benito Cereno, it is only the racist stereotype of the pleasantly affable and servile black man that the American's exceptionalist eyes allow him to see:

> There is something in the negro which, in a peculiar way, fits him for avocations about one's person. Most negroes are natural valets and hairdressers, taking to the comb and brush congenially as to the castanets, and flourishing them apparently with almost equal satisfaction. There is, too, a smooth tact about them in this employment, with a marvelous, noiseless, gliding briskness, not ungraceful in its way, singularly pleasing to behold, *and still more so to be the manipulated subject of.* And above all is the great gift of humor. Not the mere grin or laugh is here meant. Those were unsuitable. But a certain easy cheerfulness, harmonious in every glance and gesture; as *though God has set the whole negro to some pleasant tune.*
>
> *When to all this is added the docility arising from the unaspiring contentment of a limited mind, and that susceptibility of blind attachment sometimes inhering in indisputable inferiors,* one readily perceives why hypochondriacs, Johnson and Byron—it may be something like the hypochondriac, Benito Cereno—took to their hearts, almost to the exclusion of the entire white race, their serving men. . . . When at ease with respect to exterior things, Captain Delano's nature was not only benign, but familiarly and humorously so. At home, he had often taken rare satisfaction in sitting in his door, watching some free man of color at his work or play. If on a voyage he chanced to have a black sailor, invariably he was on chatty, and half-gamesome terms with him. In fact, like most men of a good, blithe heart, Captain Delano took to negroes, not philosophically, but genially, just as other men to Newfoundland dogs. (BC, 83–84; my emphasis)

As the narrator's rhetoric everywhere bears witness, what the New England captain's observant American exceptionalism ultimately blinds him to is the possibility that these black men are capable of the passion to be free of the dehumanizing degradation of slavery—their violent uprooting from a homeland, the hard labor they are forced into, their separation from families, the raping of their wives. In the secular American's tolerant exceptionalist eyes the black slaves are, as we have seen, the natural embodiment of the constituency of faithful Christian humanity that, according to the Puritan John Cotton, should freely and servilely accept the "mean and homely" vocation, however degrading, to which it has been assigned by providence:

> It is a word of consolation to every such soul as hath been acquainted with this life of faith in the calling: be thy calling never so mean and homely and never so hardly accepted, yet, if thou hast lived by faith in thy calling, it was a lively work

in the sight of God; and so it will be rewarded when thy change shall come. Many a Christian is apt to be discouraged and dismayed if crosses befall him in his calling. But be not afraid; let this cheer up thy spirit—that whatever thy calling was, yet thou camest into it honestly and hast lived in it faithfully; your course was lively and spiritual, and therefore you may with courage look up for recompense from Christ. (AP, 182)

Above all, Delano's exceptionalist oversight also blinds him to the possibility that a black man could be capable of the kind of acute intelligence that such a complex plot requires. To the American, despite his vaunted tolerance, which distinguishes him from his Old World host, the black man in the end is at best nothing more than a mindless and dependent child and, at worst, a wild animal: "bare life," in Agamben's appropriate phrase.

Not until the very end of the story proper does the visiting Captain Delano, in a seemingly epiphanic flash, see that the whole sequence of events on board the *San Dominick* has been a masquerade, that the black slave was in fact, the master:

> That moment [when the Don, having leapt into the dingy that would take Delano back to his ship to escape his captors, is assaulted by Babo with a deadly weapon], across the long-benighted mind of Captain Delano, a flash of revelation swept, illuminating in unanticipated clearness his host's whole mysterious demeanor, with every enigmatic event of the day, as well as the entire voyage of the *San Dominick*. He smote Babo's hand [which he initially thought was intended to save his master] down, but his own heart smote him harder. With infinite pity he withdrew his hold from Don Benito. Not Captain Delano, but Don Benito, the black, in leaping into the boat, had intended to stab.
>
> Both the black's hands were held, as, glancing up toward the *San Dominick*, Captain Delano, now with the scales dropped from his eyes, saw the negroes, not in misrule but in tumult, not as if frantically concerned for Don Benito, but with mask torn away, flourishing hatchets and knives, in ferocious piratical revolt. Like delirious black dervishes, the six Ashantees danced on the poop. . . .
>
> Meantime Captain Delano hailed his own vessel, ordering the ports up, and guns out. But by this time the cables of the *San Dominick* had been cut; and the fag-end, in lashing out, whipped away the canvas shroud about the beak, suddenly revealing, as the bleached hull swung round toward the open ocean, death for the figure-head, in a human skeleton; chalky comment on the chalked words below, "*Follow your leader.*" (BC, 99)

The revelation suggests that the American has been disabused of the benignity of his American exceptionalist ethos. But this inaugural denouement is not where Melville's detective story ends. Following the disclosure of the truth about the events on board the *San Dominick*, Melville attaches two addenda: the first, extracts of Benito Cereno's deposition to the official Spanish court officiating the trial of the ship's officers in the aftermath, and the second, the narrator's account of a conversation about the recent traumatic events on board the ill-fated *San Dominick* between Captain Delano and Don Benito Cereno.

In the first addendum, the don represents in minute detail the events on board the *San Dominick* and, despite a certain persistent anguished tone of ambiguity that informs his testimony, the court interprets his deposition as adequate justification for its decision to exonerate him from blame and to hang Babo. Its judgment thus ostensibly corroborates Delano's deepest exceptionalist attitude toward the black race. But in underscoring the don's ambiguities, Melville's intention is to drive home the insidious power of the redemptive American exceptionalist ethos to disavow its dark underside. He represents the don's deposition as one that, in fact, haunts the finality not only of the story's end but also of the Spanish court's judgment. This is manifestly borne witness to by two disruptive moments in his detailed account of the events on board the *San Dominick* to which the interpellated American was blinded. The first, pitted against Captain Delano's benign racist characterization, refers to the motives of the revolting slaves:

> the deponent resolved at the break of day to come up the companion-way, where the negro Babo was, being the ring leader, and Artufal, who assisted him, and . . . exhorted them to cease committing such atrocities, asking them, at the same time what they wanted and intended to do . . . that, not withstanding this, they threw, in his presence, three men alive and tied, overboard; that they told the deponent to come up, and that they would not kill him; which having done, the negro Babo asked him whether there were in those seas any negro countries where they might be carried, and he answered them, No; that the negro Babo afterwards told him to carry them to Senegal, or to the neighboring islands of St. Nicolas; and he answered, that this was impossible, on account of the great distance, the necessity involved of rounding Cape Horn, the bad conditions of the vessel, the want of provisions, sails, and water; but that the negro Babo replied to him he must carry them in anyway; that they would do and conform themselves to everything the deponent should require as to eating and drinking; that after long conference, being absolutely compelled to please them, for they threatened him to kill all the whites if they were not, at all events, carried to Senegal, he told them that what was most wanting for the voyage was water. (BC, 105)

The court reads the don's statement straightforwardly as evidence that the revolting slaves had committed an unredeemable crime. Read symptomatically, as Melville intends, however, the don's deposition undergoes an estrangement that enables the reader to *see* what is invisible to both the racist "Old World" tribunal and to the benevolent racism of the American captain. It also enables us to see the slave mutiny not as the predatory act of beasts of prey or as revenge, but as a rebellion motivated by a passionate human will to be free, whatever the cost, of the physical and mental chains of slavery, free to return to the homeland from which they were barbarically torn by the brutal white man.

The second revelatory moment of the don's deposition, pitted against Captain Delano's sense of the passive, servile mind of Benito Cereno's servant, refers to the intelligence of the leader of the slave revolt:

> They at last arrived at the island of Santa Maria . . . at about six o'clock in the afternoon, at which hour they cast anchor very near the American ship, Bachelor's Delight, which lay in the same bay, commanded by the generous Captain Amasa Delano, but at six o'clock in the morning, they had already descried the port, and the negroes became uneasy, as soon as at distance they saw the ship, not having expected to see one there; that the negro Babo pacified them, assuring them that no fear need be had; that straightway he ordered the figure on the bow [the skeleton of Alexander Aranta] to be covered with canvas, as for repairs, and had the decks a little set in order, that for a time the negro Babo and the negro Artufal conferred; that the negro Artufal was for sailing away, but the negro Babo would not, and, by himself, cast about what to do; that at last he came to the deponent, proposing to him to say and do all that the deponent declares to have said and done to the American captain; ****** that the negro Babo warned him that if he varied in the least, or uttered any word, or gave any look that should give the least intimation of the past events or present state, he would instantly kill him, with all his companions, showing a dagger which he carried hid, saying something which, as he understood it, meant that the dagger would be alert as his eye; that the negro Babo then announced the plan to all his companions, which pleased them; that he then, the better to disguise the truth, devised many expedients, in some of them uniting deceit and defense; that of this sort was the device of the six Ashantees before named, who were his braves. (BC, 108–9)

As in the case of the first passage from the don's deposition, this one too could be interpreted negatively as exemplary of the black man's instinctive penchant for violence or, with the American prior to his epiphany, as an impossibility. Read symptomatically, however, as Melville intends the reader to do, this moment in the don's deposition dwelling on Babo's systematic organization of the slaves into an active community of resistance and his projection of the intricate masquerade to deceive the intruding white American visitor takes on an entirely different meaning than it does for the hostile Old World court or for the tolerant American captain, who, as we have seen, assumed that blacks, however childlike and docile, "were too stupid" as a race (BC, 75). In this estranging light, the black leader becomes precisely the acutely intelligent mastermind that the interpellated American's exceptionalist ethos made it impossible for him to see. He becomes, as it were, the shadow that haunts the light of the redemptive American vocation.

This unsettling emergence of the specter that has always haunted the American exceptionalist ethos precisely in its disavowals is the underscoring burden of the second addendum, which consists of the narrator's account of a dialogue between Don Benito Cereno and Amasa Delano during the long voyage to Lima before the trial and the don's sudden death. In this resonant dialogue, in which Babo is an unspoken presence, the American captain, unable to understand why Don Benito feels no sense of relief at the satisfying closure of the life-threatening mutiny of the slaves, addresses the don's dark disturbance by invoking the unerring optimism intrinsic to the concept of providence—and the rejection of historical memory it entails—and recommending to the Old World don that he forget history or, we can now say more precisely, the imperatives of the time of the now that have irrupted into the Spaniard's life. Indeed, the genial American goes so far as to say, recalling to the reader the Pangloss of Voltaire's *Candide*, that the blindness of his optimistic (exceptionalist) oversight was the agency of his and the don's delivery from the mutinous slaves:

> "You generalize, Don Benito; and mournfully enough. But the past is passed; why moralize upon it? Forget it. See, yon bright sun has forgotten it all. And the blue sea, and the blue sky; these have turned over new leaves. . . ." "You are saved. . . ." "you are saved; what has cast such a shadow upon you?"

The don replies with two horrific words that bring the silenced slave to spectral presence:

> "The negro."

In a resonantly reserved way, the narrator adds:

> There was silence, while the moody man sat, slowly and unconsciously gathering his mantle about him, as if it were a pall.
> There was no more conversation that day. (BC, 116)

In that resonant silence, one infers everything about the black man that the exceptionalist American captain has disavowed.

This spectral force of the dislocating epiphany is underscored by the narrator at the end, after Babo has been hanged and his severed head mounted on a pole for all slaves to see and shudder at and Benito Cereno has died of his mysterious and incurable psychic malady:

> Some months after, dragged to the gibbet at the tail of a mule, the black met his voiceless end. The body was burned to ashes; but for many days, the head, that archive of subtlety, fixed on a pole in the Plaza, met unabashed, the gaze of the whites; and across the Plaza looked towards St. Bartholomew's church, in whose vault slept then, the covered bones of Aranda; and across the Rimac bridge looked towards the monastery, on Mount Agonia without; where, three months after being dismissed by the court, Benito Cereno, borne on a bier, did, indeed, follow his leader. (BC, 116–17)

In the end, the reader infers, the visited becomes the visitor, the seen, the see-er; and the visitor, the visited, the see-er, the seen. It is not only Benito who will follow his leader; it will also be, all things remaining the same, the America embodied in the interpellated figure of Captain Amasa Delano.[25]

6

The potential revolution implicit in the emergence to spectral presence of the passed over (preterite) to haunt the American exceptionalist ethos (and the spirit of capitalism)—the "event," in the sense of this word given to it by Alain Badiou[26]—was, as we have seen, in part heralded by the ineffable protagonist of Melville's haunting short story "Bartleby, the Scrivener: A Story of Wall Street," the reverse image of "Benito Cereno," which recounts (in his words) the increasingly bewildered reaction of a prominent, genial-spirited Wall Street lawyer to one of his employees, who suddenly, when called to copy a legal document, replies, "I would prefer not to."

For Melville, as we have seen, Captain Delano is the figure of the in-terpellated American subject. In answering the electing call of the re-demptive higher (American) cause, he becomes, like Moses in Althusser's example, a subjected subject, one who, laboring in behalf of this transcendental American *telos*, is unerringly blinded to the existential imperatives of the time of the now. Bartleby, in stark contrast, is the antithesis of this interpellated figure. In refusing to answer his "benign" Wall Street boss's call—in refusing, unlike Moses, to respond to his (identifying) name—he undermines—that is, renders inoperative—not only the latter's authority but, symbolically, also the hegemonized vocation/ethical apparatus—the "So be it!"—that sustains the entire structure of the capitalist edifice. One example of several in the lawyer's story that refer to his rejected calling of Bartleby will suffice to convey the presiding power of the (Protestant) "work ethic" and the (Franklinian) "spirit of capitalism" *that constitute his reality*—and the expectations it implies—and thus the stunning force of its disruption by this singular, indeed, "inhuman," scrivener's refusal to be answerable to his call, or, as the lawyer puts it shortly after, his "passive resistance"[27] (BS, 23):

> It was on the third day, I think, of his being with me, and before any necessity had arisen for having his own writing examined, that, being much hurried to complete a small affair I had in hand, I abruptly called to Bartleby. In my haste and natural expectancy of instant compliance, I sat with my head bent over the original on my desk, and my right hand sideways, and somewhat nervously extended with the copy, so that immediately upon emerging from his retreat, Bartleby might snatch it and proceed to business without the least delay.
>
> In this very attitude did I sit when I called to him, rapidly stating what it was I wanted him to do—namely to examine a small paper with me. Imagine my surprise, nay, consternation, when without moving from his privacy, Bartleby in a singularly mild, firm voice, replied, "I would prefer not to."
>
> I sat awhile in perfect silence, rallying my stunned faculties. Immediately it occurred to me that my ears had deceived me, or Bartleby had entirely misunderstood my meaning. I repeated my request in the clearest tone I could assume. But in quite as clear a one came the previous reply, "I would prefer not to."
>
> "Prefer not to," echoed I, rising in high excitement, and crossing the room with a stride. "What do you mean? Are you moon-struck? I want you to help me compare this sheet here—take it," and I thrust it towards him.
>
> "I would prefer not to," he said.
>
> I looked at him steadfastly. His face was leanly composed; his gray eyes dimly calm. Not a wrinkle of agitation rippled him. Had there been the least uneasiness, anger, impatience or impertinence in his manner; in other words, had there been anything ordinarily human about him, doubtless I should have violently dismissed him from the premises. But as it was, I should have as soon thought of turning my pale plaster-of-Paris bust of Cicero out of doors. I stood gazing at him awhile as he went on with his own writing, and then reseated myself at my desk. This is very strange, thought I. What had one best do? But my business hurried me. I concluded to forget the matter for the present, reserving it for my future leisure. So calling Nippers from the other room, the paper was speedily examined. (BS, 20–21)

To recall Althusser's apt model of Moses, the Wall Street lawyer is the interpellated subject who becomes the mirror image in the world of the transcendental Subject. That is to say, the lawyer represents the modern heir of Benjamin Franklin, who, as Weber shows, in secularizing the Puritan work ethic, became the figure of the "spirit of capitalism": the "truth" grounded in a worldly asceticism—that "loving the world with 'weaned affections,'" in Perry Miller's apt terms—that produced the practical, means/end or, colloquially, "can do" logic of the American people and the "reality" that "wasting time is wasting money." All this is reflected at the outset of his story, prior to and anticipating the coming of Bartleby, by way of the lawyer's lengthy account of his relations with his three employees nicknamed Turkey, Nippers, and Ginger Nut, in which, according to the dictates of his liberalism, he domesticates their time-wasting eccentricities not by force but by knowledgeable accommodation. The pacifying result of this liberal accommodational strategy is epitomized by the following conversation with Turkey, a very competent copyist, who has a drinking problem in the morning that renders his copying in the afternoon unsatisfactory and the lawyer's premises unproductively volatile, in which every response to the lawyer is preceded by the acknowledgment of his subservience:

> "With submission, sir," said Turkey on this occasion, "I consider myself your right-hand man. In the morning I marshal and deploy my columns; but in the afternoon I put myself at their head, and gallantly charge the foe, thus!"—and he made a violent thrust with the rule.
>
> "But the blots, Turkey," intimated I.
>
> "True,—but, with submission, sir, behold these hairs! I am getting old. Surely, sir, a blot or two of a warm afternoon is not to be severely urged against gray hairs. Old age–even if it blot the page—is honorable. With submission, sir, we *both* are getting old."
>
> This appeal to my fellow-feeling was hardly to be resisted. At all events, I saw that go he would not. So I made up my mind to let him stay, resolving, nevertheless, to see to it, that during the afternoon he had to do with my less important papers. (BS, 16)

To invoke Michel Foucault's critique of the modern democratic capitalist polity, the Wall Street lawyer represents a "regime of truth," the system informing the biopolitical disciplinary apparatuses the function of which is to reduce singular humans and their amorphous spectral force to "useful and docile bodies."[28]

Indeed, the lawyer inadvertently highlights this distinction between the overt use of power and the productive power that comes with knowledge about the subject (what Foucault, in identifying the difference between the power of the *ancien regime* and that of the revolutionary bourgeois/ capitalist class, calls the "repressive hypothesis")[29] by resisting the temptation to use overt (totalitarian) violence in the face of the ineffable copyist's undeviating recalcitrance in favor of the accommodational approach intrinsic to liberal democratic societies.

> I was now in such a state of nervous resentment that I thought it but prudent to check myself at present from further demonstrations. Bartleby and I were alone. I remembered the tragedy of the unfortunate Adams and still more unfortunate Colt in the solitary office of the latter; and how poor Colt, being dreadfully incensed by Adams, and imprudently permitting himself to get wildly excited, was at unawares hurried into his fatal act—an act which certainly no man could possibly deplore more than the actor himself. . . .
>
> But when this old Adam of resentment rose in me and tempted me concerning Bartleby, I grappled him and threw him. How? Why, simply by recalling the divine injunction: "A new commandment give I unto you, that ye love one another." Yes, this it was that saved me. Aside from higher considerations, charity often operates as a vastly wise and prudent principle—a great safeguard to the possessor. Men have committed murder for jealousy's sake, and anger's sake . . . but no man that ever I heard of ever committed a diabolical murder for sweet charity's sake. Mere self-interest, then, if no better motive can be enlisted, should, especially with high-tempered men, prompt all beings to charity and philanthropy. At any rate, upon the occasion in question, I strove to drown my exasperated feelings towards the scrivener by benevolently construing his conduct. Poor fellow, poor fellow! I thought, he don't mean anything; and besides, he has seen hard times, and ought to be indulged. (BS, 36)

Seen in the light of this contrapuntal reading of the Wall Street lawyer's narrative, we are enabled to understand what it is about Bartleby's "I would prefer not to" that drives his hitherto self-satisfied employer to such extraordinarily great lengths to *name* his ineffable behavior and thus maintain his authority over him. In invoking the story of Moses's calling, Althusser, to explain the insidious operations of the spirit of capitalism, added that just as the interpellated Moses (the subjected subject) needs God (the Subject), so God needs Moses (IISA, 179), implying that this is the hailing Subject's Achilles' heel. Similarly, the Wall Street lawyer needs Bartleby. From his hegemonic democratic capitalist perspective ("Amen.—So be it.") everything depends on the subject's responding to the name by which he is called—that is to say, the Wall Street lawyer's *vocational ethics are founded on a constructed identitarian system (an ideology) in which the individual is "naturally" expected to play his (non) part in the encompassing larger whole.* This is what it means to be a subjected subject understood as the truth of the way things ("really") are. When, however, the part of no part refuses to play his (no) part, to be answerable to the call of the hailing subject, the entire ideological system—the apparatus of capture—which needs the interpellated subject to maintain its power, falls apart. Though the scrivener has a name, he does not fulfill the imperatives entailed in the naming.[30] He is, as Agamben decisively puts it, proleptic of the emergent postmodern or postnational figure of the unnamable "whatever being"— the nothing, the nobody or, in the language of the American Puritans, "the preterite" or "passed over"—who "relates to singularity not in its indifference with respect to a common property (to a concept, for example, being red, being French, being Muslim), but only in its being *such as it is*" (CC, 1). And it is precisely his ineffability, his refusal to be interpellated, that is, to be identified as an individual part of the larger whole—ultimately, for being a (stateless) nomad—that the Wall Street lawyer, the interpellating Subject (the state), cannot tolerate, indeed, will go all out to identify and repress.

In Melville's story, Bartleby is eventually evicted from the Wall Street "premises" (understood as a vocational logic and bounded space) on charges of vagrancy by the officials and sent to the notorious prison called the Tombs, where he dies. And the bewildered lawyer, like Captain Delano *vis à vis* his specter, wills himself to maintain his blind tolerant attitude toward him until the very end. Nevertheless, it is precisely as the unidentifiable figure of "whatever being" that, as Agamben suggests in *The Coming Community*, Bartleby can be understood as a proleptic witness to the massacre in Tiananmen Square in 1989. I quote Agamben at length to suggest the uncanny relevance of Bartleby's "I would prefer not to" to this epochal event of contemporary history:

> What could be the politics of whatever singularity, that is, of a being whose community is mediated not by any condition of belonging (being red, being Italian, being Communist) nor by the simple absence of conditions. . . . A herald from Beijing carries the elements of a response.
>
> What was most striking about the demonstrations of the Chinese May was the relative absence of determinate contents in their demands. . . . This makes the violence of the State's reaction seem even more inexplicable. *It is likely, how-*

ever, that the disproportion is only apparent and that the Chinese leaders acted, from
their point of view, with greater lucidity than the Western observers who were exclu-
sively concerned with advancing increasingly less plausible arguments about the
opposition between democracy and communism. [My emphasis]

The novelty of the coming politics is that it will no longer be a struggle for the
conquest or control of the State, but a struggle between the State and the non-State
(humanity), an insurmountable disjunction between whatever singularity and
the State organization. This has nothing to do with the simple affirmation of the
social in opposition to the State that has often found expression in the protest
movements of recent years. Whatever singularities cannot form a *societas* because
they do not possess any identity to vindicate nor any bond of belonging for
which to seek recognition. In the final instance the State can recognize any
claim for identity—even that of a State identity within the State (the recent
history of relations between the State and terrorism is an eloquent confirmation
of this fact). What the State cannot tolerate in any way, however, is that singularities form a community without affirming an identity, that humans co-belong
without any representable condition of belonging (even in the form of a simple
presupposition). . . . For the State, therefore, what is important is never the singularity as such, but only its inclusion in some identity, whatever identity (but
the possibility of the whatever itself being taken up without an identity is a
threat the State cannot come to terms with). . . .

Whatever singularity, which wants to appropriate belonging itself, its own
being-in-language, and thus rejects all identity and every condition of belonging, is the principle enemy of the State. Wherever these singularities peacefully
demonstrate their being in common there will be a Tiananmen, and, sooner or
later, the tanks will appear. (CC, 85.6–86.7)[31]

Agamben's example of the interpellating Subject is a totalitarian/
capitalist state. But his insistent reference to the capitalist democratic polities (including the media) that self-righteously represent the massive inchoate demonstrations in Tiananmen Square as an uprising in behalf of
Western, particularly American-style, democracy, is intended, like Melville's spectral opening conclusion of *Benito Cereno,* to suggest that it is this
unnamable (spectral) "whatever being" that also haunts this very blind
exceptionalist assumption that, as his invocation of Melville's story suggests, has its origins in the Protestant work ethic. That Agamben's insight
into the modern state's response to unnamable revolutionary uprisings
does, indeed, apply to the United States is borne witness to by many
examples from modern American history. But for the sake of brevity I will
invoke one especially chilling and resonant paranoid instance from the
post–9/11 era that I have previously cited and commented on at length in

Chapter 2. I am referring to the United States' Ahabian identification of the unfathomable complexities of the Middle East—largely produced by the depredations of Western imperialism and most recently exacerbated by the Unites States' unilateral exceptionalist policies of "preemptive war" and "regime change"—with the hated figure of Osama bin Laden and then, in the name of its redemptive global errand, its mounting of a spectacular search-and-destroy mission that finally "got him," but left that fraught geopolitical world unaltered, if not more volatile.[32]

7

The counter-memory Melville inaugurated in the middle of the nineteenth century was "frozen into silence" by the dominant culture during his lifetime.[33] And although his fiction was resurrected in the 1920s, it was at the expense of its subversion of the American exceptionalist ethos and its vocational ethic. It was not until the volatile era of the Vietnam War that it resurfaced in the fiction of such postmodern American novelists as Ralph Ellison, Thomas Pynchon, Robert Coover, William Gaddis, Donald Barthelme, William Gass, Jack Kerouac, Don DeLillo, Kathy Acker, and Toni Morrison and poets such as Charles Olson and those of the Black Mountain School. Any one of these writers could be invoked to bear witness in one degree or another to the continuity of their errant *poesis*—and their preference for the nomadic "road"—with Melville's undermining of the vocational ethic intrinsic to American exceptionalism. But for the sake of economy, I will restrict my remarks to a brief commentary on Thomas Pynchon's great novel *Gravity's Rainbow*, which, more than any other literary instance of the postmodern American counter-memory, is the heir to both Melville's subversive content—its interrogation of the exceptionalist Puritan legacy—and the potentialities of his errant art. More specifically, I will focus on two uncannily revealing episodes that are central to that aspect of the novel, insufficiently addressed by the large archive of Pynchon criticism, that deals with the Puritan ancestry of Pynchon's protagonist, Tyrone Slothrop: the scene involving Slothrop's nomadic encounter with the Argentine anarchist Francisco Squalidozzi in Zurich, and the mirror scene, much later, near the end of the novel, in which Slothrop, returning one last time to his Puritan heritage, recalls the conversation with the Argentine anarchist. Indeed, when this massively commented-on postmodern American novel is read from the genealogical perspective from which I am taking my directives (it should be remembered that the term "American exceptionalism" was not current at the time of its publication) it undergoes a remarkable estrangement.

Gravity's Rainbow is, in many ways, fundamentally about the itinerary, traced by Max Weber, of the Puritan Calvinist doctrine of providential history that, in distinguishing between the elect and the damned—the chosen and the "preterite" or "passed over," in Pynchon's terms—produced the Puritan work ethic and the "spirit of capitalism." Although the mis en scène of this American novel is appropriately transnational—a devastated Europe at the close of World War II, the "zero zone" in which (remarkably reminiscent of Hannah Arendt's diagnosis of post-war Europe, not incidentally) the nation-state has been replaced by a "Zone" (un)inhabited by a multitude of stateless or displaced persons—the focus of its errant plot is on the modern American exceptionalist obsession with the high technology of the rocket, the spectacular—shock and awing—effects intrinsic to its advanced technological status,[34] and its decisive killing power. More specifically, it highlights a constituency of the American military command, to which Slothrop belongs, that works enthusiastically in behalf of a higher cause (the "They" that refers to corporate capitalism), and, in its rage for order, is engaged in a paranoid attempt to predict the pattern of the German rockets falling on London. And in the process of affiliating this distant past and immediate cataclysmic (liminal) present, it becomes manifestly clear that this paranoid modern American techno-teleological vocation in the global wilderness is the secular, capitalist allotrope of the Puritans' redemptive providential errand in the New World wilderness. That is to say, Pynchon's intention, like Melville's in *Benito Cereno* and "Bartleby, the Scrivener," is to represent the operations of the interpellative logic of the American exceptionalism vocation at its liminal point, where it self-destructs: discloses the violence its redemptive errand invariably disavows. As the novel relentlessly shows from the ominous beginning (when an incoming rocket is zeroing in on the theater housing all of humanity) to the end, the redemptive Puritan vocation ends, not in the renewal of life, but in the finality of death.

This deadly legacy of the providential history of the American Puritans—the covenantal vocation that is intrinsic to their chosen status (as opposed to the preterite, those "passed over" by their inscrutable God)—and the positive possibilities disclosed by rendering the exceptionalist logic of this legacy inoperative—are synecdochically revealed in the two episodes of the novel I referred to above. The first entails a conversation between the anarchist, Squallidozzi, a refugee from peronista Argentina, who is attempting to establish a stateless state in the zero zone that Europe has become, and Tyrone Slothrop, who, though he is now a nomadic American, between the deterministic Puritan world from which he is trying to free himself and a world struggling to be born in his mind, is too deeply inscribed (programmed) by the American exceptionalist ethos to be able to understand what the Argentine anarchist is talking about:

> "In the days of the gauchos, my country was a blank piece of paper. The pampas stretched as far as men could imagine, inexhaustible, fenceless. Wherever the gaucho could ride, the place belonged to him. But Buenos Aires sought hegemony over the provinces. All the neuroses about property gathered strength, and began to infect the countryside. Fences went up, and the gauchos became less free. It is our national tragedy. We are obsessed with building labyrinths, where before there were open plain and sky. To draw ever more complex patterns on the blank sheet. We cannot abide that *openness*; it is terror to us. Look at Borges. Look at the suburbs of Buenos Aires. The tyrant Rosas has been dead a century, but his cult flourishes. Beneath the city streets, the warrens of rooms and corridors, the fences and the networks of steel track, the Argentine heart, in its perversity and guilt, longs for a return to that first unscribbled serenity . . . that anarchic oneness of pampas and sky. . . ."
>
> "But-but bobwire," Slothrop with his mouth full of that fondue, just gobblin' away, "that's *progress*—you, you can't have open range forever, you can't just stand in the way of progress"—yes, he is actually going to go on for half an hour, quoting Saturday-afternoon western movies dedicated to Property if anything is, at this foreigner who's springing for his meal.[35]

Having learned in the process of the narrative that Slothrop is a symbolic figure of the modern American whose ancestry goes back from the practical-oriented and capitalist, through the self-reliant pioneering Leatherstocking figure of the era of westward expansion, to the austere New England Puritans of the founding moment, it is likely that Pynchon's giving Slothrop a distinctly American vernacular that, however, parodically, recalls this long tradition ("bobwire," the reference to the Saturday cowboy-and-Indian movies that he has seen) is intended to evoke this exceptionalist tradition in the reader's mind—that is to say, to suggest, however tentatively, the idea that the Argentine anarchist's account of the enclosing and domestication of the open pampas by the metropolitan Buenos Aires is intended to remind the American reader of the analogous

American errand in the wilderness that eventually included the enclosure, improvement, and settlement of the West and the extinction of the nomadic native Indians.

Be that as it may, this faint evocation of the American vocation—of the history of the "founding," "settlement," "improvement" of the "Wild West" in the name of the "errand in the wilderness"—is manifestly the decisive burden of the second episode, which harkens back to the first one. In this telling scene, Tyrone Slothrop, having finally realized that his vocation is an interpellated paranoia related to his Puritan heritage, is wandering nomadically in the zero zone (of possibility) to which the European continent has reverted. And in the process, he retrieves one of his Puritan ancestors, who, we remember, has haunted his interpellated vocation from the beginning. This spectral image from the Puritan past is William Slothrop, a member of the original Puritan covenantal community, who, having removed to the Berkshires (a deliberate echo of Melville, not incidentally), eventually refused to be answerable to the Puritan calling, becoming a heretic instead.

Sick of the Puritans' self-righteous imposition of preterition on all those who did not conform to the rigid dictates of the Puritan calling and its work ethic—their "apparatuses of capture," as it were,[36] William Slothrop, Tyrone recalls, preferred to consort with the pigs he shepherds across the wilderness of the Berkshire Mountains (not, however, without acute awareness that he is, in the end, betraying them) to the market in Boston and with the preterite natives and hill people he meets along the way:

> William Slothrop was a peculiar bird. He took off from Boston, heading west in true imperial style, in 1634 or –5, sick and tired of the Winthrop machine, convinced he could preach as well as anybody in the hierarchy even if he hadn't been officially ordained. The ramparts of the Berkshires stopped everybody else at the time, but not William. He just started climbing. He was one of the very few Europeans in. After they settled in Berkshire, he and his son John got a pig operations going—used to drive the hogs right back down the great escarpment, back over the long pike to Boston, drive them just like sheep or cows. By the time he got to the market those hogs were so skinny it was hardly worth it, but William wasn't really in it so much for the money as just for the trip itself. He enjoyed the road, the mobility, the chance encounters of the day—Indians, trappers, wenches, hill people—and most of all just being with those pigs. They were good company. Despite the folklore and the injunctions in his own Bible, William came to love their nobility and personal freedom, their gift for finding comfort in the mud, on a hot day—pigs out on the road, in company together,

were everything Boston wasn't, and you can imagine what the end of the journey, the weighing, slaughter and dreary pigless return back up into the hills must've been like for William. Of course he took it as a parable—knew that the squealing bloody horror at the end of the pike was in exact balance to all their happy sounds, their untroubled pink eyelashes and kind eyes, their smiles, their grace in cross-country movement. It was a little too early for Isaac Newton, but feelings about action and reaction were in the air. William must've been waiting for the one pig that wouldn't die, that would validate all the ones who'd had to, all the Gadarene swine who'd rushed into extinction like lemmings, possessed not by demons but by trust for men, which the men kept betraying . . . possessed by innocence they couldn't lose . . . by faith in William as another variety of pig, at home with the Earth, sharing the same gift of life. (GR, 554–55)

Eventually, William wrote a heretical tract, *On Preterition*, and, as a result of the Slothropite heresy it fomented, he was exiled ("86ed") by the presiding "saints" out of the Massachusetts Bay Colony, thus reverting to the very nomadic condition—and the profane time of the now—his covenantal community demonized in order to establish its elected identity:

It had to be published in England, and is among the first books to've been not only banned but also ceremoniously burned in Boston. Nobody wanted to hear about all the Preterite, the many God passes over when he chooses a few for salvation. William argued holiness for these "second Sheep," without whom there'd be no elect. You can bet the Elect in Boston were pissed off about that. And it got worse. William felt that what Jesus was for the elect, Judas Iscariot was for the Preterite. Everything in the Creation has its equal and opposite counterpart. How can Jesus be an exception? Could we feel for him anything but horror in the face of the unnatural, the extracreational? Well, if he is the son of man, and if what we feel is not horror but love, then we have to love Judas too. Right? How William avoided being burned for heresy, nobody knows. He must have had connections. They did finally 86 him out of Massachusetts Bay Colony—he thought about Rhode Island for a while but decided he wasn't that keen on antinomians either. So finally he sailed back to Old England, not in disgrace so much as despondency, and that's where he died, among memories of the blue hills, green maizefields, get-togethers over hemp and tobacco with the Indians, young women in upper rooms with their aprons lifted, pretty faces, hair spilling on the wood floors while underneath in the stables horses kicked and drunks hollered, the starts in the very early mornings when the backs of his herd glowed like pearl, the long, stony and surprising road to Boston, the rain on the Connecticut River, the snuffling good-nights of a hundred pigs among the new stars and long grass still warm from the sun, settling down to sleep. (GR, 555–56)

It is in the context of this intense meditation on the nomadic life in the time of the now of the open-ended zero zone—the antithesis of the concept of vocation as servitude to a higher cause—that Tyrone Slothrop suddenly but inevitably remembers the eccentric Argentine anarchist and his eloquent and impassioned account of the enclosure of the open pampas, which, at that time, Slothrop could only understand, if at all, as mere radical political diatribe. I quote at length not only to suggest how uncannily precise Slothrop's memory (not recollection but repetition)[37] of this time of the now is, but also how resonantly polyvalent its disoperating implications for the exceptionalist American vocation and the concept of national belonging it privileges:

> Could he [William Slothrop] have been the fork in the road America never took, the singular point she jumped the wrong way from? Suppose the Slothropite heresy had had the time to consolidate and prosper? Might there have been fewer crimes in the name of Jesus, and more mercy in the name of Judas Iscariot? It seems to Tyrone Slothrop that there might be a route back—maybe that anarchist he met in Zurich was right, maybe for a little while all the fences are down, one road as good as another, the whole space of the Zone cleared, depolarized, and somewhere inside the waste of it a single set of coordinates from which to proceed, without elect, without preterite, without even nationality to fuck it up. . . . Such are the vistas of thought that open up in Slothrop's head as he tags along after Ludwig. (GR, 556)

In this uncannily proleptic anarchic vision Slothrop not only renders inoperative the Puritan providential ontology, the means/end method of knowledge production, the vocational ethic (the calling) on which the American exceptionalist ethos is founded, and, not least, by way of his criticism of the enclosure movement, the logic of belonging of the modern nation-state system on which the entire political edifice of the exceptionalist United States stands. He also opens up the profane time of the now, a mode of knowledge production that protects potentiality (the question) from becoming dependent on the act, an improvisational (or nomadic) ethics, and, in so doing, anticipates a coming "depolarized" political zone, unlike the nation-state, "without elect, without preterite, without even nationality to fuck it up."

Slothrop, of course, does not make the effort to enact this revolutionary Slothropian turn in the road America had not taken. Indeed, he eventually becomes "scattered in the Zone." But from the perspective of Pynchon's novel—if, that is, it is read in the light of its insistent genealogical concerns about the origins of the American national identity—what Slothrop envisages in the "Zone," thanks to the unlikely but telling affiliation between a modern Argentine anarchist and a founding American Puritan heretic, is unforgettable in its potential, not least because it is a foreigner who enables the interpellated American subject to avow what his exceptionalism always disavows. And thus, like Melville's *Benito Cereno* and "Bartleby," "the vistas of thought that open in Slothrop's head" as he meditates on this affiliation are uncannily proleptic not only of the contemporary New Americanists' interrogation of the American exceptionalism and its work ethic, but also of the promising transnational turn of American studies. I mean by this last turn that, having broken from the nationalism of the old (myth and symbol) Americanist framework, has entered into a promising dialogic relationship with transnational intellectuals, who are, in one way or another, in Edward Said's word, the "consciousness" of the preterite victims—"the stateless" (Arendt), "the migrant" (Said), "the whatever being" (Agamben), the "uncountable" (Badiou), the "part of no part" (Rancière), "the ungrievable" (Butler)—of America's redemptive exceptionalist mission in the global wilderness. I am referring, above all, to the post–9/11 American jeremiadic initiative, activated by al Qaeda's bombing of the World Trade Center and the Pentagon, that represented the War on Terror as the war that History has called the present generation of Americans to fight.

8

In sum, what I have attempted to suggest in thus undertaking this genealogy of American exceptionalism focusing on its origins in the Puritan calling is that the prevailing understanding of the term (not only of the old Americanists, including the American political class, but even of all too many New Americanists)—that which views the United States as simply superior to the other nations of the world (old and new)—is inadequate to the task, in Noam Chomsky's apt phrase, of "deterring American democracy." On the contrary, this genealogy has shown that American exceptionalism is simultaneously an ontological, a moral, an economic, a racial, a gendered, and a political phenomenon: a deeply structured *ethos* or *ethics*—a total way of life—or, from the alienated perspective enabled by this genealogy of the calling, an apparatus of capture that saturates the American body politic right down to its capillaries. As such, its inordinate invisible power, unlike the vulnerable visible power of totalitarian states, cannot be resisted by the traditional means—that is to say, by direct confrontation undertaken in the name of an identity—working-class, a racial or gendered minority, an ethnic constituency, and so on. These identities, as we have seen, are precisely the means by which the exceptionalist state's apparatuses of capture are programmed to operate in a decisively effective way. What the exceptionalist state cannot abide, what instigates the kind of anxiety (*Angst*) that can only be assuaged by objectifying violence, as we have seen in the figure of Bartleby, is the unaccountability of the passive resister. Thus the mode of resistance against the injustices of the democratic capitalist state that this genealogy of vocation calls for is, rather, an (active) passive resistance undertaken, not by this or that identifiable constituency, but precisely by an unnamable and ineffable community representing the singular universality (or commonality) of humanity at large, the "whatever being," in Giorgio Agamben's felicitous term, that refuses to be interpellated: identified, contained, and subjected to a higher cause.

But this genealogy of the American calling not only suggests a viable mode of resisting the exceptionalist democratic capitalist state. It also, precisely in its retrieval of "whatever being," "the part of no part," "the ungrievable," "the uncounted," "the subaltern," "the preterite," from the paradoxical oblivion of naming, from the degrading servile margins to which they have been relegated by the elect, opens up a sense of a coming community of "whatever beings" replete with potentiality. This, I suggest, is the witness of Thomas Pynchon, when, in the 1970s, with the American calling—and, no doubt, Bartleby's "I would prefer not to" and Isabel's "All's o'er and ye him [Pierre] not!"—in mind, he gives the now decentered and nomadic Tyrone Slothrop to think these unforgettable—and richly potential—words: "maybe the anarchist he met in Zurich was right, maybe for a little while all the fences are down, . . . the whole space of the Zone cleared, depolarized, and somewhere inside the waste of it a single set of coordinates from which to proceed, without elect, without preterite, without even nationality to fuck it up." Given Pynchon's insistent Melvillian emphasis on the dismantling of the Puritan legacy—the rendering inoperative of the relay between, on the one hand, exceptionalism (the elect), the vocation of the calling, the sedentary (and local), and the binarist logic of belonging of the nation-state and, on the other, between the commonality of humanity, the refusal of the work ethic, the retrieval of the nomadic (and global), the time of the now, and the apotheosis of potentiality as such—it is not difficult to perceive that Pynchon's antiexceptionalist witness is remarkably proleptic of the coming community that contemporary postnationalist theoreticians—not least, Edward Said, Giorgio Agamben, Alain Badiou, Slavoj Žižek, Jacques Rancière, and Judith Butler—have been attempting to think. I end this opening genealogy of the American vocation with the strikingly exemplary witness of Giorgio Agamben. Following the directives of Hannah Arendt's diagnosis of post–World War II Europe as a space characterized by the waning of the nation-state system and the emergence of the refugee (the stateless person) as the "vanguard" of the future *polis*[38]—and echoing Edward Said's envisioning of the coming community as "'the complete consort dancing together' contrapuntally"[39]—he writes of the fraught example of contemporary Jerusalem:

> Instead of two national states separated by uncertain and threatening boundaries, it might be possible to imagine two political communities insisting on the same region and in a condition of exodus from each other—communities that would articulate each other via a series of reciprocal extraterritorialities in which the guiding concept would no longer be the *ius* (right) of the citizen but rather the *refugium* (refuge) of the singular. In an analogous way, we could conceive of Europe not as an impossible "Europe of the nations," whose catastrophe one can already foresee in the short run, but rather as an aterritorial or extraterritorial space in which all the (citizen and noncitizen) residents of the European states would be in a position of exodus or refuge; the status of European would then mean the being-in-exodus of the citizen (a condition that obviously could also be one of immobility). European space would thus mark an irreducible difference between birth [*nascita*] and nation in which the old concept of people (which, as is well known, is always a minority) could again find a political meaning, thus decidedly opposing itself to the concept of nation (which has so far unduly usurped it).
>
> This space would coincide neither with any of the homogeneous national territories nor with their *topographical* sum, but would rather act on them by articulating and perforating them *topologically* as in the Klein bottle or the Möbius strip, *where exterior and interior in-determine each other.* In this new space, European cities would rediscover their ancient vocation of cities of the world by entering into a relation of reciprocal extraterritoriality.[40]

CODA

Hi there, Madis, I'm an American poet, twentyish, early to mid-thirtyish, fortyish to seventyish. I've had poems on the *Poets Against the War* website, and in *American Poetry Review* and *Chain*, among other magazines, and I have a blog, and I really dig Arab music, and I read Adorno and Spivak, and I'm really progressive. I voted for Clinton and Gore, even though I know they bombed you a lot, too, sorry about that, and I know I live quite nicely off the fruits of a dying imperium, which includes anti-war poetry readings at the Lincoln Center and the Poetry Project, with appetizers and wine and New World Music and lots of pot. And because nothing is simple in this world, and because no one gets out unscathed, I'm going to just be completely candid with you. I'm going to box your ears with two big books of poems, one of them experimental and the other more plain speech-like, both of them hardbound and by leading academic presses, and I'm going to do it until your brain swells to the size of a basketball and you die like the fucking lion for real. You'll never make it to MI because that's the breaks; poetry is hard, and people go up in flames for lack of it every day. By the time any investigation gets to you, your grandchildren will have been dead over one thousand years, and poetry will be inhabiting regions you can't even begin to imagine. Well, we did our best; sorry we couldn't have done better. . . . I want you to take this self-righteous poem, soak it in this bedpan of crude oil, and shove it on down your pleading, screaming throat. Now, get the hood back on.

Kent Johnson, "Lyric Poetry after 'Auschwitz, or: 'Get the Hood Back On'"

Appendix

The Debate World and the Making of the American Political Class:
An Interview Conducted by Christopher Spurlock with William V. Spanos

William V. Spanos is the author of many books; he is a World War II veteran, a Distinguished Professor of English and Comparative Literature at SUNY Binghamton, and is well known in the competitive world of high school and intercollegiate academic debate. We thank Dr. Spanos so much for speaking with us. It is not often that we have such brilliant minds comment on our insular activity, and your work gets at the heart of what we do.

C.S.: When we had our discussion in Binghamton, you asked me if we, in the debate world, were ever marginalized or excluded for reading arguments based on your work. Typically a team will enact this move with an argument aptly referred to in debate as "framework" where they define and delimit their ideal world picture of a carefully crafted resolution and then explain why our argument has violated the parameters of their frame. In earlier comments on debate, you had criticized the disinterested nature of the activity and its participants—the detached model of debate where anything goes so long as you score points and detach yourself from the real (human) weight of these issues. How might debaters approach debate or relate to our resolutions in a more *interested* sense?

W.V.S.: The reason I asked you that question is because I've always thought that the debate system is a rigged process, by which I mean, in your terms, it's framed to exclude anything that the frame can't contain and domesticate. To frame also means to prearrange so that a particular outcome is assured, which also means that what's outside of the frame doesn't stand a chance: is "framed" from the beginning. It was, above all, the great neo-Marxist Louis Althusser's analysis of the problematic—the perspective or frame of reference fundamental to knowledge production in democratic-capitalist societies—that enabled me to see what the so-called disinterestedness of empirical inquiry is blind to or, more accurately, willfully represses in its Panglossian pursuit of the truth.

Althusser's analysis of the problematic is too complicated to be explained in a few words. (Anyone interested will find his extended explanation in his introduction—"From *Capital* to Marx's Philosophy"—to his and Étienne Balibar's book *Reading Capital*). It will suffice here to say that we in the modern West have been *inscribed* by our culture—ideological state apparatuses (educational institutions, media, and so on)—by a system of knowledge production that goes by the name of "disinterested inquiry," but in reality the truth at which it arrives is a construct, a fiction, and thus ideological. And this is precisely because, in distancing itself from earthly being—the transience of time—this system of knowledge production privileges the panoptic eye in the pursuit of knowledge. This is what Althusser, no doubt following Heidegger's analysis of *Ge-stell* (enframement) in "The Question Concerning Technology," means by the "problematic": a frame that allows the perceiver to see only what it wants to see. Everything that is outside the frame doesn't exist to the perceiver. He/she is blind to it. It's nothing or, at the site of humanity, it's nobody. Put alternatively, the problematic—this frame, as the very word itself suggests, *spatializes* or *reifies* time—reduces what is a living, problematic force and not a thing into a picture or thing so that it can be comprehended (taken hold of, managed), appropriated, administered, and exploited by the "disinterested" inquirer.

All that I've just said should suggest what I meant when, long ago, in response to someone in the debate world who seemed puzzled by the strong reservations I expressed on being informed that the debate community in the U.S. was appropriating my work on Heidegger, higher education, and American imperialism. I said then—and I repeat here to you—that the traditional form of the debate, that is, the hegemonic frame that rigidly determines its protocols—is *unworldly* in an ideological way. It willfully separates the debaters from the world as it actually is—by which I mean as it has been produced by the dominant democratic/capitalist culture—and it displaces them to a free-floating zone, a no place, as it were, where all things, no matter how different the authority they command in the real world, are equal. But in *this* real world produced by the combination of Protestant Christianity and democratic capitalism things—and therefore their value—are never equal. They are framed into a system of binaries—identity/difference, civilization/barbarism, men/women, whites/blacks, sedentary/nomadic, occidental/oriental, chosen/preterite (passed over), self-reliant/dependent (communal), democracy/communism, Protestant Christian/Muslim, and so on—in which the first term is not only privileged over the second term, but, in thus being privileged, is also empowered to demonize the second. Insofar as the debate world frames argument *as if* every position has equal authority (the debater can take either side), it obscures and eventually effaces awareness of the degrading imbalance of power in the real world and the terrible injustices it perpetrates. Thus framed, debate gives the false impression that it is a truly democratic institution, whereas in reality it is complicitous with the dehumanized and dehumanizing system of power that produced it. It is no accident, in my mind, that this fraudulent form of debate goes back to the founding of the U.S. as a capitalist republic and that it has produced what I call the "political class" to indicate not only the fundamental sameness between the Democratic and Republican parties but also its fundamental indifference to the plight of those who don't count in a system where what counts is determined by those who are the heirs of this quantitative system of binaries.

C.S.: I would love to hear more about what you mean by the word *interested*. In your earlier work you mentioned that it came from the Greek term for "in-the-midst." The relay between this "point of view" and your account of the bombing of Dresden in your memoir *In the Neighborhood of Zero* seems remarkable. What lessons might we take from this?

W.V.S.: Following up on what I've just said, inquiry, whether it takes the form of knowledge production or debate, cannot be disinterested. "Disinterested" inquiry is an orientation towards the truth that has been exposed as a myth by the poststructuralist revolution from Martin Heidegger through Michel Foucault to Giorgio Agamben, Alain Badiou, and Judith Butler. Inquiry is necessarily *interested* precisely in the sense that it takes place *in the world*. The word "interest" comes from the Latin (not Greek) *inter esse*, which means that we, as human beings, are "beings in-the-midst" (as opposed to beings, such as angels, who look down from a distance on or "observe" phenomena from above). As Heidegger said, following Kierkegaard, we, as human beings, have been "thrown into the world" and thus exist *inter esse*, "in-the-midst-of-being." We are, therefore, *interested*, that is, we relate to or engage phenomena with *care* precisely because everything we encounter *inter esse* is transient, uncertain, problematic, a matter of questioning. To understand human beings as *inter esse* is thus to acknowledge that we are radically free. This is not as easy as the word "freedom" implies under the aegis of American democracy. The freedom that comes with being-in-the-midst is a difficult, even agonizing freedom. We can't rely on some higher cause, whether God or a framed system (such as democratic capitalism), to choose for us. We must choose for ourselves. Being in the midst, being interested, means, as Sartre put it long ago, being "condemned to be free." But that is the price one has to pay to become free from the degradation of servitude and for the exquisitely terrible joy of being fully human. Dis-interested inquiry separates or, better, alienates the inquirer from this *inter esse*. As I said earlier, it reduces the mysterious force of being-in-the-midst to an absolutely knowable (quantifiable) thing. Put alternatively, in privileging the observing or panoptic or spatializing eye—the eye that, seeing everything in time and space at once, reduces being's dynamics to a world picture—it privileges the answer over the question. To be interested then means to beware of those who demand answers—or finality—and victory or peace, for that matter. They invariably turn out to be murderous brutes.

It was precisely this lesson about being-in-the-world that I learned in the midst of the terrorist firebombing—for that's what it was—of Dresden perpetrated by the U.S. and Britain against German civilians in World War II, after I was taken prisoner of war during the Battle of the Bulge in Belgium. All through the war I, as a young boy, was nagged by the feeling that there was something radically wrong about my being sent by an abstract "higher cause" about which I knew absolutely nothing to fight and die for my country. And the little I did know as a child of immigrant parents did not instill me with patriotic fervor for that higher cause. But I, like Huckleberry Finn in his relation to his black friend Jim, suppressed that nagging feeling by blaming myself for daring to have such heretical feelings. After all, who was I to have opinions about higher causes? In Dresden, however, under the unrelenting Allied incendiary bombs that killed over 100,000 innocent civilians in one day and night air raid, I was, as I narrate in my memoir *In the Neighborhood of Zero*, dragged into the truth. In that horrendous zero zone of mass death and mutilation—in-the-midst with a vengeance—I bore witness to the terrible end of the logic that privileges a higher cause, a *Telos*, over everything that's below, which is to say, over everything that doesn't count to those, above, who do the counting. All this, not incidentally, is encapsulated by the little poem I wrote as the epigraph to my memoir:

Hovering over
their microcosmic map,
no periplum,
They, in shining brass,
push their prosthetic armada
to its destination,
unleash its murderous load, and,
when the unexpecting city below
goes up in turbulent flames,
cry, "Good show, old chaps."

Caught in that rain of terror,
we, down here,
under Their abstract gaze,
the living and the dead,
in the midst
of fire and brimstone,
all the boundaries razed,
become
a neighborhood of zero.

c.s.: You mentioned that your work is primarily influenced (although always by many others) by Heidegger, Foucault, Arendt, Said, and now Agamben and Badiou. In focusing on the similarities between these authors and emphasizing what they have in common, how do we remain on guard against the violent processes of assimilation and homogenization?

w.v.s.: The constellation you name is, admittedly, a controversial one, especially because it includes Edward Said, who, according to "Saidians," was very critical of the poststructuralist initiative that Heidegger inaugurated. Said's criticism of this poststructuralist tradition focused primarily on two related aspects of poststructuralist theory: (1) its alleged antihumanism; and (2) its alleged denial of agency to the human subject. As for the first, it is true that the poststructuralists, especially Foucault, following Heidegger, were severely critical of the Western humanist tradition. This was because this humanist tradition privileged the concept of Man (*anthropos*) understood as a self-present and determining essence. That is, it simply substituted the word of Man (*anthropo-logos*) for the Word of God (*Theo-logos*) as the beginning and end of the truth process. To Heidegger and Foucault, for example, the so-called humanist revolution in the Renaissance that displaced God by Man was not radical, because it simply secularized the *Theo-logos*, naturalized the supernatural. This humanism, no less than the theology it replaced, remained metaphysical: an interpretation of the *being* of being *meta ta physica*: from after or beyond or above the way things actually are—that is, panoptically.

Said—and, far more, so many of his followers—felt that Foucault's privileging of *discourse* over the worldliness of the text constituted a radical denial of humanism and human agency: that man makes his/her world. In my view, however, this was not exactly true. In substituting discourse for humanism, Foucault and the poststructuralists were then confronting the problem of language—its loss of transparency—posed by Nietzsche's, Freud's, and Heidegger's inaugural interrogations of disinterested (empirical) inquiry, which they showed was metaphysical. They were not denying the human or human agency as such. They were, in fact, attempting to show that, in privileging the "observing" (panoptic) eye, the "disinterested" humanist inquiry of modern democratic capitalist or Enlightenment Western societies was no less ideological—and deterministic—than the indoctrinating language of totalitarian societies, indeed, that it was more difficult to achieve human agency under its aegis because, unlike totalitarian indoctrination, in which power is overt and manifest (and thus vulnerable), it conceals its determining power beneath the rhetoric of freedom ("knowledge will set you free from power"). In other words, Foucault and the poststructuralists overdetermined language (textuality) over the question of human agency in their critique of disinterested inquiry because it was the most pressing concern at the time when the West was proclaiming, imperially, that its imperial version of the truth was applicable to the world at large. They were not denying the humanity of man or rejecting human agency. They were—and this, I think, is what the post-poststructuralists, Agamben, Badiou, Butler, Rancière, Žižek, are all about—laying the ground for a new, radically uncentered, nonidentitarian concept of the human and humanism and the human *polis*. They were, in fact, exactly what Said, in qualifying the humanism he was committed to, called himself at the end of his life: "nonhumanist humanists."

We must, of course, be vigilant in maintaining distinctions. After all, this is the crucial imperative of the poststructuralist critique of identity (the founding principle of the West: that identity—sameness—is the condition for the possibility of difference and not the other way around). But in doing so, we must also be wary of rigidifying the "others" (temporality, affect, women, workers, blacks, gays, Muslims, Jews, nomads, and so on) decolonized by the critique of identity back into fixed essentialist identities. In my mind, the revolution in thinking inaugurated by poststructuralist theory in the 1970s was drastically set back, if not annulled, when the "worldly" (politically oriented) theorists of this revolution put themselves into a binary opposition to their textual (ontological/epistemological) affiliates, thus turning a community of nonidentical identities—what, after Antonio Gramsci, I call a revolutionary "historical bloc"—into one at war with itself.

c.s.: What does it really mean to "think difference" or "think the second term" *positively*?

w.v.s.: As I have been saying in one way or another throughout these remarks, the Western tradition, particularly in its latest (anthropological or Enlightenment) phase, has been structured according to the imperatives of a binary logic (identity/difference), in which the first term is not only privileged over the second, but is also empowered to demonize this second. It is based on a politics of enmity. Thus, Some (total) thing vs. nothing, Self vs. other, Civilization vs. barbarism, Man vs. woman, Straight vs. gay, White vs. black, Occident vs. orient, and on and on. According to this enlightened mode of knowledge production, only entities that are measurable have being; everything else is as nothing. Or to put it alternatively, only *things* count; every phenomenon that is not a thing doesn't count. But, as Heidegger says in his essay "What Is Metaphysics?," every statement that the adherents of this mode of knowledge production make about truth is necessarily accompanied by reference to this nothing: "That to which the world refers are beings themselves—and nothing besides; that from which every attitude takes its guidance are beings themselves—and nothing further; that with which the scientific confrontation in the interruption occurs are beings themselves—and beyond that nothing." And he concludes: "What about this nothing? Is it an accident that we talk this way automatically . . . ?" The implication here is that this nothing (*das Nichts*), which the West systematically has repressed, has also haunted its truth discourse from the beginning of Western civilization. Poststructuralist theory, then—which, as the etymology makes clear in questioning a mode of knowledge that spatializes or thingifies what are decisively *not* things (like time), constitutes an effort not only to retrieve the nothing that modern Western thinking will militantly have nothing to do with, but also to think this nothing positively. The question it asks—or should ask—is what would a world in which the nothing, in all its manifestations, is given its due be like? This question about the coming community is the question that, like Said at the end of his life *vis à vis* Palestine, Agamben, Badiou, Rancière, Butler, and Žižek, among others, are now asking,

C.S.: Some of the most contentious arguments in the debate community about your work revolve around questions of identity. You criticize structures of whiteness that serve to maintain the hegemony of metaphysical imperialism, but the alternative you offer of *identityless identities* in multiple places in your work, especially *America's Shadow: An Anatomy of Empire*, seems like a privileged position to take. It is certainly easy for the majority of debaters as white, privileged males to adopt a nomadic or fluid identity—but what does the strategy of *identityless identities* do for those who are facing the brunt of oppression or cultural destruction now? Is this intended to be a strategy for them?

W.V.S.: Of course, identity is crucial in the struggle of oppressed peoples against tyranny and/or degradation. Being a Palestinian, for example, is absolutely necessary to the natives of Palestine who would resist the depredations inflicted on them by the powerful Israeli regime. It enables solidarity and endows strength to the cause of resistance. But what I have been calling poststructuralist theory has also taught us that identity, as a cultural phenomenon, is a historical construct, not a fact of nature. It is, as I have been suggesting, the consequence of a mode of knowledge production structured in domination, one, that is, that reverses the primal priority of difference (the many) and identity (the One). In prioritizing identity (the One) over difference (the many) this ontological fiction thus devalues and subordinates the latter and renders it colonizable. On the surface, this disclosure, which now posits difference as ontologically prior to identity, would suggest that the relay of minority terms in this binary logic, insofar as it has been denied a natural solidarity, are rendered powerless. But this is not necessarily so, since poststructuralist theory—Gayatri Spivak comes to mind here—has also taught us that the (subaltern) identities that have been established historically (by the dominant culture) can be used *strategically* against its oppressors.

This strategic appropriation of identity in the cause of resistance is too complicated to spell out here, but its efficacy (not least for debaters who would resist the established debate frame) can be suggested briefly by my referring to a well-known literary text and a well-known (in my mind epochal) modern historical event that have something basic in common: Melville's "Bartleby, the Scrivener" and the Vietnam War. In both, the focus is on the nobodies—those who are as *nothing*, who don't count, in a binarist system in which what counts is determined by material power, Wall Street, and the forwarding American war machine. In both, as well, the weak "nobodies" defeat the powerful somebodies, not by confronting the latter head on, in the forwarding terms of encounter it assumes, but simply by *refusing to be answerable to* the "truth" of the powerful. It was Bartleby's "I would prefer not to" that disintegrated the arrogant certainty of his "liberal" lawyer boss's Wall Street (democratic/capitalist) ethos. And it was the National Liberation Front's (the Viet Cong's) refusal to fight their war of liberation according to the forwarding dictates of the American imperial regime that resulted in the disintegration of the American military juggernaut. Appropriating the very subordinate terms by which the exceptionalist dominant parties represented them, both Bartleby and the National Liberation Front were enabled to transform themselves into a weapon that defeated an infinitely more powerful aggressor. It's worth recalling, at this juncture, Edward Said's appeal (in *Culture and Imperialism*) to the "damaged life" of Theodor Adorno in his effort to envision a mode of resistance in an age when those who don't count don't otherwise stand a chance: "'In an intellectual hierarchy which constantly makes everyone answerable, unanswerability alone can call the hierarchy directly by its name.'"

C.S.: Many of the most charged criticisms of your comments on debate stem from the charge that you have had very little experience with debate and are not qualified to comment on it. We've taken the position often that our insular activity could use some outside criticism, but others remain skeptical of the view that disinterested, "switch-side" debate, where debaters can take any position on an issue, will actually produce more neoconservatives like Richard Cheney and Donald Rumsfeld. They cite policy debaters who practiced this and went on to champion rights for Guantánamo Bay detainees after debate and law school. Surely you don't believe that all debaters will become neocons simply from following this model. But what should we be most on guard against in order to avoid the worst of the imminent global disaster that the neocons are undoubtedly leading us to?

W.V.S.: The danger of being a total insider is that the eye of such a person becomes blind to alternative possibilities. The extreme manifestation of this being at one with the system, of remaining inside the frame, as it were, is, as Hannah Arendt decisively demonstrated long ago, Adolph Eichmann. That's why she and Said, among many poststructuralists, believed that to be an authentic intellectual—to see what disinterested inquiry can't see—one has to be an "exile" (or a "conscious pariah") from a homeland—one who is both a part of and apart from the dominant (exceptionalist) culture. Unlike Socrates, for example, Hippias, Socrates' interlocutor in the dialogue "Hippias Major" (he is, for Arendt, the model for Eichmann), is at one with himself. When he goes home at night "he remains one." He is, in other words, incapable of *thinking*. When Socrates, the exilic consciousness, goes home, on the other hand, he is not alone; he is "by himself." He is two-in-one. He has to face this other self. He has to *think*. Insofar as its logic is faithfully pursued, the framework of the debate system, to use your quite appropriate initial language, does, indeed, produce horrifically thoughtless Eichmanns, which is to say, an exceptionalist *political class* whose thinking, whether it's called Republican or Democratic, is thoughtless in that it is totally separated from and indifferent to the existential realities of the *world* it is representing. It's no accident, in my mind, that those who govern us in America—our alleged representatives, whether Republican, neocon, or Democrat—constitute such an exceptionalist political class. This governing class has, in large part, its origins in a preparatory relay consisting of the high school and college debate circuit, political science departments in colleges and universities, and the law profession. The moral of this story is that the debate world needs more outsiders—or, rather, inside outsiders—if its ultimate purpose is to prepare young people to change the world rather than to reproduce it.

C.S.: Lastly, and this may seem like a silly question, but many in debate do charge you as an antihumanist who has no ethical standing and, like Heidegger, would not intervene in the face of genocide—or at least that your philosophy warrants that passivity. Can you speak to this?

W.V.S.: Anyone who has read even a few sentences of my writing, including my book on Heidegger, will realize that I am radically opposed to all forms of totalitarianism. To equate my interest in Heidegger's destructive thought with Nazism is guilt by association, not encounter with my work. Everything I've taught and written since I began reading Heidegger has taken its point of departure from his interrogation of the Western metaphysical tradition, a thinking from above things-as-they-are that has as its *Telos* the coercion of everything in space and time (existence/difference) into a larger whole or totality (essence/identity/presence). That forcing of differential phenomena into taking their proper place in a larger whole is totalitarian. In reversing the traditional binary between identity and difference, I commit myself to a radically secular (worldly) perspective. He or she who subscribes to the metaphysical interpretation of being (in whatever form) is not free. On the contrary, his/her vocation (or calling) is always to serve—to be the servant of—a "higher cause." He or she who rejects the metaphysical interpretation of being, who commits him-/herself to *this* world, is radically free.

What troubles a lot of debaters about my position, however, is not so much the question of my particular politics as the fact that I don't limit totalitarianism to Nazism (or Fascism), but, following the poststructuralists' critique of the so-called Enlightenment, extend it to include liberal capitalist democracy. This, I think, is because such an inclusion subverts one of the basic—unexamined—tenets of the debate world's framework: the enabling distinction between totalitarian indoctrination and liberal democratic disinterested inquiry, a distinction that has been called into question by the poststructuralists' appropriation of Antonio Gramsci's concept of hegemony. If Spanos is against democracy, this binarist argument goes, then he must be totalitarian.

As for the question of my relation to humanism, it should be noted, in addition to what I said earlier about the "antihumanism" of the poststructuralists, that, as far as I recall, I have never referred to myself as an antihumanist. My book on *The End of Education*, where I spell out the implications of reversing the binary logic endemic to disinterested inquiry for higher education, is pointedly subtitled "Toward Posthumanism." My quarrel with humanism has to do with the way the human has been appropriated in and by and *for* the West, particularly in the wake of the so-called Renaissance, which, by the way, was not a rebirth of Greek learning—a learning grounded in the temporal (secular or, more radically, profane) world and committed to the question (to possibility), over the answer (the vocational act)—but Roman: *eruditio et institutio in bonas artes* (scholarship and training *in good conduct*). The post-theological phase of the Western tradition simply substituted the *Anthropo-logos* (the Word of Man) for *Theo-logos* (the Word of God). It thus did not radicalize humanity's relation to being; it naturalized (secularized) the supernatural. Man (with the capital letter), instead of God, became the measure of all things. His vocation—his calling—became *servitude* to the higher cause of Man, and his politics became a political theology. And, it's important to add, the word "Man" in this tradition has meant emphatically *Western* Man. The rest of the world's humanity became the Western humanist's ("white man's") burden.

In referring to posthumanism in my book on higher education, therefore, I was not suggesting that we abandon the concept of man; I was, rather, pointing to a far more radical and *inclusive* understanding of humanity's essence than that "secular" version that became hegemonic in the modern West: a profane humanity, as it were. I mean by this a radically finite humanity, a humanity, to return to the language I used earlier to criticize disinterested inquiry, that finds itself thrown in the world: always already in-the-midst (*inter esse*), always already in the time of the now, where one *must* choose. More specifically, I mean a humanity that is gifted/cursed by a finite consciousness—an animal that is simultaneously and inextricably—irreparably, Agamben puts it—outside and inside, apart from and a part of, the world he/she makes, and where, therefore, the life-enhancing question (the beginning)—is *always already* ontologically prior to the answer (the *telos*). To use the paradoxical term Edward Said adopted in his posthumously published meditation on humanism (*Humanism and Democratic Criticism*), by referring to "posthumanism," I was calling for a "nonhumanist humanism," a humanism that, unlike the essentialist humanism privileged by the West, is grounded in difference and thus constitutes a singular universal, one in which, as Said puts it quoting Aimé Cesaire, "no race possesses the monopoly of beauty / of intelligence, of force, / and there / is a place for all at the rendezvous of victory." Here, of course, "victory" means victory over (the very idea of) victory. It is the neighborhood of zero.

Notes

PREFACE

1. Martin Heidegger, "What Is Metaphysics?" in *Basic Writings*, ed. David Farrell Krell (New York: HarperCollins, 1993), 301.

2. Herman Melville, *Moby-Dick; or The Whale,* ed. Harrison Hayford, Hershel Parker, and G. Thomas Tanselle (Evanston, Ill.: Northwestern University Press; Chicago: Newberry Library, 1988), 184.

3. William V. Spanos, *Shock and Awe: American Exceptionalism and the Imperatives of the Spectacle in Mark Twain's "A Connecticut Yankee in King Arthur's Court"* (Hanover, N.H.: Dartmouth College Press, 2013), xv.

I. THE NOTHINGNESS OF BEING AND THE SPECTACLE: THE AMERICAN SUBLIME REVISITED

1. Edward W. Said, *The World, the Text, and the Critic* (Cambridge, Mass.: Harvard University Press, 1983), 158–77.

2. See Harold Bloom, *A Map of Misreading* (New York: Oxford University Press, 1975); Bloom, *Poetry and Repression* (New Haven: Yale University Press, 1976); and Bloom, *Agon: Toward a Theory of Revision* (New York: Oxford University Press, 1982). All these texts are heavily indebted to Sigmund Freud, particularly to his essay *"Das Unheimliche"* ["The Uncanny"] (1919), which proffers a psychological, as opposed to a worldly, interpretation of the uncanny. See also Thomas Weiskel, *The Romantic Sublime* (Baltimore: The John Hopkins University Press, 1978); Mary Arensberg, ed., *The American Sublime* (Albany: SUNY Press, 1986); and Rob Wilson, *American Sublime: A Genealogy of a Poetic Genre* (Madison: University of Wisconsin Press, 1991). Of these, only Wilson's genealogy addresses the worldly uses to which American writers, particularly poets, put the American sublime by way of

invoking the "technological" or "postmodern" sublime, but like the others, Wilson, too, is unaware of the relationship between the American sublime and the spectacle, not to say the American exceptionalist ethos.

3. For a significant example of this textual/universalizing reading of the American sublime, see Joseph Kronick, "On the Border of History: Whitman and the American Sublime," in Arensberg, *American Sublime*, 51–82.

4. Guy Debord, *The Society of the Spectacle* (Detroit: Black and Red, 1983); further references will be abbreviated to SS and incorporated into the text in parentheses.

5. Edmund Burke, *A Philosophical Inquiry into the Origins of the Sublime and the Beautiful* (1756); Immanuel Kant, *Observations on the Feeling of the Beautiful and the Sublime* (1764); Joseph Addison, *Pleasures of the Imagination* (*Spectator*, no. 411 [1712]); Anthony Ashley-Cooper, Third Earl of Shaftesbury, *The Moralists: A Philosophical Rhapsody* (1709).

6. *The Oxford Dictionary of English Etymology*, ed. C. T. Onions (Oxford: Clarendon Press, 1966), 199. I appropriate the word "unpresentable" from Jean-François Lyotard, *The Postmodern Condition: A Report on Knowledge,* trans. Geoff Bennington and Brian Massumi (Minneapolis: University of Minnesota Press, 1984); of all the deconstructionists, only Lyotard, as the subtitle suggests, intuited in some degree the worldly implications of the unpresentability of the sublime.

7. Heidegger, "The Age of the World Picture," in *The Question Concerning Technology and Other Essays*, trans. William Lovitt (New York: Harper and Row, 1977).

8. Heidegger, "What Is Metaphysics?," 95; further citations will be abbreviated to WM and incorporated into the text in parentheses.

9. Søren Kierkegaard, *The Concept of Dread*, trans. Walter Lowrie (Princeton: Princeton University Press, 1957).

10. Jean-Paul Sartre, *Nausea,* trans. Lloyd Alexander (New York: New Directions, 1964), 129–30.

11. Heidegger, "The Age of the World Picture," 130; further references will be abbreviated to AWP and incorporated into the text in parentheses.

12. Heidegger, "The Question Concerning Technology," in *Basic Writings*, 332; emphasis in the original.

13. Hannah Arendt, *The Human Condition* (Chicago: University of Chicago Press, 1958), 95; see also Arendt, *The Origins of Totalitarianism*, vol. 2, *Imperialism* (New York: Harcourt Brace, 1954), particularly the chapter entitled "The Decline of the Nation-State and the End of the Rights of Man," 267–304.

14. Giorgio Agamben, "Marginal Notes on *Commentaries on the Society of the Spectacle*," in *Means Without End: Notes on Politics*, trans. Vincenzo Binetti and Cesare Casarino (Minneapolis: University of Minnesota Press, 2000), 74.5; further citations will be abbreviated to MN and incorporated into the text in parentheses.

15. My appropriation of Agamben's commentary on Guy Debord's *Society of the Spectacle* is, for the limited purpose of this chapter, confined to his brief "Marginal Notes," in *Means Without End*. That Debord and *The Age of the Spectacle* are passing concerns but constitute a vital continuing presence in Agamben's estranging genealogy of democratic/capitalist modernity is borne witness to by his great recent

book *The Kingdom and the Glory: For a Theological Genealogy of Economy and Government*, trans. Lorenzo Chiesa and Matteo Mandarino (Stanford, Calif.: Stanford University Press, 2011), in which he meticulously and decisively traces the origins of the modern spectacle back to the compelling role that "glorification" or "acclamation"—the staging of the unspeakable awesomeness of the divine—played in maintaining the power of the sovereign in monarchical societies and beyond and, analogously, to the determining role glory came to play in maintaining the power of God in the process of the institutionalization of Christianity. Some minimal sense of the continuity of Agamben's "Marginal Notes" and his genealogy of modern power relations in *The Kingdom and the Glory*—and its present disclosive "threshold" or "liminal" position—should be suggested by the following brief quotation from the concluding chapter of the latter:

> In 1967, Guy Debord—in what appears to us a truism today—diagnosed the planetary transformation of capitalist politics and economy as an immense accumulation of *spectacles* [SS, 12] in which the commodity and capital itself assume the mediatic form of the image. If we link Debord's analysis with [Carl] Schmitt's thesis according to which public opinion is the modern form of acclamation, the entire problem of the contemporary spectacle of media domination over all areas of social life assumes a new guise. What is in question is nothing less than a new and unheard-of concentration, multiplication, and dissemination of the function of glory [as it played out in the Christian era] as the center of the political system. What was confined to the spheres of liturgy and ceremonials has become concentrated in the media, and, at the same time, through them it spreads and penetrates at each moment into every area of society, both public and private. Contemporary democracy is a democracy that is entirely founded upon glory, that is, on the efficacy of acclamation. . . . As had always been the case in profane and ecclesiastical liturgies, this supposedly "originary democratic phenomenon" is once again caught, orientated, and manipulated in the forms and according to the strategies of spectacular power. (55–56)

16. Sacvan Bercovitch, *The American Jeremiad* (Madison: University of Wisconsin Press, 1978), 23.

17. Tzvetan Todorov, *The Conquest of America: The Question of the Other*, trans. Richard Howard (1984; repr. Norman: Oklahoma University Press, 1999), 115; my emphasis.

18. Spanos, *The Errant Art of "Moby-Dick": The Canon, the Cold War, and the Struggle for American Literary Studies* (Durham, N.C.: Duke University Press, 1995); Spanos, *Herman Melville and the American Calling: The Fiction after "Moby-Dick," 1851–1859* (Albany: SUNY Press, 2008); and Spanos, *The Exceptionalist State and the State of Exception: Herman Melville's "Billy Budd, Sailor"* (Baltimore: The Johns Hopkins University Press, 2011).

19. See Spanos, *Shock and Awe*.

20. Sacvan Bercovitch, *American Jeremiad*, 23.

21. See, for example, Cotton Mather, *Magnalia Christi Americana*. The most telling Puritan instance of this dual-phased use of the spectacle is Mary Rowlandson's

captivity narrative *The Sovereignty and Goodness of God*, ed. Neal Salisbury (Boston: Bedford, 1997). As the Preface, written by one "*Per Amicus*," probably Increase Mather, suggests in generalizing its autobiographical intention as the working of God for the Puritan public, Rowlandson's captivity narrative immediately became a model of the Puritan jeremiad.

22. See, for example, F. O. Matthiessen, *The American Renaissance: Art and Expression in the Age of Emerson and Whitman* (Oxford: Oxford University Press, 1941); Henry Nash Smith, *The Virgin Land: The American West as Symbol and Myth* (Cambridge, Mass.: Harvard University Press, 1950); Leo Marx, *The Machine in the Garden: Technology and the Pastoral Ideal in America* (London: Oxford University Press 1964); R. W. B. Lewis, *The American Adam* (Chicago: University of Chicago Press, 1955).

23. See also Robert Montgomery Bird, *Nick of the Woods or The Jibbenainosay: A Tale of Kentucky* (1837); William Gilmore Simms, *The Yemassee* (1835); Owen Wister, *The Virginian* (1902); and Zane Gray, *Riders of the Purple Sage* (1912).

24. For extended analyses of these exemplary jeremiadic texts, see Spanos, "American Exceptionalism, the Jeremiad, and the Frontier before and after 9/11: From the Puritans to the Con-Men," in *American Exceptionalism in the Age of Globalization: The Specter of Vietnam* (Albany: SUNY Press, 2007), 187–241.

25. Because this painting is especially exemplary of the American spectacularization of the sublime in the nineteenth century, it is worth describing in some detail. I quote Anders Stephanson's excellent account because it highlights this very early American commodification of the spectacle:

> One of the most common images after the Civil War was originally an advertisement. Painted in naïve style by John Gast and entitled "American Progress, or Manifest Destiny," it was first used in 1872 to promote a book called *New Overland Tourist and Pacific Coast Guide*. At center stage appears a bright angelic woman allegorically named "Star of Empire." She holds an educational book in one hand [the Bible or Word of God?] and a telegraph wire in the other. Facing west, the ethereal figure floats toward the Rocky Mountains. Behind her at the far right, is the Brooklyn Bridge (at the time under construction). The east is light, enlightened, and civilized; the west is dark, awaiting the illumination brought by Star of Empire and her surrounding cast of settlers, stage coaches, and railroads. In the murky west, giving way to the inevitable movement of the forces of light, are a sorry-looking group of Indians and wild beasts"; Stephanson, *Manifest Destiny: American Expansion and the Empire of Right* (New York: Hill and Wang, 1995), 66.

26. See, for example, Thomas Cole's series of paintings on "'The Course of Empire': The Savage State" (1836), "Consummation" (1835–36); and "Dissolution" (1836). For a proto–New Americanist exposure of the violence the spectacular American exceptionalist cultural tradition always disavows, see the New Americanist historian Richard Slotkin's trilogy: *Rejuvenation Through Violence*; *Fatal Environment*; and *Gunslinger Nation*; see also Stephanson, *Manifest Destiny*, and Deborah Madsen, *American Exceptionalism* (1998).

27. This spectacularization of the sublime is also evident in the pop culture of this extended period: the Western tall tale, the dime novel (*Dead-Eye Dick*), the Buffalo Bill exhibitions, and not least the Hollywood westerns.

28. Thomas Jefferson, in a letter to James Madison, April 27, 1809, in *The Writings of Thomas Jefferson* (Washington, D.C.: Thomas Jefferson Memorial Association, 1904), 11–12:277.

29. See Spanos, *Herman Melville and the American Calling* and *The Exceptionalist State and the State of Exception*.

30. Melville, *Moby-Dick*, 117. Further references will be abbreviated to M-D and incorporated into the text in parentheses.

31. I use this word in Alain Badiou's sense: an event discloses the void at the foundation of the dominant discourse (the regime of truth), and, in so doing, releases "it" for positive thought; see Badiou, *Ethics: An Essay on the Understanding of Evil*, trans. Peter Hallward (London: Verso, 2001), 69.

32. The parallel between Ahab and the "Indian-hater par excellence" in Melville's *The Confidence-Man: His Masquerade* (ed. Harrison Hayford, Hershel Parker, and G. Thomas Tanselle [Evanston, Ill.: Northwestern University Press; Chicago: Newberry Library 1984]) in the chapters on "The Metaphysics of Indian-Hating" is pertinent here.

33. The name Ishmael, which the narrator, in the first enigmatic sentence of the novel, tells his reader to "call" him, here turns out to be a namesake of the Ishmael of Genesis 16:12—son of Abraham and his wife Sarah's slave, the Egyptian Hagar, whom Abraham orphans by exiling him into the desert, where he becomes the progenitor of the Arab peoples.

34. Melville, *Pierre; or The Ambiguities*, ed. Harrison Hayford, Hershel Parker, and G. Thomas Tanselle (Evanston, Ill.: Northwestern University Press; Chicago: Newberry Library, 1971), 141. Further citations will be abbreviated as P and incorporated into the text in parentheses.

35. C. L. R. James, *Mariners, Renegades, Castaways: The Story of Herman Melville and the World We Live In* (1953; repr. Hanover, N.H.: University Press of New England, 2001); see esp. Donald E. Pease's brilliant introduction, viii–xxxiii.

36. Herman Melville, *Billy Budd, Sailor*, ed. Harrison Hayford and Merton M. Sealts (Chicago: University of Chicago Press, 1962): "The symmetry of form attainable in pure fiction cannot so readily be achieved in a narration essentially having less to do with fable than with fact. Truth uncompromisingly told will always have its ragged edges; hence the conclusion of such a narration is apt to be less finished than an architectural finial"; 128.

37. George Washington Peck, review of *Pierre*, by Melville, *American Whig Review* 6 (November 1852); repr. in *Herman Melville: The Reviews*, ed. Brian Higgins and Hershel Parker (Cambridge: Cambridge University Press, 1995) , 438.

38. If one thinks of Ernest Renan's famous essay "What Is a Nation?" (trans. Martin Thom, in *Nation and Narration*, ed. Homi K. Bhabha [London: Routledge, 1990]), in which this French nationalist contemporary of Melville admits that monumentalizing—i.e., forgetting (silencing the voice of)—history—the violence at the origins of the nation state—is a necessary prerequisite of sustaining the latter's

authority in modernity, we might, according to Guy Debord, without exaggeration, say that the monument is the genealogical origin of the spectacle. This paradoxical reading of the monumental *as proto-spectacle* is anticipated and underscored by Michel Foucault's Nietzschean account of genealogy in the "parodic" mode, in which the genealogical parodist pushes the logic of monumentality to its liminal point, at which it self-destructs: "The [traditional] historian offers this confused and anonymous [modern] European, the possibility of alternate identities, more individualized and substantial than his own. But the man with historical sense [the genealogist] will see that this substitution is simply a disguise. Historians supplied the Revolution with Roman prototypes, romanticism with knight's armor, and the Wagnerian era was given the sword of a German hero—ephemeral props that point to our own unreality. . . . The new historian, the genealogist, will know what to make of this masquerade. He will not be too serious to enjoy it; on the contrary, he will push the masquerade to its limit and prepare the great carnival of time where masks are constantly reappearing. No longer the identification of our faint individuality with the solid identities of the past, but our 'unrealization' through the excessive choice of identities—Frederick of Hohenstaufen, Caesar, Jesus, Dionysus, and possibly Zarathustra. Taking up these masks, revitalizing the buffoonery of history, we adopt an identity whose unreality surpasses that of God who started the charade. 'Perhaps we can discover a realm where originality is again possible as parodists of history and buffoons of God. In this we recognize the parodic double of what the second of the *Untimely Meditations* called 'monumental history': a history given to reestablishing the high points of historical development and their maintenance in a perpetual presence, given to the recovery of works, actions, and creations through the monogram of their personal essence. *But in 1874, Nietzsche accused this history, one totally devoted to veneration, of barring access to the actual intensities and creations of life. The parody of his last texts serves to emphasize that monumental history is itself a parody. Genealogy is history in the form of a concerted carnival"*; Foucault, "Nietzsche, Genealogy, History," in *Language, Counter-Memory, Practice: Selected Essays and Interviews*, trans. Donald F. Bouchard and Sherry Simon (Oxford: Basil Blackwell, 1977), 160–62 (my emphasis).

39. Agamben, MN, 81.2–81.3.

40. Twain, *The Adventures of Huckleberry Finn*, ed. Gerald Graff and James Phelan (Boston, Mass.: Bedford, 1995), 265.

41. See, for example, Rowe, "Mark Twain's Rediscovery of America in *A Connecticut Yankee in King Arthur's Court*," in *Literary Culture and U.S. Imperialism: From the Revolution to World War II* (Oxford: Oxford University Press, 2000), 121–39.

42. Spanos, *Shock and Awe: American Exceptionalism and the Imperatives of the Spectacle in Mark Twain's "A Connecticut Yankee in King Arthur's Court"* (Hanover, N.H.: Dartmouth College Press, 2013).

43. Twain, *The Innocents Abroad or The New Pilgrims' Progress* (New York: Signet Classics. 1966), 319.

44. Twain, *A Connecticut Yankee in King Arthur's Court*, ed. Allison R. Ensor (New York: Norton Critical Editions, 1982) (further references will be abbreviated to CY, and incorporated into the text in parentheses): "I am an American. I was

born in Hartford, in the State of Connecticut. . . . So I am a Yankee of the Yankees—and practical; yes, and nearly barren of sentiment, I suppose or poetry, in other words" (8). I stress Morgan's hyperbolization of his Yankeeness (1) to suggest that Twain conceives his protagonist as the epitome of American exceptionalism, the manifestation of its unerring logic and (2) to point to the disclosive parallel and contrast with Herman Melville's "Indian-hater *par excellence*," who, unlike "the diluted Indian-hater," in whom "soft enticements of domestic life too often draw him from the ascetic trail," "the Indian-hater *par excellence* the judge defined to be one 'who having with his mother's milk drank in small love of red men, in youth or early manhood, ere the sensibilities become osseous, receives at their hand some signal outrage. . . . Now, nature all around him by her solitudes wooing or bidding him muse upon the matter, he accordingly does so, till the thought develops such attraction, that much as straggling vapors troop from all sides of a storm-cloud, so straggling thoughts of other outrages troop to the nucleus thought, assimilate with it, and swell it. At last, taking counsel with the elements, he comes to his resolution. An intenser Hannibal, he makes a vow, the hate of which is a vortex from whose suction the remotest chip of the guilty race may reasonably feel secure. . . . Last he commits himself to the forest primeval; there, so long as life shall be his, to act upon a calm, cloistered scheme of strategical, implacable, and lonesome vengeance. Ever on the noiseless trail; cool, collected, patient; less seen than felt; snuffing, smelling—a Leather-stocking Nemesis"; Melville, *Confidence-Man*, 149–50.

45. "Not incidentally," because it belies the thesis of those myth-and-symbol Americanists like Henry Nash Smith and James Cox who, in order to extricate Twain from his protagonist's action in the troublingly violent climactic Battle of the Sand Belt episode, claim he loses control of his narrative and those New Americanists like John Carlos Rowe who arbitrarily read *A Connecticut Yankee* as Twain's critique of his protagonist's American exceptionalism.

46. It is at this point that the bullet hole in the "ancient hawberk" (CY, 5), which the stranger (Hank Morgan), who accosts the American tourist "M.T." in Warwick Castle at the outset, claims to have caused is explained—another not insignificant instance of Twain's penchant for staging spectacular effects. Caught in the throes of the hyperbolic spectacle, Twain's adult protagonist, like his young ones, are immune to the pain his violence inflicts on his objects, responding instead to it as if it were a cosmic joke. This adolescence, in opposition to the alleged aged Old World consciousness, is the essence of Twain's American (Western) humor.

47. Agamben, *Homo Sacer: Sovereign Power and Bare Life,* trans. Daniel Heller-Roazen (Stanford, Calif.: Stanford University Press 1998), 122–23; further citations will be abbreviated to HS and incorporated into the text in parentheses.

48. Foucault, *Discipline and Punish: The Birth of the Prison*, trans. Alan Sheridan (New York: Pantheon, 1977), 31.

49. See especially the influential text of the policy expert Richard Haass, *The Reluctant Sheriff: The United States After the Cold War* (New York: Council on Foreign Relations, 1997).

50. Ahab's monomania is ironically articulated at the outset of his appearance in the novel in a soliloquy imagined by Ishmael; "Swerve me? Ye cannot swerve me,

else ye swerve yourselves! Man has ye there. Swerve me? The path to my fixed purpose is laid with iron rails, whereupon my soul is grooved to run. Over unsounded gorges, through the rifled hearts of mountains, under torrents' beds, unerringly I rush! Naught's an obstacle, naught's an angle to the iron way!" (M-D, 168). Neither Ahab nor, at this point, Ishmael is aware of the deadly irony of the last sentence.

51. See Spanos, *Shock and Awe*; CY.

52. Susan Faludi, *The Terror Dream: Fear and Fantasy in Post–9/11 America* (New York: Metropolitan, 2007), 4–5. I am indebted to Donald Pease for Faludi's witness to the post–9/11 occasion. He not only quotes this passage in a footnote in his groundbreaking *The New American Exceptionalism* (Minneapolis: University of Minnesota Press, 2009), 235–36; he also introduces the fantastic essence of this official post–9/11 regression to the frontier past in the terms of the spectacle: "Susan Faludi has written about the effects of this regression to the mentality of the colonial frontier as a spectacular regression to the era of Westward expansion" (235). To Faludi's list of official post–9/11 "frontier" gestures should be added the orchestration by both the Bush and the Obama administrations of the spectacular scenario of "hunting down" of Osama bin Laden; see Chapter 2 of this volume.

2. AMERICAN EXCEPTIONALISM IN THE POST–9/11 ERA: THE MYTH AND THE REALITY

1. "American Exceptionalism and the Battle for the Presidency," http://www .huffingtonpost.com/jerome-karabel/american-exceptionalism-obama-gingrich_b _1161800.html.

2. Pease, *The New American Exceptionalism* (Minneapolis: University of Minnesota Press, 2009), 10.

3. Donald Pease sees what he calls the "new American exceptionalism" as having its origins in George W. Bush's proclamation of the United States' unending War on Terror in the aftermath of al Qaeda's attacks on the World Trade Center and the Pentagon, thus overdetermining a presentist perspective at the expense of the *long durée*. See especially his chapter aptly entitled, "From Virgin Land to Ground Zero: Mythological Foundations of the Homeland Security State," in *New American Exceptionalism*, 15–179. I, on the other hand, understand President Bush's "contradictory" post–9/11 War on Terror *as the liminal point* of the development of the exceptionalist logic that had its origins in the American Puritans' belief that they had been chosen by God to fulfill his "errand in the wilderness" of the New World— that is, the historical point at which the exceptionalist ethos, in the process of fulfilling its possibilities in practice, self-de-structs: inadvertently discloses what its successes had hitherto enabled it to disavow. The difference between Pease's interpretation of American exceptionalist history and mine is, thus, not radical, but a matter of emphasis.

4. Bercovitch, *American Jeremiad*, 23; my emphasis.

5. Spanos, "American Exceptionalism, the Jeremiad, and the Frontier, Before and After 9/11: From the Puritans to the Neo-Con Men," in *American Exceptionalism in the Age of Globalization: The Specter of Vietnam* (Albany: SUNY Press, 2008), 194–98.

6. Richard Slotkin, *Rejuvenation through Violence: The Mythology of the Frontier, 1600–1860* (Hanover, N.H.: Wesleyan University Press, 1973).

7. Twain, *Connecticut Yankee in King Arthur's Court*, 8.

8. Melville, *Moby-Dick*, 168.

9. See, for example, Henry Nash Smith, *Mark Twain's Fable of Progress* (New Brunswick, N.J.: Rutgers University Press, 1964), 65; and James M. Cox, "A Connecticut Yankee in King Arthur's Court: The Machinery of Self-Preservation," *Yale Review* 50 (1960): 125–26.

10. Michael Herr, *Dispatches* (New York: Vintage, 1991), 71.

11. George W. Bush, State of the Union Address, January 29, 2002: "History has called America and our allies to action, and it is both our responsibility and our privilege to fight freedom's fight"; http://stateoftheunionaddress.org/2002-george -w-bush.

12. Agamben, *Homo Sacer*.

13. As Edward Said has shown, Huntington appropriated the phrase from the Orientalist Bernard Lewis; see Said, "The Clash of Civilizations," in *Reflections on Exile and Other Essays* (Cambridge, Mass.: Harvard University Press, 2000), 571–72.

14. Samuel P. Huntington, *Who Are We?: Challenges to America's National Identity* (New York: Simon and Schuster, 2004), 64; further references will be abbreviated to WAW and incorporated into the text in parentheses.

15. In invoking the term "spectacle," I am not simply referring to the use to which Guy Debord puts it in *Society of the Spectacle*, but also the meaning it accrues in the era of the "American Century," when the spectacle-inducing exceptionalism of American exceptionalism comes to its fulfillment, when, more specifically, the early use of spectacular effects of modern weaponry—guns, for example—by the "advanced" American colonists "to strike the inferior natives dumb"—deprive them of language—becomes the effects of the high-tech "shock and awe" tactics of the Bush administrations' invasion of Iraq and Afghanistan; see Section 4 of this chapter.

16. John McCain speech at 2012 Republican National Convention, http://www .foxnews.com/polititcs/2012/08/29/transcript-john-mccain-speech-at-rnc/.

17. Scott Shane, "The Opiate of Exceptionalism," *New York Times*, October 17, 2012. I am indebted to Adam Spanos for pointing this essay out to me. For an extended and scholarly version of this incommensurability between the alleged achievement of the American exceptionalist ethos in the domestic sphere and the historical reality, see William V. Spanos, "Redeemer Nation and Apocalypse: Thinking the Exceptionalism of American Exceptionalism," in *Literature, Interpretation Theory* 25, no. 2 (Spring 2014): 174–200.

18. Marco Rubio speech at 2012 Republican National Convention, http:// foxnews.com/politics/2012/08/30transcript-marco-rubio-speech-at-rnc/.

19. I invoke here as a synecdoche of the interpellated Others of America the tragic figure of Jay Gatsby in F. Scott Fitzgerald's early modern meditation on the exceptionalist American dream. I am indebted to my colleague Susan Strehle for reminding me of this resonant parallel.

20. The membership of this influential neoconservative group of policy experts included William J. Bennett, Jeb Bush, Eliot Cohen, Dick Cheney, Francis Fukuyama, Donald Kagan, William Kristol, Norman Podhoretz, Donald Rumsfeld, Paul Wolfowitz, and John Bolton. Their notorious white paper, "Rebuilding America's Defenses," sponsored a unipolar world under the aegis of the United States—indeed, a *Pax Americana*.

21. "Transcript of John Kerry's Speech to the Democratic National Convention," *Boston Globe*, September 6, 2012; further references will be abbreviated to JK and incorporated into the text in parentheses.

22. Behind this rhetorical apotheosis of American-style leadership is the image of the self-reliant, trail-blazing pioneer mythologized by the novelist James Fenimore Cooper in the figure of Natty Bumppo—"He had gone far towards the setting sun, the foremost in the band of Pioneers, who are opening the way for the march of the nation across the continent"; Cooper, *The Pioneers* (Oxford: Oxford University Press, 1991), 456—and the artist George Caleb Bingham in the painting entitled "Daniel Boone Escorting Settlers through the Cumberland Gap, 1851–52."

23. On being informed by President Obama that Osama bin Laden was dead, George W. Bush said, "This momentous achievement marks a victory for America, for all people who seek peace around the world, and for all those who lost loved ones on September 11, 2001. . . . The fight against terror goes on but tonight America has sent an unmistakable message. No matter how long it takes, justice will be done"; CBS News, May 2, 2011, 4:41 p.m.

24. This Democratic rhetoric, which spectacularizes the United States' techno-scientific superiority over its backward enemy, it should not be overlooked, has its immediate source in the "shock and awe" tactics of the Bush administration. Its ultimate source, however, resides in the absolute certitude of America's History-ordained "errand" to domesticate the world's wilderness: the unerring certitude of the American exceptionalist ethos Herman Melville calls radically into question by way of his portrayal of Captain Ahab's unerring pursuit of the white whale in *Moby-Dick*; see below.

25. Not incidentally, President Obama did invoke the term, indeed, in a dramatic way, in his victory speech after his election to a second term. Careful to minimize the imperial implications and the politically conservative domestic of the Republican version of American exceptionalism, Obama said, "This country has more wealth than any nation, but that's not what makes us rich. We have the most powerful military in history, but that's not what makes us strong. Our university, our culture are the envy of the world, but that's not what keeps the world coming to our shores. What makes America exceptional are the bonds that hold together the most diverse nation on earth, the belief that our destiny is shared— (CHEERS, APPLAUSE)—that this country only works when we accept certain obligations to one another and to future generations, so that the freedom which so many Americans have fought for and died for come with responsibilities as well as rights, and among those are love and charity and duty and patriotism. That's what makes America great (CHEERS, APPLAUSE)"; *New York Times*, November 7, 2012.

26. I am referring to George W. Bush's speech to the sailors on board the aircraft carrier U.S.S. *Abraham Lincoln* in the Persian Gulf, in which, standing in front of a banner entitled "Mission Accomplished," he announces the (radically premature) end of the Gulf War on May 3, 2003.

27. Walter Benjamin, "Theses on the Concept of History." Despite the fact that Benjamin's thesis is now quite familiar, the American context of this essay warrants quoting it here: "Whoever has emerged victorious participates to this day in the triumphalist procession. According to traditional practice, the spoils are carried along in the procession. They are called cultural treasures, and a historical materialist views them with cautious detachment. For without exception the cultural treasures he surveys have an origin which he cannot contemplate without horror. They owe their existence not only to the efforts of the great minds and talents who have created them, but also to the anonymous toil of their contemporaries. There is no document of civilization which is not at the same time a document of barbarism. And just as such a document is not free of barbarism, barbarism taints also the manner in which it was transmitted from one owner to another. A historical materialist therefore dissociates himself from it as far as possible. He regards it as his task to brush history against the grain"; http://www.afj.ca/~andrewf/CONCEPT2 .html.

28. Melville, *Moby-Dick*, 184; my emphasis.

29. Melville, *Confidence-Man*, 149–50; my emphasis. In this passage, Melville, via Judge James Hall, is alluding to a pervasive figure in early America, but, above all, I think, to the Indian killer par excellence, Nathan Slaughter, in Robert Montgomery Bird's novel *Nick of the Woods or The Jibbenainosay: Tale of Kentucky* (New York: Redfield, 1854).

30. By "self-de-struction" I mean, with Heidegger and the poststructuralists, not self-annihilation, but, according to the dictates of the etymology, the liberation for positive thought of the dynamic historicity that structure has colonized.

31. See Anne McClintock's brilliant analysis of the George W. Bush administration's paranoid (Ahabian) means of identifying (seeing) the invisible enemy in the aftermath of the bombings of the World Trade Center and the Pentagon in her essay "Paranoid Empire: Specters from Guantanamo and Abu Ghraib," in *States of Emergency: The Object of American Studies*, ed. Russ Castronovo and Susan Gillman (Chapel Hill: University of North Carolina Press, 2009): "The suicide attackers, deliberately flying passenger planes into buildings as they did, instantly obliterated themselves in the fiery cataclysm, removing their bodies from the realm of visible retribution and thereby removing all means for the Bush administration to be seen to recuperate its wounded potency. The state was faced with an immediate dilemma: how to *embody* the invisible enemy and *be visibly seen* to punish it? The U.S. state had to turn ordinary people into enemy bodies and put them on display for retaliation. In the humiliated aftermath of 9/11, the Bush administration set out to embody the enemy in three ways. First, the enemy was *individualized* as a recognizable *face*—the epic, male, archenemy bin Laden, a strategically disastrous tactic, for the administration could not put bin Laden on display, either dead or alive. Second, the dispersed forces of al Qaeda, traversing as they do over sixty countries, were

nationalized, equated with two nation-states. The invasion of Afghanistan was justified by identifying Afghanistan as a nation-state that had given sanctuary to al Qaeda, which would present a critical contradiction, for the men later imprisoned at Guantánamo were defined as lying outside the protection of the Geneva Conventions on precisely contradictory grounds that Afghanistan was a failed nonstate. Iraq presented an even deeper problem: there was no *casus belli* for the invasion and (following the lessons of Vietnam) the illegitimate war would need to be kept as invisible as possible from public scrutiny. As conservative commentator David Brooks asked: 'How are we going to wage war anymore, with everyone watching?' The third solution was to produce the enemy *as bodies* under U.S. supervision, subjecting them to dreadful revenge in the labyrinths of torture" (95); I will elaborate on McClintock's essay in Chapter 3. See also Emily Apter, "Paranoid Globalism," in *Against World Literature* (London: Verso, 2013), 70–98.

32. DeBord, *Society of the Spectacle*, rev. trans. (Detroit: Red and Black, 1983), no. 18.

33. Agamben, MN, 82.2.

34. Todorov, *Conquest of America*, 115. For a classic American version of this domesticating spectacular tactic, which relies on the superior technoscientific knowledge of the colonizer over the brutal native, see Twain, *Connecticut Yankee in King Arthur's Court*: "You see, it was the eclipse. It came into my mind, in the nick of time, how Columbus, or Cortez, or one of those people, played an eclipse as a saving trump once, on savages, and I saw my chance. I could play it myself, now, and it wouldn't be plagiarism, either, because I should get it in nearly a thousand years ahead of those parties"; 9–10. For an extended analysis of this spectacular tactics, see Spanos, *Shock and Awe*.

35. For an amplified analysis of Hannah Arendt's understanding "polity," see Spanos, *Exiles in the City: Hannah Arendt and Edward W. Said in Counterpoint* (Columbus: Ohio State University Press, 2012), 188–205.

36. Agamben pursues the train of this thought more fully in *The Coming Community* (Minneapolis: University of Minnesota Press, 1993).

37. Agamben, "Beyond Human Rights," in *Means without End*, 24.5; my emphasis.

3. "THE CENTER WILL NOT HOLD": THE WIDENING GYRE OF THE NEW, NEW AMERICANIST STUDIES

1. Pease and Robyn Wiegman, *The Futures of American Studies* (Durham, N.C.: Duke University Press, 2002).

2. Francis Fukuyama, *The End of History and the Last Man* (New York: Free Press, 1992), 45; my emphasis.

3. Spanos, "American Studies in the Age of the World Picture," in Pease and Wiegman, *Futures of American Studies*, 390. The quotation from Bercovitch is from the afterword to *Ideology and Classic American Literature*, ed. Bercovitch and Myra Jehlen (Cambridge: Cambridge University Press, 1986), 438. The quotation from

Paul Bové is from "Notes toward a Politics of 'American' Criticism," in *In the Wake of Theory* (Middletown, Conn.: Wesleyan University Press, 1992), 52–60.

4. Herr, *Dispatches*, 71; originally published by Alfred A. Knopf, 1977. For an amplified account of the self-destruction of the American exceptionalist ethos during the Vietnam War (and its recuperation in the aftermath), see Spanos, *American Exceptionalism in the Age of Globalization: The Specter of Vietnam* (Albany: SUNY Press, 2007).

5. George Bush, to a group of state legislators, reported in *Newsweek*, March 11, 1991.

6. Janice Radway, Kevin Gaines, Barry Shank, and Penny von Eschen, *American Studies: An Anthology* (Hoboken, N.J.: Wiley Blackwell, 2009).

7. Donald E. Pease, Winfried Fluck, and John Carlos Rowe, *Re-Framing the Transnational Turn in American Studies* (Hanover, N.H.: Dartmouth College Press, 2011).

8. Paul Giles, *Virtual America: Transnational Fictions and the Transatlantic Imaginary* (Durham, N.C.: Duke University Press, 2002).

9. Paul Jay, *Global Matters: The Transnational Turn in Literary Studies* (Ithaca, N.Y.: Cornell University Press, 2010).

10. The work of Donald E. Pease constitutes a significant exception to this tendency to overdetermine the global, as his magisterial *New American Exceptionalism* testifies; see also "Re-Mapping the Transnational Turn," his introduction to Rowe's *Re-Framing the Transnational Turn in American Studies*. Though ostensibly a summary of the various itineraries of this transnational turn, it is evident from his insistence on the fundamental centrality of the George W. Bush administration's War on Terror, the exceptionalism of which has normalized the state of exception, that Pease discriminates qualitatively between those post–9/11 New Americanists who focus on the critique of American exceptionalism and those who do not: "In calling for a wholesale dismantling of American exceptionalism, transnational Americanists have failed to see that transnational American studies produced the version of American exceptionalism without exceptionalists that the transnational state of exception required. Transnational Americanists' generalized disavowal of the state of exception became especially discernible in their anti-exceptionalist explanations of the transition from Cold War American studies to transnational American studies" (23).

11. Dipesh Chakrabarty, *Provincializing Europe: Postcolonial Thought and Historical Difference* (Princeton: Princeton University Press, 2000).

12. This trinity defining the essence of the nation-state system was first posited by Hannah Arendt in *Origins of Totalitarianism*, vol. 2, and later appropriated by Giorgio Agamben in *Means Without End*.

13. See Chapter 2.

14. Jacques Derrida, "Structure, Sign, and Play in the Discourse of the Human Sciences," in *Writing and Difference*, trans. Alan Bass (Chicago: University of Chicago Press, 1978): "It has always been thought that the center, which is by definition unique, constituted the very thing within structure while governing structure which escapes structurality. This is why classical thought concerning structure

could say that the center is, paradoxically, *within* the structure and *outside* it. The center is at the center of the totality, and yet, since the center does not belong to the totality (is not part of the totality), the totality *has its center elsewhere*. The center is not the center. The concept of centered structure—although it represents coherence itself, the condition of the *epistémé* as philosophy or science—is contradictorily coherent. And, as always, coherence in contradiction expresses the force of a desire. The concept of centered structure is in fact the concept of play based on a fundamental ground, a play constituted on the basis of a fundamental immobility and a reassuring certitude, which itself is beyond the reach of free play. And on the basis of this certitude anxiety can be mastered" (279).

15. W. B. Yeats, "The Second Coming," in *The Collected Poems of W. B Yeats* (New York: Macmillan, 1956), 183.

16. Louis Althusser explains the operations of the problematic in "From *Capital* to Marx's Philosophy," in *Reading "Capital,"* by Althusser and Étienne Balibar (London: Verso, 1979), 24–30. For my analysis of the problematic, see Spanos, "Althusser's 'Problematic': Vision and the Vietnam War," in *American Exceptionalism in the Age of Globalization*, 35–57.

17. Titles: *The World Republic of Letters*; *What Is World Literature?*; *Modern Epic*; and *The Idea of World Literature*, respectively.

18. For a persuasive early critique of the general tendency of recent transnationalist scholars to overdetermine the global, see Timothy Brennan, "Cosmo-Theory," *South Atlantic Quarterly* 100, no. 3 (Summer 2001): 659–91.

19. Paul Giles, "The Deterritorialization of American Literature," in *Shades of the Planet*, ed. Wei Chee Dimock and Lawrence Buell (Princeton: Princeton University Press, 2007), 39–61. This essay is reprinted with some revisions from Giles's *The Global Re-Mapping of American Literature* (Princeton: Princeton University Press, 2011). Further citations of the latter will be abbreviated to GR and incorporated into the text in parentheses.

20. "The National Security Strategy of the United States of America." Though the second paragraph of this quotation disclaims the Bush administration's willful resort to military force to achieve its preemptive defense, the truth is that the Bush administration justified its preemptive war against Saddam Hussein's Iraq by falsely representing it as manufacturing weapons of mass destruction.

21. Robert Marzec, "Introduction to Environmentality: MEDEA, the SAGEs of the Earth and the Environmental Politics of Adaptation," in *Environmentality* (Minneapolis: University of Minnesota Press, forthcoming).

22. See "Rebuilding America's Defenses: Strategies, Forces, and Resources For a New Century," the white paper of the influential neoconservative group called "Project for New American Century" (PNAC) that became the ideological blueprint for the George W. Bush administration's foreign policy.

23. Agamben, *Homo Sacer*, 114–15.

24. Enacted by Congress following the directives of the Bush administration's post–9/11 declaration of policy entitled "The National Security Strategy of the United States of America."

25. The recent exposures by Bradley Manning and Edward Snowden of the disturbing degree to which the state operates according to the imperatives of the state of exception bear witness to this.

26. Jerome Karabel, "American Exceptionalism and the Battle for the Presidency," http://www.huffingtonpost.com/jerome-karabel/american-exceptionalism-obama-gingrich_b_1161800.html.

27. Senator John Kerry used the term "exceptionalism" nine times in his speech.

28. John Kerry, http:foxnewsinsdier.com/2012/09/06/read-john-kerrys-address-to-the-democractic-national-convention/.

29. Melville, *Moby-Dick*, 184; my emphasis. The unintended ironic parallel between the spectacular high-tech ("shock and awe") metaphor Senator Kerry uses to characterize Obama's assault on Osama bin Laden ("like a laser") and the spectacular high-tech metaphor Melville uses to characterize Ahab's assault on the white whale ("and then, as if his chest had been a mortar, he burst his hot heart's shell upon it") should not be overlooked.

30. See Preface.

31. Raymond Williams, *Marxism and Literature* (Oxford: Oxford University Press, 1977), 109–10.

32. Edward W. Said, *Culture and Imperialism* (New York: Vintage, 1993), 332; see also Arendt, "We Refugees," in *The Jew as Pariah: Jewish Identity and Politics in the Modern Age*, ed. Ron H. Feldman (New York: Grove Press, 1978); and Agamben, "Beyond Human Rights," 15–28. I amplify the liberating potential of the figure of the contemporary figure of the refugee in Spanos, *Exile in the City: Hannah Arendt and Edward W. Said in Counterpoint* (Columbus: Ohio State University Press, 2013), 165–74.

33. This, not incidentally, is, consciously or not, an echo of Martin Heidegger's phenomenological analysis of the de-structive by which the "ordinary" becomes "extraordinary."

34. See Agamben, *The Time That Remains: A Commentary of the Letter to the Romans*, trans. Patricia Daily (Stanford, Calif.: Stanford University Press, 2005), 23.

35. Dimock, "Introduction: Planet and America, Set and Subset," in Dimock and Buell, *Shades of the Planet*, 1; further references will be abbreviated to PA and incorporated into the text in parentheses.

36. The dearth of reference to American exceptionalism in Dimock and Buell's *Shades of the Planet*, which is a volume of thirteen essays, is evidenced in the Index. Under the heading "American studies, and exceptionalism," the Index lists six single-page entries; under the heading "exceptionalism: American," it lists five single-page entries.

37. See Marzec, "Environmentality: The War Machine and the Struggle for Inhabitancy in the Age of Climate Change," in *Environmentality*.

38. Brian T. Edwards and Dilip Parameshwar Gaonkar, "Introduction: Globalizing American Studies," in *Globalizing American Studies*, edited by Edwards and Gaonkar, 4–5 (Chicago: University of Chicago Press, 2010); further references will be abbreviated to GAS and incorporated into the text in parentheses.

39. Edwards and Gaonkar, *Globalizing American Studies*. The editors refer twice more to "the closing of the American Century" as if it were a *fait accompli*. A page later, for example, they write, "We briefly defer the question of what sort of American studies emerges after the American Century by asking what sort of disciplinary anxiety our time—the end of the 'American Century'—present" (6); see also 30 and 39.

40. McClintock, "Paranoid Empire: Specters from Guantánamo and Abu Ghraib," in Castronovo and Gilman, *States of Emergency*, 91; further references will be abbreviated to PE and incorporated into the text in parentheses.

41. See Slotkin, *Rejuvenation Through Violence*.

42. Bercovitch, *American Jeremiad*, 23; my emphasis. Further references to *American Jeremiad* will be abbreviated as AJ and inserted into the text in parentheses. For an extended account of the relationship between the Puritan understanding of the enemy and the later American understanding of the frontier, see Spanos, "American Exceptionalism, the Jeremiad, and the Frontier before and after 9/11: From the Puritans to the Neo-Con Men," in *American Exceptionalism in the Age of Globalization*, 187–242.

43. I put "nomadic" and "sedentary" in parentheses to suggest that Baucom could have extended his genealogy beyond Cicero's argument against Mark Antony to include the fundamental distinction, extending throughout the history of Western colonialism to the present day, that justified Rome's conquest and occupation of the *terra incognita* beyond the *terra orbis*: that between a sedentary (agricultural and thus "civilized") people and a nomadic (and thus "barbarian") people. Had Baucom included this aspect of Rome's justification of war against an "unjust enemy," it would have enabled him to be more historically accurate about the genealogy of post–9/11 America's version of the "unjust" or "inimical" enemy. For this distinction was absolutely central in the establishment of the American exceptionalism ethos, which in the period of westward expansion was expressed in the vernacular as the opposition between the Americans' "betterment" or "settlement" of the land and the natives' merely "roaming on" the land.

44. Ian Baucom, "Cicero's Ghost: The Atlantic, the Enemy, and the Laws of War," in Castronovo and Gillman, *States of Emergency*, 131; further references will be abbreviated to CG and incorporated into the text in parentheses.

45. Huntington, *Who Are We?* Baucom refers to Huntington in his essay "Cicero's Ghost" (137), but it is Huntington who is identified with the "clash of civilizations" thesis of his earlier book, *The Clash of Civilizations and the Remaking of World Order* (New York: Simon and Schuster, 1996).

46. Fukuyama, *End of History*.

47. Spanos, "American Exceptionalism and the State of Exception after 9/11: Melville's Proleptic Witness," in *State of Exception and the Exceptionalist State: Herman Melville's "Billy Budd, Sailor,"* 157.

48. Ezra Pound, "Canto LIX," in *The Cantos* (New York: New Directions, 1970), 324.

49. Charles Olson, "On First Looking Out through Juan de la Cosa's Eyes," in *The Maximus Poems*, ed. George Butterick (Berkeley: University of California Press,

1983), 81–84. For Pound and Olson the periplus is an immediate expression of being-there, in the midst. As such their peripluses are more true to the reality of the world than the earlier maps of sedentary academics, such as the map of the world of Martin Behaim (1492), which shows no land between Europe and Cipangu (Japan), but also earlier maps of the world based on Mercator's projections. For an expanded commentary on this issue of cartography, see Spanos, "The Ontological Origins of Occidental Imperialism: Thinking the *Meta* of Metaphysics," in *America's Shadow: An Anatomy of Empire* (Minneapolis: University of Minnesota Press, 2000), 39–52.

50. See Spanos, "American Exceptionalism, the Jeremiad, and the Frontier, before and after 9/11," 167–242.

51. Eric Auerbach, "Figura," in *Scenes from the Drama of European Literature: Six Essays* (New York: Meridian, 1959), 53–54.

52. What I have said about Giles's reading of Cotton Mather's *Magnalia Christi* can also be applied to his reading of Timothy Dwight's *Conquest of Canäan*.

4. AMERICAN EXCEPTIONALISM AND THE CALLING: A GENEALOGY OF THE VOCATIONAL ETHIC

1. George W. Bush, "State of the Union Address 2002," http://stateoftheunion address.org/2002-george-w-bush; my emphasis.

2. For an amplification of this criticism, see Chapter 3.

3. Max Weber, *The Protestant Ethic and the Spirit of Capitalism*, trans. Talcott Parsons (New York: Scribner's, 1958), 104; further citations will be abbreviated to PR and incorporated into the text in parentheses.

4. Perry Miller, ed., *The American Puritans: Their Poetry and Prose* (New York: Anchor, 1956), 172; further citations will be abbreviated to AP and incorporated into the text in parentheses.

5. The disavowed ideological function of this "warrantable calling"—acquiescing to the higher powers that be—is epitomized in the conclusion of Cotton's treatise on "The Christian Calling" not only by the content but also by the metaphorics of panoptic vision: "It is a word of consolation to every such soul as hath been acquainted with this life of faith in his calling: be thy calling never so mean and homely and never so hardly accepted, yet, if thou hast lived by faith in thy calling, it was a lively work in the sight of God; and so it will be rewarded when thy change shall come. Many a Christian is apt to be discouraged and dismayed if crosses befall him in his calling. But be not afraid; let this cheer up thy spirit—that whatever thy calling was, yet thou camest into it honestly and hast lived in it faithfully; your course was lively and spiritual, and therefore you may with courage look up for recompense from Christ" (AP, 182).

6. Antonio Gramsci, *Selections from the Prison Notebooks*, ed. and trans. Quentin Hoare and Geoffrey Nowell Smith (New York: International Publishers, 1971), 12–13.

7. Althusser, "Ideology and Ideological State Apparatuses: Notes towards an Investigation," in *Lenin and Philosophy and Other Essays*, trans. Ben Brewster (London: Monthly Review Press, 1971), 179; emphasis in the original. Further citations will be abbreviated to IISA and incorporated into the text in parentheses.

8. This important qualification is an allusion to Gramsci's means of exposing the violence that is otherwise hidden in democratic societies. It is only when a constituency of civil society refuses its "spontaneous consent" to the hegemonic discourse that the police, who are normally hidden, become visible: "These [the private and the political realms of the state] comprise (1) The 'spontaneous' consent given by the great masses of the population to the general direction imposed on social life by the dominant fundamental group; this consent is 'historically' caused by the prestige (and consequent confidence) which the dominant group enjoys because of its position and function in the world of production; (2) The apparatuses of the state coercive power which 'legally' enforces discipline on those groups who do not 'consent' either actively or passively. This apparatus is, however, constituted for the whole of society in anticipation of moments of crisis of command and direction when spontaneous consent has failed"; Gramsci, *Selections from the Prison Notebooks*, 12.

9. Raymond Williams, "Hegemony," *in Marxism and Literature*, 110.

10. Agamben, *The Time That Remains*, 95; further citation will be abbreviated to TR and incorporated into the text in parentheses.

11. See Agamben, *The State of Exception*, trans. Kevin Attell (Chicago: University of Chicago Press, 2005).

12. Agamben, *The Coming Community*, trans. Michael Hardt (1990; repr. Minneapolis: University of Minnesota Press, 1993), 42.3; further citations will be abbreviated to CC and incorporated into the text in parentheses.

13. Agamben, "What Is the Contemporary?," in *What Is an Apparatus? And Other Essays*, trans. Davis Kishik and Stefan Pedatella (Stanford, Calif.: Stanford University Press, 2009), 40; see also Apter, *Against World Literature*.

14. To be more specific, Agamben goes on to suggest the similarity of the "remnant" with Marx's Proletariat—"in the latter's noncoinciding with itself as class and in its necessarily exceeding the state and social dialectic of *Stände*—which underwent '*no particular wrong* but *wrong absolutely*,'" and with Jacques Rancière's concept of the people understood as the "part of those who have no part," meaning a supernumerary party, the bearer of a wrong that established democracy as a "community of dispute" (TR, 57).

15. See Maurice Blanchot, *The Writing of Disaster*, trans. Ann Smock (Lincoln: University of Nebraska Press, 1986); Gilles Deleuze, "Bartleby; or, the Formula," in *Essays Critical and Clinical*, trans. Daniel W. Smith and Michael A. Greco (Minneapolis: University of Minnesota Press, 1997); and Michael Hardt and Antonio Negri, *Empire* (Cambridge, Mass.: Harvard University Press, 2003), 203–4.

16. For a suggestive discussion of Agamben's appeal to Melville's "Bartleby, the Scrivener," see Leland de la Durantaye, *Giorgio Agamben: A Critical Introduction* (Stanford, Calif.: Stanford University Press, 2009), 164–72.

17. Agamben's critique of the means/end logic, particularly in the essays in *Means without End*, derives in part from Heidegger's interrogation of metaphysical (teleological) time and in part from Hannah Arendt's critique of *homo faber* (modern man, the maker), in *Human Condition*.

18. For an amplified version of Agamben's meditation on the relationship between Aristotle's analysis of the potentiality/act dyad and Bartleby's "I prefer not

to," see Agamben, "Bartleby, or On Contingency," in *Potentialities: Collected Essays in Philosophy*, trans. and ed. Daniel Heller-Roazen (Stanford, Calif.: Stanford University Press, 1999), 243–74; see also Rancière, *Dis-agreement: Politics and Philosophy*, trans. Julie Rose (Minneapolis: University of Minnesota Press, 2004), 11–12.

19. See Agamben, "Bartleby, or On Contingency," 253–54.

20. See de la Durantaye's excellent reading of the Tiananmen Square chapter of *Giorgio Agamben*, 164–72.

21. See Spanos, *Herman Melville and the American Calling*.

22. See note 6.

23. As Michael Paul Rogin resonantly noted a long time ago, Melville changed the name of the ship under the command of Captain Amasa Delano from the *Tryal* to the *San Dominick* to call attention "to the slave seizure of power on Santo Domingo in the wake of the French Revolution. That slave uprising spread terror throughout the American South"; Rogin, *Subversive Genealogy: The Politics and Art of Herman Melville* (New York: Alfred Knopf, 1983), 213. See also Melville, "Benito Cereno," in *Piazza Tales* (Evanston, Ill.: Northwestern University Press; Chicago: Newberry Library, 1987), 83–84. Further References are abbreviated as BC and incorporated into the text in parentheses.

24. Melville insistently refers to Captain Delano and his American crew as "visitors," by which I take him to mean, as the etymology suggests, the privileged ones who come to *see* those who are not. As the story unfolds, however, the visitors become the visited, in the second sense of "visit": as visitation, a haunting that undermines the hierarchical binary of the visitor/visited opposition; see Derrida, *Specters of Marx: The State of the Debt, the Work of Mourning, and the New International*, trans. Peggy Kamuf (New York: Routledge, 1994).

25. For further evidence that the black man in Melville's texts haunts the American exceptionalist ethos, see James, *Mariners, Renegades and Castaways: The Story of Melville and the World We Live In* (1953; repr. Hanover, N.H.: University Press of New England, 2001). Donald E. Pease's "Introduction" to this volume is especially pertinent to my argument.

26. Badiou, *Being and Event*, trans. Oliver Feltham (London: Continuum, 2005). For a brief definition of the event (*événement*), see Badiou, *Ethics*:

> We might say that since a situation is composed by the knowledge circulating within it, the event names the void inasmuch as it names the unknown of the situation.
>
> To take a well-known example, Marx is an event for political thought because he designates, under the name "proletariat," the central void of early bourgeois societies. For the proletariat—being entirely dispossessed, and absent from the political stage—is that around which is organized the complacent plenitude established by the rule of those who possess capital.
>
> To sum up: the fundamental ontological characteristic of an event is to inscribe, to name, the situated void of that for which it is an event. (69)

27. Melville, "Bartleby, the Scrivener," in *Piazza Tales*, 23.

28. Foucault, *Discipline and Punish: The Birth of the Prison*, trans. Alan Sheridan (New York: Pantheon, 1977), 137–38.

29. Foucault, *The History of Sexuality*, vol. 1, *An Introduction*, trans. Robert Hurley (New York: Pantheon, 1978), 17–49.

30. For a similar analysis of naming, see Badiou, *The Rebirth of History: Time of Riots and Uprisings*, trans. Gregory Elliott (London: Verso, 1212), 92–95.

31. See Badiou's remarkably parallel reading of the Arab Spring uprising of 2011 in *Rebirth of History*; see also Spanos, "Arab Spring, 1211: A Symptomatic Reading of the Revolution," *Symploké* 21–22 (2012).

32. My reference to "Ahabism" is intended to recall Captain Ahab's monomaniacal naming of the white whale (the unidentifiable and irreparable contingencies of being that reaped his leg from his body) "Moby Dick" to render "it" "practically assailable" (M-D, 184).

33. George Washington Peck, Review of *Pierre; Or the Ambiguities*, by Melville, *New York Herald*, September 18, 1852; reprinted in *Herman Melville: The Contemporary Reviews*, ed. Brian Higgins and Hershel Parker (Cambridge: Cambridge University Press, 1995): "We can afford Mr. Melville full license to do what he likes with 'Omoo' and its inhabitants; it is only when he presumes to thrust his tragic *Fantoccini* upon us, as representatives of our race, that we feel compelled to turn our critical Aegis upon him, and freeze him into silence" (438).

34. I am referring to the essential strategy of the European colonizers of the New World in their effort to subdue the natives: their advanced scientific knowledge that was staged to achieve spectacular—"shock and awe"—effects on the benighted; see Todorov, *Conquest of America*, 115. For my amplification of this spectacular strategy of conquest, see also Chapter 1.

35. Thomas Pynchon, *Gravity's Rainbow* (New York: Penguin, 1973), 264.

36. I am using this Deleuzian term in the sense to which Giorgio Agamben gives it by way of his tracing its genealogy back from Deleuze and Foucault through Heidegger and Hegel to its origins in the Christian theological concept of the economy (*oikonomia*, the law of the household): "What is common to all these terms ["dispositive," "*Ge-stell*," "apparatus"] is that they refer back to this *oikonomia*, that is, to a set of practices, bodies of knowledge, measures, and institutions that aim to manage, govern, control, and orient—in a way that purports to be useful—the behaviors, gestures and thoughts of human beings"; Agamben, "What Is an Apparatus?", in *What Is an Apparatus?*. Agamben expands on this genealogy in *Kingdom and the Glory*.

37. I am referring to the distinction Heidegger, following Kierkegaard, makes between recollection, which *recuperates* a past, and repetition (*Wiederholung*) which *retrieves* a meaning of the past that was not available at the time as a possibility in the present; see Heidegger, *Being and Time*, trans. John Macquarrie and Edward Robinson (New York: Harper and Row, 1962), 437–38.

38. See Arendt, *Origins of Totalitarianism*, particularly Chapter 9, "The Decline of the Nation-State and the End of the Rights of Man," 2:267–302; and Arendt, "We Refugees."

39. Said, *Culture and Imperialism* (New York: Alfred A. Knopf, 1993), 332.

40. Agamben, "Beyond Human Rights," 23.4–24.5; my emphasis. For an extended analysis of this passage from Agamben, see Spanos, *Exiles in the City*, 198–204.

Index

9/11: errand in the wilderness, xvii, xviii, 61; exceptionalism in post–9/11 era, 42–73; New Americanism post–9/11, 77; normalization of state of exception, xii, 39–40, 66–67; post–9/11 distortion in New Americanist studies, 87; as turning point in American studies history, 87–88; *Who Are We?: Challenges to America's National Identity* (Huntington), 51–53

Abu Ghraib, 54; paranoia and, 92; photos of torture, 91–92
academic discourse: American studies, 42; New Americanist studies, 43
Addison, Joseph, 3
Agamben, Giorgio, 107; I Corinthians, 117–18; apostle, 118; calling as political, 117; capitalist work ethic, 113–14; *The Coming Community,* 114–15; Debord and, 11–13; ethics of vocation, 115–16; operational time, 118; Paul's Epistle and, 114–15, 115–16; polity and Möbius strip, 72; potentiality/act dyad, 119–20; radical democracy, 114; the remnant, 118–19; the spectacle and capitalism, 11–12; spectacularity of the spectacle, 72; Tiananmen Square, 132–3; *The Time the Remains,* 115–16; vocation, 114

"The Age of the World Picture" (Heidegger), 9
Althusser, Louis, 107; the calling, 111–13; capitalism, 111–12; "Ideology and Ideological state Apparatuses: Notes towards an Investigation," 111–12; interpellation, 110–11; Moses's calling, 130; Weber comparison, 111–12
American Adam, 16–17
American as synomym for exceptionalism, 15
American Century, 89; closing of, 90–91
American Communist Party, 44–45
American exceptionalism, 2; bin Laden assassination and, 64, 66–67, 84; celebratory use of term, 83; first usage of term, 44–45; as hegemonic discourse, 85; as ideology, 85; the spectacle and, 13; spectacle-oriented logic, 19; staged use of term, 44; the wilderness and, 14–15
American jeremiad, 14, 17–18; American national identity and, 95–96; Huntington, 52–53; Huntington and, 96–97; Kerry, John, at DNC 2012, 62–63; McCain, John, 55–58; perpetual enemy and, 93; Puritans' ritualization, 46–47; Twain and, 31
American Jeremiad (Bercovitch), 46

American studies, 42–43; 9/11 turning point, 87–88; GLAS (Global American Studies) project, 89; transformation, 77–78; transnationalization, 77–79, 88–89

"American Studies after American Exceptionalism:? Toward a Comparative Analysis of Imperial State Exceptionalism" (Pease), 89–91

American sublime: apparatus of capture, 15; Cold War and, 2; concept's origins, 1–2; cultural history, 14–18; ineffable sublime to effable spectacle, 16; Puritans and, 16–17; as the spectacular, 14–15; worldly implications, 3

American vocation, 106–7

Americanism, 3

anthropological knowledge production, 4

Anthropologos, 3

anxiety: climate of, 58; *versus* fear, 4, 5; the nothing and, 5; over loss of enemy, 92–93; the sublime nothing and, 6; sublime wilderness, 16

apotheosis of man, 3

argos, 114

Aristotle, potentiality, 120

Ashley-Cooper, Anthony, 3

author interview, 145–56

axis of evil, 106

bare life, 29; capture and, 9; concentration camps and, 54; Connecticut Yankee, 37; Nazi biopolitics, 82–83; shock-and-awe tactics, 51

"Bartleby, the Scrivener: A Story of Wall Street" (Melville), 119–20, 121, 128–34

Bataille, Georges, 113–14

Baucom, Ian: "Cicero's Ghost: The Atlantic, the Enemy, and the Laws of War," 91, 94–95; European origins of unlawful combatants, 94; unjust enemy, 94–95

Being, the nothing and, 4

being: re-presentation and, 10; the sublime and, 7; thought and, 8–9

Being and Time (Heidegger), 4

belonging, logic of, 120

Benito Cereno (Melville), 121–28

Benjamin, Walter: historical materialism, 67; *Jetztzeit*, 118

Bercovitch, Sacvan, 14; *American Jeremiad*, 46; McClintock and, 93–94

bereavement of speech, 11

bin Laden, Osama, 84; execution, promises and, 66–67, 84; frontier narrative and, 67; as personification of Islam, 53; spectacle of DNC 2012, 64; surgical execution, 64–65

biopolitics, 37–38; *A Connecticut Yankee in King Arthur's Court*, 37–38; Nazi, 82–83; U.S. detention camps, 54

Bloom, Harold, 3; the sublime, 2

Burke, Edmund, 3

Bush, George H. W., Vietnam Syndrome, 77

Bush, George W.: response to bin Laden assassination, 166n23; State of the Union 2002, 105–6

Bush (George W.) administration: appropriation of the spectacle, 70–71; homeland security state, 54; preemptive war doctrine, 81–82; U.S. as homeland security state, 81–82

call of History, 106

calling: Althusser, 111–13; becoming ethics, 113; continued influence, 109–10; messianic call, 118–19; Mosaic law and, 118; negative consequences, 107; Paul's Epistle to the Romans and, 115–16; as political, 117; predetermination and, 108; servitude and, 111; spirit of capitalism and, 108, 109, 113; subjected subjects and, 111; Weber's interpretation, 116–17. *See also* vocation

Calvinists: predestination, 108–9; providential view of history, 45

capitalism: Agamben, 113–14; Althusser, 111–12; Republican National Convention 2012, 59; the spectacle and, 11–12;

spirit of, predestination and, 108; work ethic and, 108–10. *See also* spirit of capitalism

capture, the spectacle and, 8–9

cartography metaphor in Giles, 98–100

Castronovo, Russ, *States of Emergency: The Object of American Studies,* 91

Cavafy, Constatine, "Waiting for the Barbarians," 92

celebratory expressions, 43–44

centered circle. *See* exceptionalist center/origin

chosen culture, 14

chosenness, Puritan calling and, 110

"Cicero's Ghost: The Atlantic, the Enemy, and the Laws of War" (Baucom), 91, 94–95

the class of civilization, 51

climate of anxiety, 58

Cold War, 43; American sublime and, 2; end as threat to exceptionalism, 52

The Coming Community (Agamben), 114–15

commodity fetishism, 9–10; Crystal Palace Exhibition and, 11–12

communism, Lovestoneites, 44–45

community: Said, Edward, 142; unhomed homeland, 72

concentration camps, bare life and, 54

The Confidence-Man: His Masquerade (Melville), 68–69

A Connecticut Yankee in King Arthur's Court (Twain), 18, 32–38, 162n44; frontier closing and, 47–51

The Conquest of the Americas (Todorov), 15

Constitution (U.S.), separation of church and state, 47

Continental thinkers, 107

contrapuntal reading, 44

Cortés, Hernando, 15

Cotton, John, 110; "The Christian Calling," 173n5

Crystal Palace Exhibition, capitalism and the spectacle, 11–12

Debord, Guy, 2; commodity fetishism, 11–12; society of the spectacle, 10

decentered speech of the sublime, 7–8

Democratic National Convention 2012: Kerry, John, 61–63; Middle East violence, 64–65; Obama, Barack, 65–66; promises, 63–65; recidivism of Republicans, 62–63; staged spectacle, 71–72

detention camps, bare life and, 54

de-territorialization, 98–99

Dimock, Wai Chee: *Shades of the Planet: American Literature as World Literature,* 87; transnationalization of American studies, 87–89

domestic policy, John McCain, 56–57

ecos, militarization, 89

Edwards, Brian T., *The Globalization of American Studies,* 89

election by God, 43

end of History, 75–76

enemies: anxiety over loss, 92–93; climate of anxiety, 58; perpetual, 53, 57, 929–8; unjust, 94–95

enemy in common, need for, 47

establishment clause of Constitution, 47

ethics, Agamben, 114–16

European origins of unjust enemy, 94

exceptionalist center/origin, 79–80; interregnum and, 86–97

exceptionalist logic, 32

exceptionalist Western metaphysical tradition, 3

exilic consciousness, 80; now time, 86

extraordinary rendition, 54, 82

extremity as value, 70–71

Faludi, Susan, 40–41

fear *versus* anxiety, 4, 5

foreign policy, John McCain, 56–57

Foucault, Michel, 129; repressive hypothesis, 130

Franklin, Benjamin, work ethic, 117

Freud, Sigmund, 3

frontier: *A Connecticut Yankee in King Arthur's Court,* 47–51; need for, 47
frontier narrative, bin Laden execution, 67
frontier thesis, 46–47
The Futures of American Studies (Pease and Wiegman, eds.), 75

Gaonkar, Dilip Parameshwar, *The Globalization of American Studies,* 89
Giles, Paul, *The Re-Mapping of American Literature,* 98–103
Gillman, Susan, *States of Emergency: The Object of American Studies,* 91
GLAS (Global American Studies) project, 89
global normalization of the state of exception, 82–83
global state of emergency, 82
global warming, planetization of American studies, 89
global wilderness, Islam and, 53
globalization, viability of American exceptionalism, 89–91
The Globalization of American Studies (Edwards and Gaonkar, eds.), 89
God, election by, 43
Gramsci, Antonio, 85–86
Gravity's Rainbow (Pynchon), 134–40
Guantánamo, 54

Heidegger, Martin, 3; anxiety robs us of speech, 6; *Being and Time,* 4; destructive heremeneutics, 114; "The Age of the World Picture," 9; "The Question Concerning Technology," 9; world picture, 8–9
Herr, Michael, 50–1; Tet Offensive account, 76
historical materialism, 67
History: call of, 106; end of, 75–76; Manifest Destiny, 47; Western interpretation, 78
The Homeland Security Act, 82
homeland security state, 54

homocide. *See* bare life
Huntington, Samuel P., 51–52; American jeremiad and, 96–97; perpetual enemy, 97–98; War on Terror defense, 96–97; *Who Are We?: Challenges to America's National Identity,* 51–52
Hurricane Katrina, transnationalization of American studies, 88–89
Hussein, Saddam, 77

ideology: the calling in capitalism, 112–13; as culture, 113; *versus* hegemonic discource of American exceptionalist ethos, 85–86
"Ideology and Ideological State Apparatuses: Notes towards an Investigation" (Althusser), 111–12
imperial logic, 79
The Innocents Abroad (Twain, Mark), 31
interpellation, 107, 110–11; Bartlleby as interpellating subject, 128–34
interregnum, 80, 86; historical reality, 91; vocation of the intellectual, 87
iron cage, spirit of capitalism and, 111
Islam: enemy qualifications, 53; global wilderness and, 53; personification in Osama bin Laden, 53

Jay Gatsby, 165n19
Jerusalem, Said on, 142
Jetztzeit (Benjamin), 118
Johnson, Kent, 143

Kant, Immanuel, 3
Karabel, Jerome, 42–43; popularization of exceptionalism terminology, 83
Kerry, John, 84–85; Democratic National Convention 2012, 61–63; spectacular use of exceptionalism terminology, 84
Kierkegaard, Søren, 5

language: *Moby-Dick,* 24; the sublime nothing and, 6, 7; Twain's American vernacular, 31
logic of belonging, 120

Longinus, 3
Lovestoneites, 44–45

Manifest Destiny, 43, 107; History and, 47
McCain, John, Republican National Convention 2012, 55–59
McClintock, Anne: Bercovitch and, 93–94; "Paranoid Empire: Specters from Guantánamo and Abu Ghraib," 91–93
means/end ethics of the vocation, 107
Melville, Herman, 16, 67–68; "Bartleby, the Scrivener: A Story of Wall Street," 119–21, 128–34; *Benito Cereno,* 121–28; *The Confidence-Man: His Masquerade,* 68–69; global age and, 38; *Moby-Dick,* 18; *Pierre: Or the Ambiguities,* 25–30; the spectacle in, 19–20
messianic call, 118–19
metaphysics, 4
Middle East: violence against, 64; Western colonialist exceptionalism and, 65
militarization of ecos, 89
Moby-Dick (Melville), 18, 67–68; language, 24–25; the spectacle in, 19–23
monomania, 4–5
monomaniacal worldly violence, 69
monumentalizing history, 161n38

Nancy, Jean-Luc, 114
nation-state, New Americanists and, 77–81
Native Americans, extermination, 96
Natty Bumppo, 166n22
Nausea (Sartre), 6–7
New Americanism: global *versus* local, 78, 79–81; post–9/11, 77; scholarship, 77–78
New Americanist studies, 43; contrapuntal reading, 44; globalism *versus* localism, 75–76; overdetermination of the global, 87; post–9/11 distortion, 87
nihilism *versus* the nothing, 6
normalization of the state of exception, 89; *States of Emergency,* 91–92

the nothing: anxiety and, 5; Being and, 3–4; indeterminateness, objectification of, 5–6; infinite finitude, 6; monomania and, 4–5; *versus* nihilism, 6; as rhetorical phenomenon, 2; Western knowledge production and, 4–5; Western man and, 4. *See also* the sublime

Obama, Barack: American jeremiad of John McCain, 58; DNC 2012, 65–66; victory speech at second term, 166n25
Obama administration's lack of change, 82–83
official paranoia, 91–92
Old World, exceptionalism to distinguish from, 52
ontologic of exceptionalism, Kerry, John, 84–85
onto-theological tradition, xv; the sublime and, 7
The Oregon Trail (Twain, Mark), 31
the Other, 14–15; anxiety and, 96; imperialism and, 79; perennial (America's), 60; violence against, 43–47
overcivilization, 47
overdetermination of the global, 78–79, 87; Hurricane Katrina and, 88–89
overdetermining of rejuvenation, 18

paranoia, official, 91–92
"Paranoid Empire: Specters from Guantánamo and Abu Ghraib" (McClintock), 91–93
paranoid imperial syndrome, 91–93
passive resistance, 141
Paul, Saint: Agamben, 114–16; Puritan calling and, 115–16; Weber's interpretation, 116–17
peace in the aftermath of violence, 65–66
Pease, Donald, 44–45; "American Studies after American Exceptionalism:? Toward a Comparative Analysis of Imperial State Exceptionalism," 89–91; *The Futures of American Studies,* 75; long durée, 164n3

Pentagon Papers leak, 76
perpetual enemies, 53, 57, 92–98
Pierre: Or the Ambiguities (Melville), 25–30
political conventions, 43–44
polity, unhomed homeland, 72
postmodern novelists, 134
potentiality/act dyad, Agamben, 119–20
predestination, 107–9
preemptive wars, 2, 134; Bush adminis-
    tration, 81–82
promises: bin Laden execution and,
    66–67; DNC 2012, 63–65, 84
Protestant work ethic, 107; spirit of capi-
    talism and, 108–10
*The Protestant Work Ethic and the Spirit of
    Capitalism* (Weber), 116–17
providence, 107–8; Calvinists, 45; slaves
    and, 123–24
Puritan calling. *See* calling
Puritans, 14; American sublime and,
    16–17; errand in the wilderness,
    45–46; exceptionalism paradox,
    46–47; exodus to New World, 45;
    good works, 108–9; Huntington on,
    51–52; New World wilderness and,
    16–17; overcivilization and, 47; pre-
    destination, 107–9; providence,
    107–8; recidivism, 46; Twain and, 30;
    violence against "other," 43–44
Pynchon, Thomas, *Gravity's Rainbow,*
    134–40

"The Question Concerning Technology"
    (Heidegger), 9

radical democracy, 114
the real, as a simulacrum, 10
recidivism, 14; Puritans, 46; Republicans
    accusing Democrats, 56–58
redeemer nation, 2; America's election by
    History, 58
refugees, 142
regime change, 2, 134; ventriloquized
    governments, 53–54
rejuvenation through violence, 47–48

The Re-Mapping of American Literature
    (Giles), 98–103
the remnant, 118–19
re-presentation, being and, 10
Republican National Convention 2012:
    McCain, John, 55–59; Rubio, Marco,
    59–61; staged spectacle, 71–72
resistance, passive, 141
rhetoric, the nothing and, 2
Roughing It (Twain, Mark), 31
Rubio, Marco, Republican National
    Convention 2012, 59–61

Said, Edward, 39–40; Jerusalem, 142
Sartre, Jean-Paul, *Nausea,* 6–7
"Second Coming" (Yeats), 79–80
self-de-struction of American exception-
    alism, 71–72; theoretical, 81
self-righteousness of modern societies,
    39–40
separation of church and state, 47
September 11th bombings. *See* World
    Trade Center bombings
servitude as result of calling, 111
*Shades of the Planet: American Literature
    as World Literature* (Dimock), 87
Shane, Scott, 56–57
"The Significance of the Frontier in
    American History" (Turner), 47
simulacrum, as the real, 10
slaves, providence and, 123–24
Slotkin, Richard, 47–48
society of the spectacle, 10
"The Society of the Spectacle," 2
sovereign logic, 79
the spectacle, 8, 69–70, 165n15; achieving
    power, 18; American exceptionalism
    and, 13; American sublime and, 10;
    American sublime as, 14–15; appropri-
    ation by Bush administration, 70–71;
    capitalism and, 11–12; capture and,
    8–9, 12–13; climate of anxiety and, 58;
    contemporary global politics, 70;
    extremity as value, 70–71; in *Moby-
    Dick,* 19–23; promises, 63–65; real of,

10; society of the spectacle, 10; staged in presidential conventions, 71–72; transformation from sublime, 9–10; Twain and, 31–32

speech: act and, 11; bereavement, 11

spirit of capitalism: Bartleby, 129; iron cage, 111; predestination and, 108; Puritan calling and, 108, 109; work ethic and, 108–10, 113

staged spectacle, presidential conventions 2012, 71–72

staged use of "American exceptionalism" terminology, 44

Stalin, Joseph, 44–45

state of emergency: as global rule, 91; as norm, 54

States of Emergency: The Object of American Studies (Castronovo and Gillman, eds.), 91

subjected subjects, 111; Captain Delano, 122; democratic capitalist exceptionalism, 112–13

the sublime: anxiety and, 6; being and, 7; Bloom, Harold, and, 2; comprehensibility, 5–6; decentered speech, 7–8; Heidegger, Martin, 3; infinite finitude, 6; language and, 6, 7; Melville and, 25; onto-theological tradition and, 7; secular ontological condition, 5; transformation to spectacle, 9–10. *See also* American sublime; the nothing

thought and being, 8–9

Tiananmen Square, 132–33

The Time the Remains (Agamben), 115–16

Todorov, Tzvetan, *The Conquest of the Americas,* 15

transnationalization of American studies, 77–79; anti-exceptionalism and, 79; global warming and, 88–89; Hurricane Katrina and, 88–89

Turner, Frederick Jackson, "The Significance of the Frontier in American History," 46–47

Twain, Mark (Samuel Langhorne Clemens), 16, 30–31; American jeremiad and, 31; *A Connecticut Yankee in King Arthur's Court,* 18, 32–38, 162n44; global age and, 38; *The Innocents Abroad,* 31; *The Oregon Trail,* 31; *Roughing It,* 31; the spectacle and, 31–32

unlawful combatants, 95; European origins, 94

ventriloquized governments, 53–54

Vietnam Syndrome, 77

Vietnam War, 50–51; forgetting of violence, 76–77

violence: against Middle East, 64; monomaniacal worldly violence, 69; national forgetting, 76–77; against "others," 43–45; peace in the aftermath, 65–66; rejuvenation through violence, 47–48; wilderness and, 53–54

vocation: Agamben, 114–15; ethics of, 115–16; means/end logic, 120

"Waiting for the Barbarians" (Cavafy), 92

War on Terror, 2, 38–9, 43, 50; Huntington on, 96–97; justification, establishment, 77; Obama administration, 83; redemptive exceptionalism, 88; unjust enemy and, 94–95

warrantable calling of the Puritans, 110

Weber, Max, 107; Althusser comparison, 111–12; Catholic tradition, 108; consciously held ideology *versus* lived ethos, 111; *The Protestant Work Ethic and the Spirit of Capitalism,* 116–17; spirit of capitalism, Puritans and, 108–10

Who Are We?: Challenges to America's National Identity (Huntington), 51–52

Wiegman, Robyn, *The Futures of American Studies,* 75

wilderness: exceptionalism and, 14–15; Puritans and, 16–17; sublime, 16; violence and, 53–54. *See also* global wilderness, Islam and

Williams, Raymond, Gramsci and, 85–86

work ethic: Agamben, 113–14; Bartleby, 129; Franklin, Benjamin, 117; spirit of capitalism and, 113. *See also* Protestant work ethic

world picture, 8–9

World Trade Center bombings, 43. *See also* 9/11

Yeats, W. B., "Second Coming," 79–80